To: ELAINE YARBROUGH

To whom Madeleine and I feel deeply indebted for having introduced us to Westminster Village — and whom we value highly as a special person and true friend.

Warren T. Kingsbury
9/7/90

a man of many letters

the "mam" letters, 1911-1921

Lilburn Adkin Kingsbury 1884 - 1983

Joys and sorrows of life in Missouri's fascinating Boonslick County as reported by its premier historian and genealogist in letters written between 1911-1922

Edited by
Warren Kingsbury, Ed. D.

Published by
Roberta Burnett
Communications, Inc.
Tempe, Arizona 1990

Copyright © 1990 Warren T. Kingsbury, Ed.D.

All rights reserved. No part of this publication may be reproduced or transmitted in any form or by any means, electronic or mechanical, including photocopy, recording, or any information storage or retrieval system without permission in writing from the publisher. Inquiries should be addressed to:

> Roberta Burnett Communications, Inc.
> 607 E. Loyola Drive
> Tempe, Arizona 85282-3834
>
> 602 966-7277

Printed in the United States of America,
by Classy Copy Center Inc.

ISBN 1-879046-00-8

Library of Congress Catalog Card Number: 90-084353

Cover design by Andrew Weed, Tempe, Arizona

DEDICATION

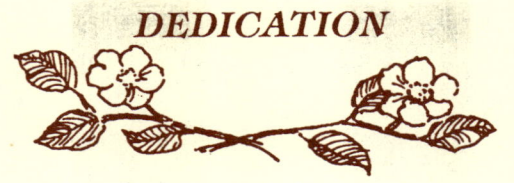

To the memory of
Lilburn Adkin Kingsbury
MAN OF MANY LETTERS
Who enriched the lives of so many
This book is gratefully dedicated

INTRODUCTION

Not many of us leave behind a detailed and accurate account of our life and times. Biographies frequently reveal a point of view, with undue emphasis on either our good or our less than good qualities. Even those who write autobiographies may find it difficult to be completely objective. How refreshing it is to read this *"Man of Many Letters,"* lovingly compiled by Warren Kingsbury from a remarkable collection of letters written by his uncle, Lilburn Kingsbury.

Just who was this man, Lilburn Kingsbury? Because my great-grandmother was Lucina Kingsbury, I came to know him as "Cousin Lilburn." But it was soon apparent that respect and affection was not limited to kinfolk. Contrary to the usual qualifications for laudatory accolades, Lilburn spent almost all of his ten decades in the small town of New Franklin, Missouri, in the heart of Boonslick Country. Yet he was recognized for his skills as a farmer, fruit grower, musician, composer, author, collector, banker, historian, churchman, insurance agent, and goodness knows what else. All without benefit of media hype, which he did not seek.

"Man of Many Letters" is an intimate record of a unique time and place. The time is shortly after the turn of our 20th century, in the early days of our amazing era of technology. The gasoline engine was in its early stages of development, scarcely hinting of the coming revolution in the way we would live and travel. Radio and television were not yet a dream of scientists who would later mold our national character. The Wright brothers had demonstrated that man could fly but who could envision the jet age, let alone space exploration?

The place was Boonslick Country, along the Missouri River in Central Missouri. Shortly after the turn of the 19th century, this was the Western frontier for the young nation that more than doubled in size with the Louisiana Purchase. First settled by intrepid pioneer families from Virginia and Kentucky for the most part, the ill-fated settlement of Franklin played a key role in the great Western Migration. Here came the sons of Daniel Boone to make salt by boiling down the briny spring water of the region. From here William Becknell launched his famed overland trip to Santa Fe in Mexican territory. And in its early days of statehood Missouri benefitted from leadership provided by Boonslick citizens.

A gracious style of country living blossomed here. Today spacious brick homes have survived to speak of an era of farm prosperity, aided somewhat by cheap slave labor. This era carried over into the early part of the next century, and Lilburn's account provides glimpses of the lifestyles of the modestly affluent families of the area. His grandfather, Jere, had profited by growing apples on the Missouri River hills of southern Howard County. Apples were processed into vinegar, a prized frontier food preservative and condiment.

Family get-togethers, weddings, church services, courtships (failed or otherwise) and comings and goings were faithfully chronicled for the homebound "Mam" of these letters. Never mind that momentous events were shaping up the world outside and overseas.

All of this was written in the gentle, down-home style that made Lilburn's writings so pleasing and easy to read. He made liberal use of rural colloquialisms, sometimes even inventing new words to fit the situation.

Later, his writings were not confined to the almost daily letters to Mrs. Tom Smith, called Ida by her friends, and "Mam" by Lilburn. His contributions to Boonslick history and lore were eagerly sought by area newspapers and historical societies. He became known as "Mr. Boonslick," and served the Boonslick Historical Society as its first and now-and-again president. Some of his contributions to history preserved were somewhat off-beat: He recorded names and locations in Howard County family cemeteries, a demanding task. He also had an extensive collection of old buttons.

His wry sense of humor that so enlightened his writings made Lilburn a popular speaker, and he was generous with his time and talents. How could he maintain his lifelong modesty? On the occasion of his 93rd birthday, the Boonslick Historical Society honored him with a banquet at Central Methodist College in nearby Fayette. When it finally came his time to respond to all the glowing things being said about him (including flowery resolutions from both houses of the Missouri General Assembly), he said, "This beats anything I have ever heard of anybody having," and then proceeded to speak of his "abject failures." These included composing a ragtime song that sold only three copies at the local drugstore. Moreover, he dedicated the song to a girlfriend who married someone else.

The letters here cover only a little more than one decade of his long life. He remained alert up to the night before his death in his sleep at the age of 99. And so the laborious task of editing his letters, so that all of us can have the opportunity of enjoying the accounts of his gentle life has been assumed by his nephew, Warren Kingsbury. It truly has been a labor of love. Only someone who was on hand at the time and who has committed himself to preserving his letters could capture, as this book does, the flavor of the "Man of Many Letters."

Lilburn and his nephew were good friends as well as relatives. Warren went along on one of Lilburn's great adventures, a trip on a mule boat to Spain. But that's another story, one that Warren intends to include in subsequent volumes. Lacking direct descendants, it is up to admirers and relatives to preserve the memory of this remarkable man. Fortunately, he, himself, provided the means to do just this. But what a pity to have lost the line of genes that resulted in such a true country gentleman! A man of his time, yes, but have the people in any time really changed that much? We can only hope they have not.

–Cordell W. Tindall

[Editor's note: Mr. Tindall is a native of Boonslick country and today owns the farm given to his great-grandmother, Lucina Kingsbury by her father, Jere. Now retired, his career was spent in agricultural journalsim after graduating from the University of Missouri. He is a past president of the UMC National Alumni Association. He is a past editor of the Missouri Ruralist and Editorial Vice President of the Harvest Publishing Company and was later its Director of Public Affairs. He is currently President of the Boonslick Heritage Association, in Fayette, and has published extensively in his own right.]

ACKNOWLEDGMENTS

These excerpts of Lilburn's letters would never have appeared in book form, had not many of Lilburn's friends and relatives, knowing them to be in my possession, besieged me to do something about publishing them. These special people include Elaine Derendinger, Emily Norbury, Gene Owen, and Jewell Vivian of the South Howard County Historical Society. They have not only provided constant encouragement, but also have devoted much time and effort to searching out pictures and verifying data. This has also been true of three of Lilburn's nieces, Alice Burrows, Kermit, Texas, Jean Edmonston, Moberly, Mo., and Alice Terry, Mobile, Alabama. Without them, this book would not be.

My immediate family has contributed much. Madeleine, my tolerant wife for sixty years, helped in selection of excerpts, and saw that I was free from distracting interruptions; my daughter, Carol Weed, helped eliminate irrelevant paragraphs; and my grandson, Andrew Kingsbury Weed, designed the cover and the area map; my son, Bill Kingsbury and his wife, Linda, provided special pictures.

I am indebted to Cousin Cordell Tindall of Fayette, Missouri, for the sensitive introduction which gives the reader interesting perspective to *Man of Many Letters*. I am grateful for the cooperation of the State Historical Society of Missouri: especially to Randy Roberts, Senior Manuscript Specialist of the Western Historical Manuscript Division, for helping to locate and make available for use photographs in the Lilburn Kingsbury files.

I am indebted to and deeply appreciate the sensitive insight and skillful editorial assistance provided by Roberta Burnett, and her talented assistant, Terri Macdonald.

We are grateful for permission to use invaluable photographs from archives of the following:

State Historical Society of Missouri, Western Historical Manuscripts, University of Missouri-Columbia, for photographs 2, p. viii; 10, p. xviii; 14, p. 3; 18, p. 20; and 19, p.26; 26, p. 91.

South Howard County Historical Society, New Franklin, Missouri, for photographs 3, p. viii; 12, p. xxiv; 7, p. xv; 8, p. xvi; 7, p. xv; 16, p. 14; 17, p. 16; 25, p. 74; and 30, p. 129; and to

Bill and Linda Kingsbury, San Francisco, Ca., for photographs 5, p. xii; 11, p. xxiv; and 6, p. xv .

Jean Edmonston, Moberly, Mo., for photograph 13, p. 3.

Photographs 15. p. 5; 21, p. 49; 22, p. 49; 23, p. 64; 24, p. 70; 27, p. 92; 28, p. 101; 29, p. 124; 30, p. 129 and 31, p. 161, are from the editor's files.

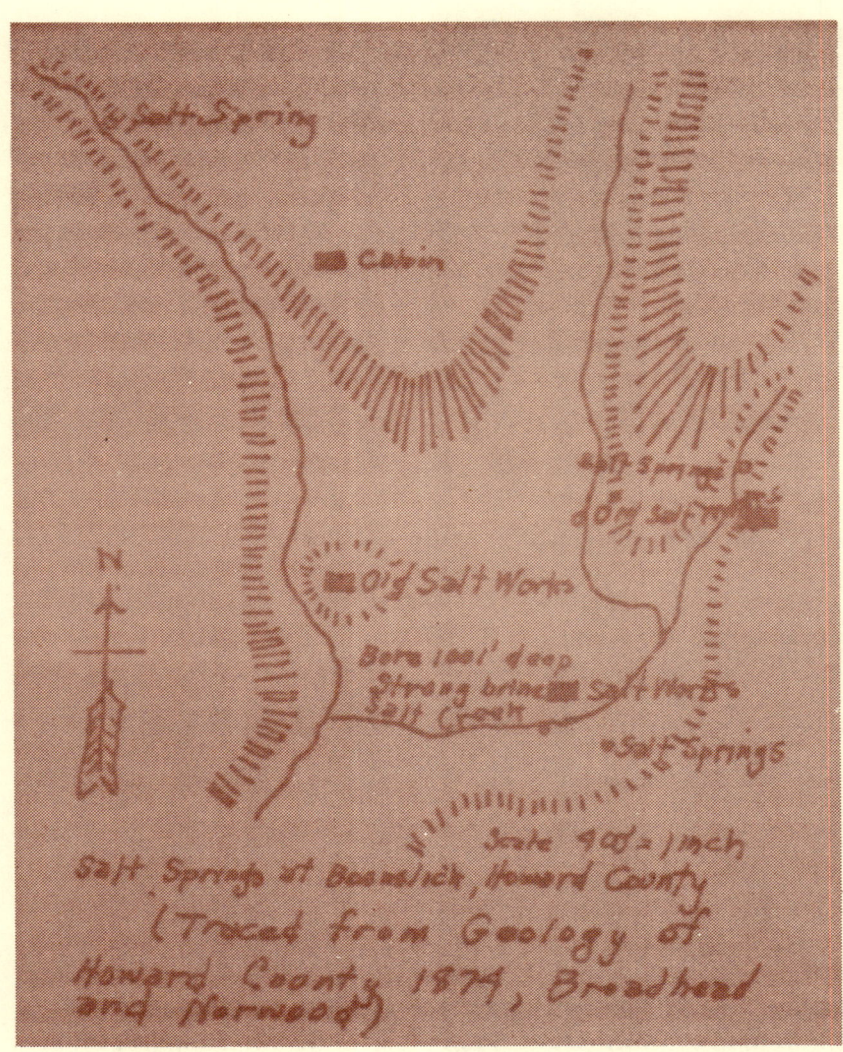

Map of Boonslick Salt Springs 1874

In 1869 the Boonslick Salt Manufacturing Company was organized. A well six inches in diameter was drilled to a depth of 1000 feet to produce a greater volume of salt water. The 1874 map shows the site of the well and the works, as well as the location of the natural springs. A combination of water not sufficiently saline and the lick being too far from commercial markets, resulted in the Company's liquidation in 1879.

Boonslick, 1959

Lilburn Kingsbury shows his Cousin Theodora Brill Tindall the site of the Boonslick well.

TABLE OF CONTENTS

Dedication .... p.   iii

Introduction .... p.   v

Acknowledgments .... p.   vii

List of Illustrations .... p.   xi

Prologue .... p.   xiii

1911 .... p.   1

1912 .... p.   11

1913 .... p.   35

1914 .... p.   51

1915 .... p.   71

1916 .... p.   85

1917 .... p.   113

1918 .... p.   129

1919 .... p.   137

1920 .... p.   143

1921 .... p.   161

Epilogue .... p.   175

Footnotes .... p.   179

Appendices
    I   Lilburn's Boonslick Folks .... p.   181
    II Mam's Marriage .... p.   185

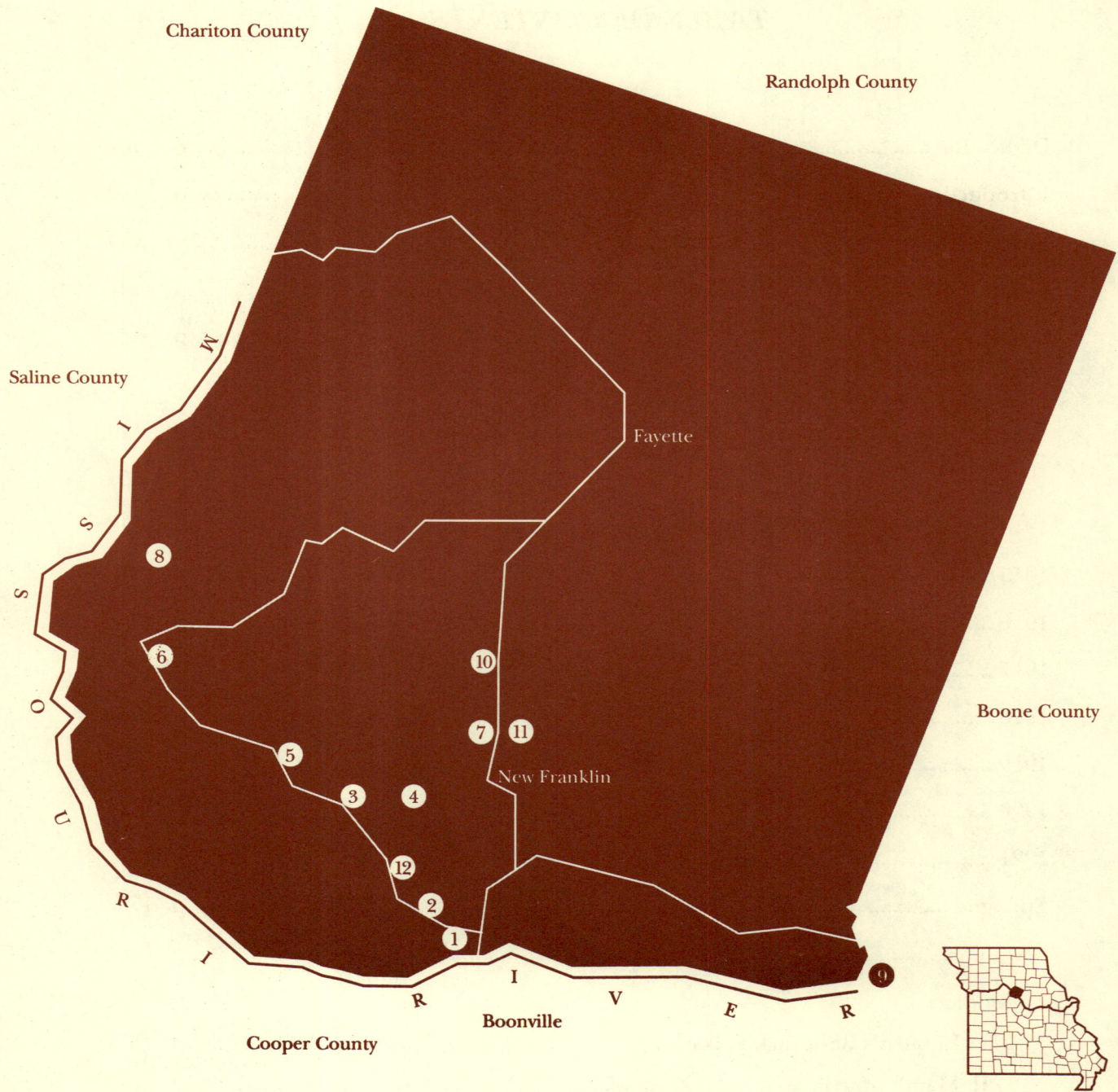

1 Old Franklin
2 Kingsbury Siding (Elevator)
3 Clark's Chapel
4 Sunnyside (William Jefferson Smith —C.I. Smith, Sr., C.I. Smith, Jr.)
5 Cedar Grove—Nicholes Amick —Dr. Horace Kingsbury
6 Glenida (Razed)—Home of Thomas and Ida Smith
7 Fairview (Lilburn's Home)
8 Boones Lick State Site
9 Rocheport (Boone Co.)
10 Woodlawn
11 Mt. Pleasant Cemetary
12 William Wallace Smith Home

HOWARD COUNTY

LIST OF ILLUSTRATIONS

1.	Boonslick Salt Works	Cover
2.	1874 Map of Boonslick Salt Springs	p. viii
3.	Boonslick, 1959	p. viii
4.	Map of Howard County	p. x
5.	Summer Socializing	p. xii
6.	Jere Kingsbury	p. xv
7.	Dr. Horace Kingsbury	p. xv
8.	Cedar Grove	p. xvi
9.	Taylor Kingsbury	p. xvii
10.	Fairview	p. xviii
11.	Pump House and Filling Station	p. xxiv
12.	Temperance Rally	p. xxiv
13.	Lillian Kingsbury in her Wedding Dress	p. 3
14.	Lillian and Carl Edmonston Going Away	p. 3
15.	"Us Winton Six"	p. 5
16.	Lilburn Kingsbury and his mother, Alice, dressed for church	p. 14
17.	Alice Virginia and Warren Kingsbury	p. 16
18.	Lilburn Kingsbury and Helen Smith	p. 20
19.	"Wonderful Party"	p. 26
20.	Gathering at the River	p. 48
21.	Christmas at the Billies	p. 49
22.	Arrow Rock Tavern	p. 63
23.	The Billies and Nanny Estill	p. 64
24.	Winter Wonderland—Fairview	p. 70
25.	Sunnyside	p. 74
26.	Clark's Chapel	p. 91
27.	Lilburn at Clark's Chapel Cemetery	p. 92
28.	Lilburn and "A Girl Called Josephine"	p. 101
29.	Alice and Taylor Kingsbury	p. 124
30.	Lilburn at Mount Ranier	p. 129
31.	New United Methodist Church	p. 161
32.	Josephine Pritchett	p. 162

Summer Socializing

Intersection of Broadway and Missouri, looking east from Bank of New Franklin (not shown). Town pump can barely be seen in front of buggies. Loafers, left to right: Norb Alsop, Sonny McCauley, Kelly Turner, Ed Crews, Pete Wayland, Augustus Turner, John Wayland, and unidentified.

PROLOGUE

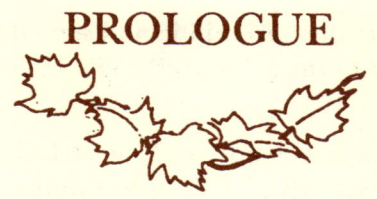

by

Warren Taylor Kingsbury, Ed.D.

Boonslick Country gets its name from Daniel Boone and his two sons, Nathan and Daniel Morgan. The elder Boone, feeling Kentucky was over-populated, had moved to Missouri with his family, about 1798, settling near St. Charles, a short distance up the Missouri river from St. Louis.[1] In 1806, Boone and his sons made their way along the north side of the Missouri river into the central part of the state. At the base of a bluff, rising from the heavily wooded bottom land on the river's north side, the Boones found a spring with a substantial flow of salt water. The Boone brothers joined forces with James and Jesse Morrison and became the primary salt producers for St. Louis and early settlements along the river.[2]

For several years Daniel Boone lived in a cabin near the salt lick, which was known as Boonslick. He died in 1820.[3]

In those times, salt was a precious commodity in great demand. Much was used by fur trappers in curing and preserving pelts for the market as well as meat from the game they killed for food. In 1807, the Boones transported huge iron kettles to this spring. The salt was produced by pouring salt water, or brine, into the kettles, heated over a stone furnace. As the brine boiled, the water evaporated, leaving a salt crystal residue. Approximately 300 gallons of water was required to produce 60 pounds of salt. Much of the salt was packed into hollowed out logs, rafting it down the Missouri to the St. Louis market.[4]

Boone's son, Nathan, apparently had a relationship with the Cooper family of Culpepper, Virginia.[5] He is credited with persuading the Coopers to emigrate to Missouri. Between 1810 and 1812, the Coopers established the first permanent settlements, which attracted other families to the area.[6] The trail they followed along the Missouri river into Howard County became known as the Boonslick Trail.

The Boonslick Country of Missouri was the third area of the state to attract permanent white settlers. St. Louis, at the confluence of the Missouri and Mississippi rivers, and St. Genevieve, on the Mississippi about 50 miles below St. Louis, were settled earlier by the French. By 1830, Boonslick Country residents numbered about a third of the state's population. Events in the area from 1800 until after the Civil War were important to the state's early history.

The increasing threat to the early settlers by Indians, incited by the British in their effort to obtain control of the Mississipi-Missouri River valley, caused them to establish forts to defend themselves. The largest of these was Fort Cooper which housed some twenty families and a number of bachelors. Here the defense efforts of the pioneers in the War of 1812 was coordinated by Colonel Benjamin Cooper. Trouble with the Indians caused the two Boone sons to sell out to the Morrisons. The Morrisons continued salt-making at the lick until 1833.

The Boones became Majors in the Missouri militia and served under Colonel Cooper throughout the war. Nathan Boone was in and out of the army until 1853. He was a member of Missouri's first Constitutional Convention.

In addition to identifying this area of Missouri as Boonslick Country, the Boone name was given to Boonville, a town just across the Missouri river in Cooper County; to Boone County to the east, whose county seat, Columbia, is site of the University of Missouri; and to the small village of Boonsboro, a short distance from the salt springs. The salt springs and the surrounding area became the Boonslick State Park in 1960.

The Boones, Coopers, and other pioneer families who fought off the British and Indians soon after the peace treaty was signed in 1815 were followed by an influx of settlers from Virginia, the Carolinas, Tennessee and Kentucky. Many of them contributed significantly to the development of the area and state. Most came over the Boonslick Trail and settled near or in Franklin.[7]

The town, named for Benjamin Franklin, was established in 1816 on the north bank of the river a few miles to the east of the salt springs. It was designated as the Howard County seat of government. Franklin quickly became a thriving community of about 1700 people. Its growth was stimulated by the developing steamboat traffic which, abetted by trading expeditions to Santa Fe, New Mexico, beginning in 1821, made Franklin the "commercial emporium" of Central Missouri.[8]

Franklin's bid to become a metropolis was short-lived, for the great Missouri river flood of 1826 changed the river channel and directed the force of the swift main stream current against the north bank. The river began cutting away at the bank on which the town was built, and within two years most of the homes, business buildings, and streets had tumbled into the river. Some of the home and building owners, recognizing Franklin was doomed, managed to have their buildings moved about two miles up on the hills which rose up from the river bottom. In 1828, they organized a town they called New Franklin. A new county seat was established at Fayette in the center of the county.[9]

Franklin in its brief existence made significant contributions to Missouri's development and history. It was the first county seat of Howard County, known as "Mother of Counties," as 37 of the state's present counties were carved from its original boundaries. Four of Missouri's early governors were one time residents of the town. The first newspaper published west of St. Louis, *The Missouri Intelligencer and Boonslick Advertiser*, began publication there April 13, 1819. The first federal land office west of St. Louis was established there. The first Missouri circuit court session met there in 1817. The famous frontier scout and trail-blazer, Kit Carson, for whom Carson City, Nevada, is named, lived there as a boy.[10]

It was into this historical country, Lilburn Adkin Kingsbury was born. His great grandfather, Jeremiah Kingsbury, was one of its early settlers. Jere, as he was always called, came in 1816 with his wife and two children from Randolph County, North Carolina. They made their way through the Cumberland Gap into Kentucky and on into Missouri. Like many other pioneers, the Kingsburys followed the Boonslick Trail to Howard County. Here Jere bought 480 acres of land about four miles east of Fort Hempstead. This he cleared and farmed. As the years passed, Jere prospered. He expanded his holdings until a legend grew up, not entirely accurate, that he could walk the six miles from his home to Franklin and never set foot on any land but his own. In addition to his large land-holdings, Jere acquired many slaves and was involved in a number of successful commercial enterprises. He became one of Boonslick Country's most prosperous and influential citizens.[11]

After their arrival in Missouri, nine more children were born to Jere and his wife. Only two of the eleven died before adulthood. When the others married, Jere gave them property. At his death, all of his still sizeable holdings of land, slaves, and other property was equitably distributed among the surviving children. The descendants of Jere and their spouses (children of other Boonslick pioneers)

xiv

Jere Kingsbury

Dr. Horace Kingsbury

were from families that frequently intermarried. As a consequence, the Kingsburys, Smiths, Gearharts, Blankenbakers, Lees, Whittens, Chandlers, and Chancellors found themselves with ties of relationship almost as closely entwined as the roots of many plants growing in one large pot.[12]

These families were lovers of the land and prideful of the richly productive acres they had cleared from the bottom land wilderness. The big homes they built to replace original log cabins were testaments to their achievements. Most homes were given names such as Cedar Grove, Sunnyside, Woodlawn, Fairview and Glenida.[13]

Cedar Grove, now on the National Register of Historic Places, was the home of Jere Kingsbury's oldest son, Dr. Horace Kingsbury, Lilburn Kingsbury's grandfather. Dr. Kingsbury was married three times. There were eight children by his first wife and two each by his second and third. The last wife survived him and upon her death Cedar Grove was inherited by her daughter and son-in-law, Elizabeth and Frank Blankenbaker. Blankenbaker descendants of Horace Kingsbury, my great grandfather, continued living in the home until 1962 when it was sold out of the family.[14] (The last Blankenbaker owner, my cousin, Robert, was a schoolmate of mine at Central Methodist College.)

When I was about 12, I remember a big family picnic gathering at Cedar Grove. The large home is on a hillside, rising from the Missouri river bottom lands. Lilburn's father, Taylor Kingsbury (my grandfather), was born at Cedar Groves. He lived there until he took his bride to Fairview, given to him by his father as a wedding present.

After the abundant picnic spread, featuring plenty of country ham, fried chicken, corn on the cob, a variety of vegetables and salads, and the luscious cakes and pies, produced by the women of the family, Grandfather thought a walk in order. He took my older brother, Bill, and me for a hike up the hill back of the house. From a clearing in the cedars, he pointed out across the colorful cultivated fields of lush alfalfa and wheat in the river bottom to a cluster of trees where Jere Kingsbury's home had been. Grandfather told us, when he was a boy living at Cedar Grove, most of the bottom land we could see was owned by his grandfather Jere, and was thick with walnut, pecan, and towering cottonwood and sycamore trees. Some of these trees were more than 100 feet high. As a boy, he helped with the lumbering. One huge

The house at Cedar Grove

Built by Dr. Horace Kingsbury in 1856. In picture (about 1890), left to right, Franklin Blankenbaker, Clarence McGrew, Ada Blankenbaker, and Elizabeth Kingsbury Blankenbaker.

walnut tree was nearly seven feet in diameter. Some of the trees were cut into planks for housing and barns. More were split into rails to fence the cleared land. Most of the trunks were corded and sold to stoke fires of steamboat engine furnaces.

Grandfather went on to tell us he used to pick blackberries, gooseberries, and strawberries in the woods. The woods then were full of game: squirrels, rabbits, possums, foxes, coons, minks and weasels. Deer were plentiful. "There was many a night," he said, "we could hear wolves howl and sometimes a painter [panther] scream would sound like a distressed woman's voice."

Grandfather recalled that, standing where we were, he had frequently seen flights of migrating passenger pigeons so large and dense they blocked sight of the sun for as long as an hour as they streamed by overhead. He remembered the wood duck as the bird having the most beautiful plumage. These ducks, he said, nested high up in the sycamore trees. When the eggs hatched, the hens would bring each chick down in her bill and launch it on the water.

Grandfather recalled the long days of hard work which went into clearing the wilderness land and creating the prosperous farms with their substantial homes. When he lived at Cedar Grove, there was little communication with the outside world. Homes were heated by fire places and stoves and lighted by candles and oil lamps. Such roads as existed were dirt. People traveled from place to place on horseback, in buggies, or mule-drawn wagons. Oxen were used to pull plows to break the ground and haul the heavy loads of timber. These farms produced bountiful crops of corn and wheat, as well as raising cattle, chickens, and hogs. Their owners prospered. Their families ate well, canning and preserving fruit and vegetables for winter consumption, butchering hogs and steers to provide meat for seasoning in the smoke houses. Most clothing worn prior to the Civil War was made in the home. For miles around, the owners of these Boonslick homes were related and, frequently visiting among themselves as they did, formed what amounted to an extended family. They shared the social customs, traditions, beliefs, attitudes, and values their forefathers brought from the South.

Although the end of the Civil War freed Boonslick family slaves, Boonslickians still depended heavily upon Negroes (many of them descendants of family slaves) for their household servants and farm labor. Though farm owners were generally kind to Negroes who worked for them, they thought them inferior in intelligence and irresponsible in much of their behavior. As was general in the South at that time, Negroes were expected to know and "keep their place," as the commonly-used phrase of the times described. Nevertheless, some warm, affectionate relationships developed between the principal Boonslick landowners and their Negro retainers. These Negroes were frequently referred to as Aunt Annie, Uncle Jo, etc. Some had taken white family names. Negro women took much responsibility for bringing up the children, and running the household. Negro straw-bosses supervised the farm hands. But for Negroes to eat at the same table with "their white folks" or come into the family section of the house except in performing their duties as servants was unthinkable. A Negro "Auntie" could cuddle and rock one of the white children to sleep but would not think of coming into physical contact with the child's mother. The white citizenry would never shake hands with a Negro or address him or her as "Mr." or "Mrs."

No provision was made for education of Negro children. It was not thought they would ever need more learning than picked up from association with their white family.

Boonslick white families banded together and subscribed funds to provide education for their children. For many years the Clark's Chapel was also used as a school for the children of the area. The teacher, often a man, would board in a nearby home. Later a one room school house was erected near the Chapel. When the children outgrew this school, they were sent to private schools and colleges in nearby towns. Letters in my possession, written by Taylor and Alice Kingsbury, Lilburn's father and mother, testify excellent instruction in penmanship and composition was provided in those one-room rural schools.

(Robert) Taylor Kingsbury

Boonslick families prided themselves upon their Southern hospitality. The "latch-string was always out" at these homes. (That expression developed in the log cabin days before locks. A wooden bar with a pin holding it on the inside of the door could be raised and extended over and lowered into a wooden wall bracket a few inches from the door. This kept the door closed. To the bar was attached a leather thong. This could be inserted through a hole in the door. To enter from the outside, one pulled up the thong which "latched" the door. When family members were home and did not wish visitors, the latch could be pulled inside. Thus to have the "latch string out" was a sign of hospitality.)

I remember on one of my childhood visits to Fairview, Grandfather Kingsbury boasted that in the fifty years he had owned the place, the front door had never been locked and no one seeking shelter had ever been turned away. Hospitality was always extended. Visitors were warmly welcomed whether expected or not. Most families were large and the daily preparation of food for them by Negro house servants meant there was always plenty for guests who dropped in. Almost always there was a boiled country ham on the pantry shelf and a butter-cake in the tin box used to keep it moist. Blankets, quilts, feather-beds, comfortables for "bedding down" guests forced to stay overnight by weather or some other exigency seemed inexhaustible. I remember several times that I as a family member slept on a palette on the floor so an unexpected or expected guest might have a feather-bed which was much more comfortable.

Such hospitality and other gracious Southern customs and traditions were still the norm of family life in Boonslick Country when Lilburn Kingsbury was born to Taylor and Alice Smith Kingsbury, October 14, 1884. A Negro midwife assisted at Lilburn's birth at Fairview, as she had with the birth of his four older brothers.

FAIRVIEW

Fairview was on the crest of a hill which sloped gently in all four directions. When I knew it as a child, back of the big house was a three-room cottage. First built for Lilburn's four older brothers and frequent visitors, it was then occupied by the family's long-time handyman, Louis Williams. To the rear of the big house were a chickenhouse, icehouse, outhouse (with a 50-foot plank walkway to the kitchen entrance), smokehouse, and fruit and vegetable cellar. To one side was a cistern and pump. Water run-off from the roof into the cistern provided water for the house.

The house at Fairview

Lilburn's home all his life. The original structure was built by slave labor in the 1830's.

Across the road (now State Highway 5) which cut through the farm about 200 yards in front of the house was a large white, red-roofed barn with a red silo at its side. The upper portion of the barn provided storage for hay and grain to feed the working stock. The lower section had a harness room and stalls for the horses and mules. The barnyard pasture sloped down to a large willow-rimmed pond where the stock watered and the grandchildren caught catfish. Adjoining the barnyard were an apple-packing shed, a sizeable barn to shelter farm equipment, and another for the blacksmith shop and barrel-making areas.

As a child growing up at Fairview, Lilburn Kingsbury came to know the place well. His love for the beauty and fragrance of the snowy white apple blossoms of orchards in the spring, the smell of fresh cut clover hay, and the savory aroma of bread, pies and cakes baking in the kitchen is ever present in his letters. He heard the plaintive cry of whippoorwills, the hooting of barnyard owls at night, the soaring song of meadowlarks as the new day dawns, and the cheery "bob white" call of the quail. He was often awakened by the crowing of the roosters and frequently noted the lowing of the cattle making their way to the feeding pen as dusk approached.

Lilburn could look east across the rolling green pastures to the left of the lane leading to Mount Pleasant Cemetery where his grandfather Jere's tall white monument was visible and many kinfolk were buried. To the right of the lane, behind the barnyard compound, was the principal apple orchard extending out to the Bon Femme Creek where he fished and picnicked with his friends. About a quarter of a mile to the South was his brother Robert's substantial home, appropriately called "The Maples" for the trees which shaded it.

To the west, a Fairview grain field stretched to the Missouri, Kansas, and Texas Railroad branch-line that ran from New Franklin east to the Mississippi river at Hannibal. On one side of the field near a spring was the tenant house. North of the big house was a large garden with a vegetable patch, vineyard, berry plants and bushes and the bee hives which not only pollinated the orchard but also provided honey for sale and the table. Further north was yet another apple orchard.

These and a myriad of other sights, sounds, and smells of this busy, self-sufficient orchard/farm were absorbed by Lilburn, becoming a part of the growing boy who along the way learned to feed the chickens and animals, to milk, plow, and put up hay, to spray and prune the orchard, to slaughter and butcher hogs and steers, and to take up ice from the pond in the winter. These and other necessary tasks kept Fairview productive and profitable throughout the lifetime Lilburn had in under his care.

Lilburn attended public schools in New Franklin and Fayette. He had two years at Central College (now Central Methodist College) at Fayette. In 1905, when his father suffered a financial setback, he sacrificed his ambition to finish college and went to work as cashier of the Bank of New Franklin. He continued with the bank until January 1, 1918, and spent several months visiting with relatives in California, Washington and Montana. Some months after his return, he was prevailed upon to buy stock and participate in reorganization of the bank. and for several years took the major responsibility for its operation.

Over time it became apparent to Lilburn and his siblings that management of Fairview Farm/Orchard was becoming a heavy burden for his father. They agreed to waive their interests in the property in return for Lilburn's running it and looking after the parents for the remainder of their lives. To implement this, he sold his interest in the bank, opened an insurance office in town and divided his time between it and Fairview. Few parents have ever been blessed in their declining years with the kind of devoted, loving care and attention Taylor and Alice Kingsbury received from their son, Lilburn.

Lilburn's office building was in the center of the principal business block of New Franklin's Main Street. The office had a large plate glass window out of which one could easily see the goings and comings of the people of the town. When Lilburn was "in" (which he usually managed for a few hours most days), he had frequent callers. Many came not only to discuss their insurance needs, but also to pay their utility bills (Lilburn's contract arrangement with the utilities companies), have help with the drawing of their wills, papers notarized, or just to chat about the news and exchange views and information about the current gossip of the community. Lilburn was on a first name basis with nearly all the town's residents as well as those of the surrounding countryside who came to town to shop. Many of these were related. Infinitely agreeable, he always seemed to be able to find time to visit with them.

Life in Boonslick Country was absorbing and richly rewarding to Lilburn. Increasingly, he became interested in its history. He savored and absorbed the stories about his great grandparents, grandparents and other pioneer relatives as related by his parents sitting around the parlor fireplace in the long winter evenings before the flickering flames of the burning apple logs.

Lilburn was an embodiment of what Walt Whitman said so poetically:

> *"There was a child went forth every day,*
> *And the first object he look'd upon, that object he became,*
> *And that object became part of him for the day or a certain part of the day,*
> *Or for many years or stretching cycles of years."*

> Walt Whitman. "There Was a Child Went Forth," 1855-1871

The special character of the Boonslick Country truly became part of Lilburn Adkin Kingsbury, shaping his values, beliefs, attitudes and behavior throughout a long productive life. This is shown in more than 1100 preserved letters, which are his legacy to me. The originals are now housed in the State of Missouri Historical Society Library at the University of Missouri-Columbia for their archives.

The letters, written between 1911 and 1983, report his uniquely interesting experiences and adventures as an enthusiastic collector, travelling to out of the way places in search of antique furniture, early American glassware, lustreware, china, old clocks, bottles, and buttons. He writes both of his pleasures and the trials and tribulations which the changing seasons and times brought to his life as a farmer and orchardist. Nothing seems to escape his attention, and he writes of anything catching his fancy, including the amusing, whimsical, and sometimes vexing and patience-testing problems occurring with hired help.

Collectively, the letters give a fascinating, insightful portrayal of the social and economic life of the Boonslick Country. Lilburn Kingsbury writes of the long-established, successful Southern-rooted families of the area and how they lived. He tells of courtships, weddings, births and deaths; the homes people lived in; what they ate; how they dressed; their social conventions, religious convictions and practices; how they made their living; and how they conducted themselves in the presence of sickness and death. Lilburn writes of joyous celebrations, of neighborly misunderstandings, and of the ways people found to entertain themselves in the days before automobiles, radio and television. Community life of the time is touched upon lovingly.

Often the letters are humorous; sometimes they express sorrow and deep feeling; but always they candidly and realistically report Lilburn's activities, and his observations and perceptions of the people and happenings in the community. It should be remembered life in the Boonslick Country when Lilburn was born in 1884 was not much different from what it had been fifty years earlier. American industry was just beginning to develop the things we take for granted today. The year of Lilburn's birth brought the first modern bicycle, the safety razor, the fountain pen, and the first practical steam engine. The first automobile, the single cylinder Benz, made its appearance the following year. Necessities such as the telephone and electric fan hadn't been around long. Tom Edison's phonograph was just a new toy for a few and his incandescent light bulb was lighting up only the homes of the well to do. It would be more than thirty years before it was widely used in Boonslick farm homes.

The nearly one hundred years Lilburn lived included two World Wars, the Great Depression, the New Deal, and the Great Society, the Motor Age, and the beginning of the Space Age. Revolutionary developments in technology and communications brought great changes in the social, economic and cultural life of the Boonslick Country. Their impact is reflected in Lilburn's letters and writings until the last month of his life.

I first remember Lilburn when he was about 27 and a frequent visitor to our home in Boonville. My mother called Lilburn "Uncle Cyc" because he whirled from place to place and from girl to girl with almost cyclonic velocity and movement.

He would sweep into the house, toss us children into the air, catch us, set us gently down, and swiftly embrace our parents. Then he would reach into his coat pockets and pull candy out for us, usually foil-wrapped Hershey kisses, or little wax-paper enclosed butter-scotch squares. Occasionally he would bring a treasured box of Whitman's Sampler. We looked forward eagerly to his visits. They were usually short, principally given over to telling our parents how wonderful was his latest "Dream Girl." Sometimes, when he was not in too big a hurry to get to his current "little bit of loveliness," he would have supper with us and play the piano before or after dinner. He could play almost anything and frequently would improvise or play a rag-time tune of his own composition.

I remember my Uncle Lilburn then as a slender but well-built man, about six feet tall. His hair was reddish and wavy, cut and brushed into the then prevailing pompadour style. His eyes were a bright blue; his features, symmetrical, and his smile infectious. There was a winning warmth and gaiety to his voice which drew people to him. His way of saying things was different and amusing. He was always interested in his nieces and nephews and frequently before our bedtime would regale us with with fantastic stories about the peculiar Porter family whose little girl, Sodie "liked to wash her feet in soda water." Our family adored him as did his parents, brothers, sisters and all his nieces and nephews.

I thought I had come to know my uncle well before his death, but it was not until I began to read the letters he gave me, at first casually, then with growing absorption and fascination, that I realized what an extraordinary person he was. The letters are a story of life - both Lilburn Kingsbury's, his family's, and that of the Boonslick community. They record the places he went, the people he saw and related to, the things he did, and what was in his mind.

Lilburn was an inveterate letter-writer. Some people found his letters so interesting they could not bear to destroy them. Because so numerous letters were preserved, covering so many years, they in effect form a small but very precious library.

That library is Lilburn's legacy. The rich detail given of Boonslick Country life provides unique insights into social, cultural, and economic life of the area, and make a rich contribution to the social history of America.

The prolific, tasty fruit of Lilburn's letter-orchard of prose will provide many hours of delightful reading for readers who are not Kingsbury related. For the Kingsbury relationship, they constitute additionally a treasure to be prized, and savored (hopefully) by generations of Kingsburys yet to come.

How sad and what a loss it is that most people who live long, adventurous, interesting, lives, and contribute notably to their families and communities, die leaving little or no record of their presence and accomplishments for the enlightenment of those who follow.

"THE MAM LETTERS"

As a child of eight or nine, Lilburn attracted the attention of his Aunt Ida Smith, wife of one of his Mother's brothers, Tom Smith. Lilburn and Alma, the Tom Smith's youngest child, were born a month apart in 1884. They grew up, developing an affectionate brother-sister relationship, and both participated actively in social activities of the young people of the Boonslick community. Lilburn, in accordance with Southern custom, was taught to address women as "Ma'am," although he often used other endearing salutations. [Lilburn's spelling of "Mam" is adhered to throughout this book.]

When Alma married Homer Armstrong in 1911 and accompanied him to his ranch in Montana, Lilburn promised her he would keep her house-bound mother informed of the "goings on" of the young people of the community. Rural telephone service was then limited to "party lines." Lilburn didn't fancy entertaining listening in busy-bodies with accounts of his many social activities, so chose to write about them to Mam. He could write a letter at the bank, drop it in the Post Office that evening, and the rural route mail carrier would deliver it to Mam at Glenida the next day. Thus began a mutually pleasurable correspondence with Mam. When the Smiths sold Glenida and moved west to be with their children, Lilburn continued writing his Aunt Ida until her death in August 1921.

I was completely unaware of this close, affectionate relationship until 1980, when Lilburn gave me some of his memorabilia. Among these was a shoe-box full of letters with salutations such as "Golden Lamb," "My dearest Mam," "Dearest Little Mam Lady," and "Niftiest Nectarine." The first of these letters was written in August 1911; the last, July 14, 1921. Often the letters were signed "Your Loving Son." All were addressed to "Mam."

Lilburn confessed that during the early correspondence,

"I didn't know Mam as well as the letters would indicate until I began to write to her.

"Sometime before the turn of the century, I remember we went to visit at Glenida [the Tom Smith home] in preparation for a wedding at Cooper's Chapel. I was dressed for the affair and told to go outdoors and keep clean. I proceeded to trip and fall into the slop bucket outside the kitchen door. A tragedy, but I was laundered in time to go to the wedding. Alma, the daughter, and I became good friends. We were born Cousins the same year as were Albert Smith and Rose Dye, four babies to sisters and brothers in the Smith family."

Lilburn's writing Mam was more than courtesy; it was an act of humanitarianism, for she spent most of her life in a wheelchair, her activities circumscribed by a housebound world. Lilburn wrote,

"Mam, Aunt Ida Smith, Tom's wife, was shot accidentally by Earl, the oldest of the two sons, and became crippled from it so she was confined to her home. Not until automobile days did she ever get away from home. Then they could put her in a car. I was fond of Alma and went to her home every chance I got.

"Somehow, 'Mam' aroused my sympathy. She was an outgoing person. We used to think she poured apple sauce on everybody, but it was good to the feelings. She was so interested in what was going on outside and seemed interested in all my goings and comings, especially with the girls. I fell into the habit or way of writing to her. My inherent interest in writing letters first manifested itself in my letters to her. Unknown to me, she kept all the letters and returned them to me when she went west to be closer to her children."

A year or so later when I was visiting Lilburn, we drove up the Howard County Missouri river bottom road about nine miles above Boonville where Glenida had been. (It was razed about 1974.) From there one could look out over the river bottom to the bluffs of Arrow Rock. A beautiful view. According to Lilburn, Glenida was a 12-room, two storey natural brick house with outside woodwork painted white. He remembered it fondly as a comfortable, hospitable home which he always enjoyed visiting before his Uncle Tom and Aunt Ida moved west.

From the 291 letters which Lilburn wrote to "Mam" in this period, most are *not* included in their entirety but are excerpted in passages of greatest insight into the activities and personalities of Lilburn Kingsbury and the Boonslick Country people of whom he writes. During the time of their writing, Lilburn was a young man (aged 27 to 37) and was cashier of the Bank of New Franklin. He had started working at the bank in 1905 and was generally considered one of the community's most eligible young bachelors. In 1911, he became 27 years old, and had at least three serious love affairs, the last of which he reported to Mam was still "hanging by a string." He was, however, never heartbroken. Apparently the pain of one maiden's refusal was quickly alleviated by his discovery of another "little bit of loveliness." His letters indicate that it was a rare evening when he was not out with some girl "sweeter than the last."

Lilburn's Mam letters generally followed a pattern of reporting on his dating and social activities, the health and well-being of parents and relatives (including nieces and nephews), and such gossip and scandal as he had gleaned from bank clients transacting business at the cashier's window, or picked up as he made his business and social rounds. People loved to talk with him. Some seemed to bare their souls. The letters reveal a romantic young man, much more interested in girls than in his banking duties.

In this book the excerpts are grouped by year written. Many of his letters were not dated. In such cases, having been living in the area at the time the events written about occurred, I have usually been able to determine from content of the letter, the year and sometimes the month the letter was written. In some instances excerpts dealing with a specific topic have been placed together. For the most part, however, they are arranged in chronological or developmental sequence. In most cases I have omitted salutations and closes. Any necessary explanatory information has been bracketed [ ]. Unless in brackets, or otherwise identified, the textual material is taken verbatim from a Lilburn letter. Punctuation such as the use of parentheses, where Lilburn used double dashes, has been contemporized.

Readers of Lilburn's total letter output and these excerpts will find Lilburn occasionally using pejorative terms such as "niggers," "coons," "pickaninnies," and "darkies" as synonyms for Negroes. He calls Negroes who "know their place," "colored people." Some of the jokes he tells about Negroes are offensive for their condescending reflection upon Negro intelligence, capability, and morality. It should be explained that although this era in no way accepts or condones these things (and certainly neither the publisher nor I do), Lilburn was a product of the Boonslick culture and attitudes of the time, and thus unknowingly and unquestioningly Lilburn accepted Boonslick beliefs about, attitudes towards, and treatment of Negroes. These mores had been firmly ingrained in the emigrants from the deep South and were brought by them into the area, often along with their slaves. These folkways persisted tenaciously in Boonslick Country well into Lilburn's adulthood, and it was not until the later years of his life that Lilburn's attitudes and beliefs changed significantly—and that they finally did.

Despite such attitudes, Lilburn was highly regarded by the Negroes who worked for him and turned to him for assistance. If his departed spirit had been able to look down upon the funeral service held for him at the Clark's Chapel Cemetery, I believe nothing would have pleased him more than to see the placing of a rose on his casket by the son of long time Negro occupants of Fairview's tenant cottage who had named their boy, Lilburn Kingsbury Junior Shirley.

It gives me the greatest pleasure to imagine your enjoyment of these excerpts from my Uncle Lilburn's "Mam Letters," which are

Acts of kindness and care from
Lilburn Adkin Kingsbury to
Ida Casey Smith

— Warren Taylor Kingsbury, Ed. D.
Professor Emeritus, Arizona State University

Scottsdale, Arizona
September 1, 1990

Pump House and Filling Station—*About a year after the photo on page xii ("Summer Socializing") was taken, the pump was enclosed in the brick building shown. Gasoline pumps are at the two sides.*

Temperance Rally—*Under Missouri's "Local Option Law," an attempt was made to legalize the sale of liquor. The rally expressed opposition. The Citizens Bank Building seen in the background was bought by Lilburn for his office in the early twenties.*

1911

[Undoubtedly there were earlier letters, but the first one in the shoe-box Lilburn gave me described his Sister Lillian's wedding ceremony at Fairview.]

August 11 "THE DEED IS DONE, THE KNOT IS TIED!"

The quotation is one I read in the *Democrat Leader* in the write-up of a Boonsboro wedding, but it applies just as well to what happened at our house last Wednesday at half after two in the afternoon.

We were busy for a week or ten days getting ready for the big event. There was the front yard to water so we would have a little grass for the occasion. I transplanted the ferns that grew over in the big hollow into the beds around the porch and made big swinging baskets full of them to hang up. But there were big doings on the night before the eventful day and on that morning we had the decorating to finish up. We made a railing of asparagus fern all around the porch about two and a half feet high, wrapped the columns of the porch with it and had big bunches of it branching out at the top of the columns. We made it just thick enough to let the white columns show through. Our porch swing was outlined with asparagus greens, and we stuck a lot of it in the shutters of the windows on the porch. In the middle of the ceiling of the porch we made a sort of canopy of green under which the ceremony was performed. We concealed a contraption up there which contained about a pound of rice. On the porch we put a big green rug and several little ones to match it, with one covering the steps leading down into the yard. We put little chairs around for the "dear halt," the "dear lame," the "dear blind," the "dear aged," and the "dear young ones," too, who cared to sit down. The porch swing was reserved for Father and Mother.

Right back of the hall, a part of the back porch was screened off with green and white, and here Anna Rose *[Lillian and Lilburn's attractive, vivacious youngest sister, then 17 years old]* elected herself to serve punch, but she would forget it was her job time and hike off to see what was doing elsewhere. Therefore everybody served himself, and it was so good and there was so much of it one could drink as much as he liked without being halted. Mary Dimmitt of Fayette mixed it, and she is so good and sweet herself her punch was bound to be fine. In the dining room we used branches of wild cherries, banked the mantle, the side board and made them stick up above the lace curtains. Then we put asparagus green in to make a more graceful effect. In the center of the long table we had a big cut glass bowl full of bride's roses, resting on a big mirror, and around the edge of the table cloth we had a lot of hot-house greenery.

The wedding gifts were displayed on this table which was lit by white candles with green shades in cut glass and brass candlesticks. The guests were served here in the dining room or out on the porch, and the brick ice cream was white with the green heart in the center. Angel food cake was served with the cream.

We did not try to entertain or take care of any of the guests who came from a distance as we knew there was not as much room in our house as there is in our hearts. Cousin Nell and Cousin Ada took some and another lady in town cared for the rest. It was for only a short time, however, as most of them came on the 6:30 a.m. train and left at 4 p.m. Mary Dimmitt and Jane Carol came to our house that morning. I went to the depot in a big white car which crept along pretty fast and scared all the horses and buggies into their places before Mary, Jane, Carl and I came out home for breakfast. It was sure hot and before seven in the morning we were all wearing chains of perspiration beads. Lillian was up and doing and so was Anna Rose, but the latter spent the preceding day at Sulphur Springs and Rocheport and had had only a little peck at sleep. Mother was having hot spells and was all excited and working herself up to a fine pitch, so we gave her Alice Virginia and Baby Jean to keep out in the yard and they kept her so busy she almost forgot Lillian was going away with Carl. By noon everything was ready. We ate fried chicken and sandwiches out of our hands out in the yard and sweltered. Pretty soon after one we got into our best togs, and it was none too soon for the crowd began to come early, as if to get good seats. Aunt Lena and Ida and her family of two and the Tom Smiths were the first to arrive. *[Apparently Lilburn wrote this letter as a general letter for the information of out of state relatives, making carbon copies. And so he recorded the arrival of Mam, Mrs. Tom Smith, in a letter she received. It is notable, too, for this probably was Mam's first automobile ride.]* It was good to see Aunt Ida in her chair and Grannie too. They came down in an automobile in about two jiffies but were nearly cooked by the sun and hot wind along the road. It was moderately cool on the porch though, or perhaps the greenery made it look that way. The bride was ready an hour before time and was wondering why the groom did not appear. We had arranged for a Boonville machine to come across the first trip of the ferry after dinner and bring him and some of the guests out. At two o'clock the big Winton [automobile] carrying the Billie Kingsburys had a tire puncture just below Rob's house, and the next car which came along picked up Sister Julia who came on to bear the tale of woe that the machine engaged by Carl was not coming at all and that something must be done quickly to get him out in time for the wedding. It seems that the Billie Kingsburys were all coming in the machine that was to carry the wedding party. They had been ready for an hour to start and were "up on their ear" when the phone rang, and someone told them that they had been asked by Gillis Windsor, Lillian's old flame, to notify them that if they expected to go over to the wedding, they would have to go some other way as the Viertel machine was not going over. Whether Gillis found it out and called up through kindness of heart or whether he was merely playing the devil, we do not know. We have never heard any explanation from the Viertel garage and there surely could not have been a misunderstanding, for Lillian phoned the garage that morning and gave instructions for the driver. It lends a romantic flavor to think that Gillis did spite work, but I believe he just found out that that machine was not coming and someone had to call Billie, for Gillis has always shown himself to be a gentleman, and I do not think he would resort to a dirty trick, especially after Lillian had granted his last request that he not be mailed a wedding invitation.

We sent a couple of machines that were there at the house to town quickly and got everyone out in good time. But to go back. Billie phoned to the other garage which had not been engaged because of a stiff double charge for coming across the river. The man had not had his dinner and was sore because he had not been given the job, but Billie argued with him and got him strung out on the road to our place as quickly as possible. Mrs. Charlie Leonard came over to Billie's and offered her limousine which is sure a rich folk's thing, but Billie had made the other arrangement. I am sorry the limousine was not forthcoming because I would have had a ride in it with the bride and groom. As it is, I never expect to press my backbone against the gorgeous cushions of that machine.

Rev. Stout drove up in a big red car and brought his part of the crowd. Why, there was such a honking and snorting around of the machines in the yard, I hesitated to step off the porch lest I should be mangled.

Billie's William had talked all the way over, and for several days previous about how he wanted to "see Aunt Lillian in her bridal gown" and he kept on, so Sister Julia brought him upstairs and told him to behold the fair lady. He just stood and looked and Lillian said, "Bless your heart, come give me a kiss." He stepped back and continued to stare at her and his eyes filled and tears streamed down his cheeks. Lillian said everybody in the room then "broke down." This was my first weak spot. She made us all skin out of the room so she wouldn't spoil her best face. I went on down the steps and there was *[my first cousin]* Helen *[Smith]* on the stairs and tears streaming down her face. I hadn't seen the little child for five weeks, and she had been entirely out of touch with all the wedding plans of her dearest pal. Well, we kissed each other and I cried on her shoulder at the risk of getting a scarlet fever germ. She had stopped on the steps a little while trying to get her face straight so she could go up and see Lillian, but she couldn't get a clutch on herself. Finally we both went upstairs and neither of us had any more sinking spells.

Jane Carroll played the wedding march, "Lohengrin's," and the accompaniment for "Call Me Thine Own" which Ida Kardell sang very sweetly. Brother Stout used the ring ceremony very impressively as the fine looking pair stood beneath the canopy of asparagus. Immediately after the ceremony the groom took a kiss and at that moment the pound of rice from above showered over them. They both had been warned of it but had forgotten and they jumped as if they had been shot. This stunt proved interesting to all, and they wanted to know how it happened. Sister Minnie had pulled small invisible wires which ran to the "trip-latch." Then there was a general kissing all around as is usual at affairs of this kind.

There was just an hour and fifteen minutes from the time of the ceremony until their train departed so things were quite rushed for Lillian. She looked right stunning when she came down in her going away clothes. Her suit was of dark blue voile over messaline. It had black bands around the collar and sleeves and black satin buttons. The waist was of white lace with the blue thin stuff over it. Her hat was a big one of white felt with just a band of brown velvet on it. Her hair looked so pretty in contrast with the dark blue. Brown suede shoes and a brown suede bag. Carl gave her a beautiful pendant of pearls with a cameo in the center. But the principal thing she wore was the smile from head to foot it seemed, and so did the groom. Anna Rose, Helen and I rode in the machine with them to the train, and the other machines filled with as many as could get in, and we all went down to wave them out of sight.

Lillian in her Wedding Dress

Newlyweds Lillian and Carl Edmonston "going away."

Anna Rose had boasted that she was one who would not weep at a wedding. She saw William "weep," and it must have started a weep for her as she cried the whole time and was the only one who did shed tears on the porch. I was glad no-one else felt glad to over-flowing. Mother got through as chipper as you please, and one of Carl's sisters-in-law on whom we had depended to furnish a regular flood just stood and bit her lip and didn't cry a drop. I don't want to attend another wedding where there is so much crying the bride gets to going, too. We were talking at home last night and all of us said it was just like Lillian had gone away for a visit somewhere. She and Carl have rooms at 609 West Broadway in Sedalia and will play at house-keeping this winter. His work keeps him in Moberly about half the time.

We, the brothers, and Father gave them the knives, forks, tea spoons, and bullion spoons and a steak set in the Paul Revere pattern. Aunt Ida and Uncle Tom and Grannie, the salad forks; the Tindalls the chocolate spoons and Aunt Lill the dessert spoons in that pattern. They got a number of odd pieces. The Canterbury spoons are much like them. There were two other sets of spoons in beautiful patterns and a whole lot of things like berry and sugar spoons and salad and cold meat servers. Ida and Mr. Kardell and the Bells gave them a set of cut glass tumblers and a pitcher in the thistle pattern on a big round mirror. Lots of other cut glass, bowls, a jelly stand, one small vase, a large one and napkins galore. A clock, some china, a set of Haviland China from the Edmonstons, electric iron, pearl-handled butter spreaders, a whole table full of linens, some beautiful embroidery, and a hand made quilt from an old lady friend of Carl's who is 80 years old. Mr. and Mrs. Wallace Estill gave them a solid silver bread tray. There was a lemon set in glass and silver filigree. And a lot of things I don't recall. Uncle A.W. Kingsbury sent a check for $25.00.

Miss Berndt made some beautiful things for Lillian's trousseau. One brown dress I thought the prettiest of all, with such beautiful trimming on it. The blue dress was handsome, trimmed in white messaline and black velvet. Those things all looked pretty hot in August but fall will soon be here.

I wish everyone of you could have been here. Everybody had a good time and things happened on schedule except the Gillis Windsor episode. It was a happy solemn occasion, and the memory of it will be with me for years. I was as tired as a dog after it was over, but every lick I hit was a love lick and I had the time of my life fixing up for it.

THE COMING OF THE MACHINE

["Machines," as Lilburn referred to automobiles for some time, were still a rarity in 1911. Some years later, when he had become interested in Boonslick Country History and was reading early New Franklin News *files, he noted several interesting references to early "machines."]*

1904   An automobile passed through New Franklin last week. Most everybody got a sight of the auto as it passed.

1906   Ferd Arn came over from Boonville Tuesday afternoon with Jim Butler's automobile. He had been repairing it for Mr. Butler of Fayette who came down on the train the same afternoon and took the automobile from here to Fayette.

Homer Wade has ordered an automobile and expects to get it in about two weeks. This makes two of the machines for New Franklin. Homer says he is tired seeing Will Boggs *[the bachelor bank President]* sailing around with a horse and buggy making "goo goo" eyes at the girls while he has to walk along and look down his nose. Already the young ladies of marriageable age are smiling at Homer as he passes by and eagerly speak to him across the street. It's as exciting as a piano contest to see who gets the first ride.

[A few months later]

Homer Wade had a bad breakdown on the engine of his automobile Tuesday and he informs us he will not attempt to have it repaired, at least for the present.

WINTON SIX

[Shortly after Lillian's wedding. Lilburn writes:]

Saturday night I went over to Billie's and we got in the Winton Six and rode until the rain drove us into a picture show which was real good. Sister Julia said your house *[Glenida]* was one of the first places she wanted to ride to in that car. She sure has got the riding bee. The car eats up more gasoline in proportion to its size than I do *grub*. It has been in commission three weeks and 65 gallons of gasoline has been fizzled away. When Billie told me that, I just begged him to go right to the garage, that maybe I was riding more than my share and should get out. But the Billies are so nice, they let me go right on riding.

Sunday it just poured company. By the time we got through dinner, the Winton Six was at the door with Mr. Taylor *[Mrs. W.W. Kingsbury's father]*, Billie, Julia, and all the kiddies. And Billie reloaded the car with Mother, Father, Rob, Margeret, Alice Virginia, Jean, and Baby Julia and took them for a ride up to Fayette. While they were gone, a load of the Billie Smiths drove up in their new Cadillac and when we got together after the return from Fayette, some of us had to sit outdoors. Albert Smith took Anna Rose, Miss Biddle and me riding late in the afternoon, and we speeded up to 35 to 40 miles an hour on one straight stretch. That was exciting and fast enough to begin with.

"Us Winton Six," as Baby Julia has always called it, is a dark green car with red lines, and a neat little monogram, "J.T.K.," adorns the back doors. The monogram is red like the lines. Mr. Taylor gave the car to Julia for her birthday. Billie told me the car cost Mr. Taylor more than $3000.00.

"Us Winton Six"

I went over to Boonville last night and we went out on the Santa Fe Trail past Lamine for a delightful drive, and I can't find any fault with "Us Winton Six" at all. It went right up the steepest and longest hills "on high." You know, the more hills you can make "on high," the more you congratulate yourself for owning that kind of car. It is pretty special. It has little seats for two between the big seats. The car contains the Billies exactly, counting Nurse Bales.

The new concrete driveway at the Billies is finished and the garage of red brick with concrete floor will soon be ready. Billie has had a pit built in the floor so he can get under the car to grease it. The garage is built like a bungalow with overhanging roof of green shingles and colonial doors. It nestles back amongst the apple trees on the lot and is big enough to hold two Wintons. I sure enjoyed my visit and ride last night.

FAIRVIEW "KETCHED ON FIRE"

Don't you know we have something to be thankful for today? We barely missed being out in all this rain with nothing but a rag here and there adorning us, for our roof tree "ketched on fire" last night about half past nine while all the "men folks" were in town. Mother, Anna Rose, and Ruth *[the dress-maker who had come in to make Anna Rose's college wardrobe]* had the time of their lives playing Fire Department. If I were Carnegie, I would give Anna Rose a medal. But she is quite as happy to have all her new school clothes intact.

Anna Rose was in bed asleep. Ruth was sitting up reading (both upstairs), and Mother was doing her Saturday night "rinsing" in her room below. Just at that time when she went back to the time she was born, and didn't have a raveling of clothes on, she aimed to set the lamp on the table and missed the table, and the lamp hit the floor, exploded, and Mom was 'most eating fire. She called for clothes to cover her, and blankets to smother the fire. Ruth and Anna Rose came pouring down the steps and Ruth commenced screaming. She thought Mother was on fire and ran from house to the front road with her curdling cries which nobody heard. A.R. beat it to the cistern, found a tub under the spout, and pumped and hollered, "Oh! Won't somebody come, ditto-ditto!"—carried the water in by herself and turned it on the flames. Then she "flew" upstairs and got the new dresses and as many more as she could and put them outside in safety, returned to the tub and brought more water in, phoned to Phone Office and "done real noble." All this time poor Mother was hunting a fig leaf, wringing her hands and giving distress signals, and had Ruth hunting for some clothes. Ruth brought her a cloak, or I should say, jacket, which wouldn't do at all. Father, Horace, Sister Minnie, Louis and I were on the street in front of the Phone Office when Central called out the window that A.R. had phoned that Kingsbury's house was burning. We beat it, Mam, it was the quickest trip and seemingly the longest we ever made, and we kept watching the horizon for the blaze. When we got in sight of home, there wasn't a speck of light, so we knew the fire was out. About twenty men got there about the time we did to view the ruins: lace curtains, window shades, dresses, table, chairs, rug, bed clothes, clothing, and pictures and wall paper burned off one side clear to the ceiling. Anna Rose certainly did wonderfully to extinguish it.

There is always a funny side, and we have laughed at Ruth for thinking Mother was afire when she was real nude. Anna Rose had a big cry as soon as I got there with my shoulder. The weeping ceased abruptly when all the men came trooping in, and she realized she was standing there barefoot in her night gown. She hurried upstairs for more clothing. We tease Mother about not putting on clothes when Ruth brought her a jacket. I'd better tell you she did find something before we got there, and oh, such a kissing around. Kissing sure seemed to come natural, for we were all so thankful that nobody was burned. (A.R. stepped in fire once but didn't burn much.) All the stuff is insured, but money don't comfort when the loved ones get hurt, and that was what we had feared might happen while we were rushing home. Mother is in bed, and Ruth is all scattered around. She says she is certainly going away, a fire and "pizenin" are enough for her.

ta ta ta ta ta

September 15   "ALL SWEATED DOWN AND ASMELLING"

This is a railroad payday and time has to be spread around a hundred different places, so I will just type a note today.

[New Franklin was a division point, where express trains switched crews and locomotives for the Missouri, Kansas, and Texas Railroad, with approximately 300 employees there.]

I do so hope the "storm within" has subsided and left a most happy calm by this time. Inside unhappiness is the worst that is. And this is such bad weather to entertain it. When the weather is like this, I sure do work off a lot of fuss on that old broom that cleans out this bank. That broom could tell things worse than the dog did in the book we read. By the time I get all cleaned out and dusted, I am wet all over, and the dust in the air settles on me, and when the ladies come in, it is mortifying to be all sweated down and asmelling. When I get to be President, I am going to have a boy to sweep out. I may have to go to Mary Cary's Asylum for Boys to get him. I would rather sweep than raise one.

When Lillian and Anna Rose both left, our upstairs looked like the "folks had moved out." They took all the furnishings. It is so still after evening creeps around us, that it is almost lonesome. As Mother says, she and Father are almost to the place where they started in to raise a family.

The insurance adjuster has not yet come, and everything is as it was the night of the fire. We are weary waiting for him, as we would like to go ahead with the repairs.

Brother Horace lost a fine mule yesterday from over-heating, and we lost a fine hog the same way. I don't know what Horace did with his mule, but we are eating our hog and pork chops do taste so good. We needed the meat anyway to feed the six negroes and more who eat in the kitchen. Mayme sure sets a good table for the coons. Her Montgomery man has lit here, and Mayme is all smiles. Mother did not "low" to take any roomers, but Mayme 'lowed she would take one. She does the work very nicely, and the back end of the house is "a-goin" fine now.

ﻊ ﻊ ﻊ ﻊ ﻊ

October 14   "STRIKEY NEGROES ACCEPTED ANYWAY"

It is still as night today, so I will just do a little writing while nobody needs such a thing as a banker and his wares.

The insurance company has made its settlement for the fire damage, the building is under way, rather the foundation, and I hope the cellar foundation can be completed by tomorrow so the part of the house that sticks up in the air can be commenced. The men seem to work so slow and the dollars count up so fast.

I started to read Gibbie to Mother, and she snored right out loud in such an interrupting manner that I had to poke her with my foot and wake her up. And when I examined her to find where she "let off" and quit hearing, she had missed five pages and me with weak eyes and poor voice!!! Mother and I have been keeping ourselves cheerful for nearly a week now since Father went to Texas. Poor Mother gets so lonesome without her beau. Father's absences always give Mother a chance to feel how it would be like if he should die. Father went to Texas to dispose of the apples, but since his departure we have made several sales, and we wrote him today to come on in as we think we can place everything.

Last night the negroes we have to feed at the house got kinda "strikey" about the barn beds they have to sleep on and right after supper, every copper or ink-skinned face disappeared out of the kitchen.

We thought the whole population had gone, but Mayme came back and said to Mother: "Mrs. K., if Irv goes, I'll have to go, too." Now when the cook talks of going, the thought of Mother having all that work to do just paralyzes me, and I wondered if things were going to the bad, but this a.m. the quivering of their stomachs brought them back. Mayme saves all the chicken livers and pieces of cake for Irv. He eats either before or after the colored "riff-raff," and she gives him Post Toasties and Mam, we don't even have them either. Yesterday Mother was putting pineapple in the canned apples, and Mayme saved about half a can of it for her beau. You could just laugh until you hurt to see Mother cabbage on to me and pull me out of sight into some room or corner and hear her say, "Don't you know Mayme cut off most of that best steak for Irv?" or, "Let me tell you something, Mayme gave Irv nearly half a box of raisins." And then Mother says, "Oh! well, it's all right. I couldn't get along without her." I never get the choicest delicacies because I know Irv gets them. Mother will sure have a new tale to tell me tonight, and we just say, how awful it is, and then say it is all right.

October 25   DONATION PARTY

My lunch is setting so heavy I wish I were a boa constrictor snake so I could crawl off and take a nap. When I left home, Mother was asthmatic, and I told her not to pester herself about lunch for me. I went by Margaret's, and she fixed one for me. Later, Mother had a chance to send along her "few bites." When I opened it all out, it looked like I had been given a "donation party." *[Church congregations in small rural towns were not able to pay their preachers well. In addition to supplying them with a parsonage, from time to time the congregation would have a "donation party" with members donating to the preachers family canned goods and fruit, preserves, jam, and jelly, etc.]* I wonder if preacher folks gorge themselves after one like I did today. I never like to take anything home in my lunch box. The fixers seem to regard any "leavins" as a warning that I "ain't got no taste" for their special little grublet. I feel like I have a tumor.

My pin that Clara sent from Japan came through all right in the queerest little "do-up" —a little handmade wooden box and stuck inside was the quaintest little pad. It is what I thought it was, a chrysanthemum of gold and silver inlaid on a base metal. Then there is a little gold rim around that. The petals of flowers are of silver and the centers, leaves, and stalks are in gold. It is so odd, and I am very glad to possess it. I selected Clara's Christmas present and have sent it on to the Santa Claus transport. She should have it by December 10th, an early celebration. It was a very pretty pendant in gold with some real pearls pasted on it and an amethyst drop dangling off. It looked classy to me. My most bothersome Christmas shopping is done.

"CHESTER WHITE PIG"

All the Billies are well. There are so many children over there, and do you know I forgot all about the baby until they called him "Jere." They spoke of him as the "Chester White Pig" and asked me if I had seen it. I couldn't find my recollection for a minute or two. Jere is a healthy looking little piece—white as snow with prettiest rosy cheeks. They call him Jere Lilburn when I am there and maybe after I leave. I never stayed to hear.

November 22   REMODELING

I do not know when we will get through with our remodeling. It is no use to plan to be "finished" by any time. The water tank that is to be buried has not come, nor the bath fixtures, so Mr. Geiger has nothing to come over for. He has finished the sewers. We had some more plastering done yesterday and have to wait until it dries good before John Long can finish papering. We are having all the woodwork in the upstairs rooms painted white and enameled, but the painter seems to get along very well. I am sick talking house, and all the men tell tales on the others until I think I have a real nest of rascals, and it is a nuisance.

Anna Rose has not been home and says she could stay until Christmas if she had to. However, she is planning to bring her new girl friends and new beaux home with her the Saturday after Thanksgiving for a weekend party if the house is finished. Next Sunday, if the day is pretty, we look for some of the Brothers and Sisters and their children to spend the day. Mother has been holding them off for about as long as she can.

GINGER'S APOLOGY

I do not think I told you how Alice Virginia apologized to Mother, did I? Ginger had sat on the chair long enough to repent but would not beg Mother's pardon, so of course, she and the chair did not part company. In due time, Alice said, "I beg your pardon, Grandmother Kingsbury, you nasty stinking thing." Then Mother said she would have to apologize again, and she said: "I've begged your pardon once and that's enough." She stayed on the chair a long, long time. I think she will be the story teller of the family as her imagination is the rankest growing thing I ever saw. I try to tell her a wonderful made up story and she adds a little more to it after I get through.

December 11   DECISIONS! DECISIONS!

Well, we ain't never going to get in the straight life again, it seems. After one has lived crooked so long, it is hard to be a real new person. We won't be done before Christmas. Ain't that the limit? That Groundhog, John Finn, is going right through to China, and we will soon have our new cistern. I'm all bum-fuddled about the chandeliers. I don't know whether we want Belle Davis's old truck or not. I change my mind after every conversation with anyone about them. Some say that glass prisms are just heavenly homes for flies. So I have not placed the fixtures order yet.

"CLIPPETY-CLIPPED"

Rob and Mag have begun their remodeling, and the upstairs of their house is being pushed to a finish. Mother has charge of the daughters of the household, and Sunday morning Billie K. heard a racket in Mother's room and went in. A.V. had Jean backed into a corner by the dresser and was saying, "Now little sister, be still just a minute. I'll be through pretty soon." And as she gathered bunches of Jean's hair with her left hand, she clippety-clipped a pair of scissors in the right. Baby Jean was fast becoming bald. A.V. had already shorn herself of all curls around her face and had put all the hair, as she whacked it off, into a little drawer of the dresser. We have two pretty kids? Nix! They look like hoodlums.

THE STAIRWAY'S GONE

Billie and Julia were over yesterday between trains and liked our house very much. They said they could appreciate Warren's comments—"Well, Grandmother, everything is just beautiful, but the stairway's gone!" Warren thought it was a very long way upstairs now, and the night he was over and he knew it was getting bedtime, he kept looking at the corner where the old lift used to be, no doubt thinking he used to be safer when he could go straight up. Neither he nor William would say he was sleepy, although their eyes stuck out, until Grandmother said she would go upstairs with them.

I have found a rug, a Kalliston, which is reversible and about an inch thick. It is a solid grayish blue with a tan strip around the border. Wish you could see Grandfather Horace K's old bookcase. It has had one coat of shellac, and it shines like a mirror. Next, it gets a coat of crystal varnish, then a rub-down with oil and pumice stone, then a little waxing, and it promises to look so good none of Grandfather's three wives would know it, if they should see it. I am still scraping hall woodwork, and the end of that is afar off.

NO CHRISTMAS PARTY

Two weeks from today and Santa's whiskers will be froze off—maybe. We are not planning a Christmas party this year, and Anna Rose and I will probably be the only ones at home. I wish we had our good Christmas times of a few years ago to do over again. Christmas doesn't mean as much to me as it used to. I'm glad Sunday and Christmas come together, so I'll have two days to do nothing.

1912

BANKING

[Lilburn went to work in 1905 as Cashier of the Bank of New Franklin.

At that time the bank was open week days from 8:00 a.m. until 4:00 p.m. and, on Saturdays, from 8 until noon. Lilburn, a woman clerk, and the President, his cousin Will Boggs, the principal stockholder, were the only employees. Because of this, Lilburn performed most of the routine chores such as dusting the fixtures, sweeping out, fetching a bucket of the bachelor President's favorite drinking water from a friendly widow's cistern a half block away, unlocking the vault and safe doors, bringing out the books and the money to be ready for business at eight o'clock. In cold weather he also had to start the coal fire to warm the place up. To get to the bank by seven a.m., in order to do all this, he had to get up at five-thirty, fix his breakfast and lunch, and walk from Fairview into town.

He writes of the surprise he experienced one morning in late November.]

As I inserted my key in the front door to admit myself, I noticed through the glass that everything was gray with dust. Strange! What in the world? When I stepped inside a peculiar odor permeated the air. This was stranger still. Then I saw the vault door wide open with hammer, an auger, steel drills and the empty money rack on the floor in front of it. Inside the vault was a tangled mass of gunny sacks, timothy hay, and straw. The money safe, cleared of debris, had its door blown open and was empty.

He quotes from the New Franklin News *of Nov. 29, 1907:*

"From the best evidence at hand, it seems the burglars went to the New Franklin depot and took a wheelbarrow. With this they hauled a load of hay, straw and sacks from the mill. These were spread over the safe before the shot was fired to deaden the noise of the explosion. From the mill they came up Howard Street to Merchants Street, thence to the bank. They entered through the side door.

This door was locked with the key left in the key hole on the inside, so they must have had some instrument to get hold of the key and unlock the door.

"Before entering the bank, they had gone across the street to McKinley's blacksmith shop and secured an auger brace, several steel drills and a large hammer. They tried to break the combination lock off the vault door but gave that up and drilled a hole just opposite the bolt which held the door shut. The drill partially cut this bolt in two and it was then broken with a hammer and punch. Every movement showed the work of experts. The charge tore the door completely off the safe but didn't harm the vault to any considerable extent. Except for a hole or two in the plaster of the ceiling, one would not notice after the debris was removed that an explosion had occurred within the vault."

The loss was fully covered by insurance, but despite substantial rewards offered, the guilty parties were never found.

April 3

Yesterday was election day in town. There is another little bank in this "Human Ant Hill," and until last year they had all the school moneys and funds of the city, and had handled it for years, and we could not get it divided with us for love nor money. Last year we put up a little fight, and it resulted in the accounts being brought to us. This year our worthy competitor was "going to do us up," and for weeks he had some man smelling the situation and has been working hide, meat, hair, tooth and toe-nail, skin and bones, to get school directors and city aldermen elected who would favor him. I am informed they put out cigars, fifty cent pieces, and somebody dispensed thirst swigs and other grand inducements to the nigger element especially. We did not make a fight except in a quiet way, and all who applied here for "vote money" were not encouraged enough to vote for the men who would help us most. Those who voted for the men who are our friends did so because they believed in those men. It was a very close contest, and I had to phone Mother to send every pair of suffraged breeches on the place to town, and the four votes from there saved us one director. We won two out of three to elect and that gives us a majority on the board. In the city election, we also got what we wanted. Cousin Will and I are mighty proud this morning that we got it without it costing a cent, and we did not do anything unfair. I never saw so many nigger bucks lined up against us, with their "big seegars." Some we have befriended had better pray for hard times to let up, for they fell into the hands of the Philistines, and Cousin Boggs done said he is goin' to fix 'em. This morning at dawn I crowed, and I have been cackling all morning. I think you will cackle, too, and that is why I must tell you right away. Just cackle cause the voters left them golden eggs in me and Cousin Bogg's nest. All during the day we felt like our nest was being robbed, and if we did not squawk and peck as much as a settin' hen, we had her feeling.

"JUST STATING THE FACTS"

This is Saturday, the end of the week. Which reminds me with exception of two days when I was sick last Christmas, I have not failed to work out the daily balance sheet every day since a year ago today. I have used the tail-end of a few days, but after my regular work was laid away. I don't know that this stick-it-outness has been any benefit to me either, so I'm not boasting of the record. I am just stating the facts.

May 28 WEATHER

The wind tore through the west side of New Franklin last night and blew all the telephone poles down, tangling wires very badly. Trees came to pieces and in some places they came out by the roots. It tore a lot of limbs off trees in our yard but it lasted just a jiff, and we didn't have time to get apprehensive. About ten o'clock, Louis went out to see about the chickens, and one coop containing 105 month-old chicks was without a roof, and don't you know how I made a fire in our range in a hurry. We actually filled the floor of the oven and the warming closet with the practically dead chicken bodies and het them back to consciousness. The last tubful were hopeless looking, for they had been floating around in the water without life preservers. All but three "come to" after we gave first aid to the injured. They were all we lost. All were Black Minorcas in that lot and worth saving.

More rain, more rain, but "Some days must be dark and dreary!" I never will forget what a doleful hole was dug into my sensibilities when I heard a girl recite that piece in school when I was at an *impressionable age.*

RELIGION

[The Kingsburys were Southern Methodists. Lilburn's parents were "pillars of the Church." As such they attended church regularly and eschewed liquor, card-playing and dancing which the Methodists adamantly opposed at that time. It was customary when a church member was a bank officer to have him as a member of the Board of Stewards and as church treasurer. Thus Lilburn found himself serving in that capacity, as well as regularly playing the piano or organ. Services were then conducted Sunday mornings and evening. Prayer meetings were held Wednesday evenings and several times during the year there would be revival meetings featuring visiting evangelists who held services daily. Occasionally there would be a "Protracted Meeting" that might continue two weeks or more. Lilburn frequently found himself torn between his desire to comport himself in accordance with parental and church teachings and participation in frowned-upon social activities of his peers. This conflict is evident in some of the excerpts describing religious activities.]

BLESSED OUT

There isn't much news up to date, for we have done nothing but go to church every blessed night, and get blessed out for not coming every blessed afternoon. Preacher Crowe said the business men of this place remind him of a lot of little ants, too much important business to leave for an hour in which to worship God. He said last night this was the first place he has preached where officers of the church had not been inside the church in a month of protracted meetings, and one official was out every Friday night, to the tango, he supposes. I got credit for being *it*, as the only one who leans toward things terpsichorean, and I got warmer inside than the tango ever made me, for I have not been away from church on Friday night, the only tango night in town, since the Crowe came. And what is more, I haven't indulged any other night. Heretofore, I have had the idea that Crowe always knew what he was talking about, but I have my doubts now. He says if we say anything against him, we sin against God, so I guess I better talk about something else.

Baby Jean is all time nearly breaking up the meeting. Yesterday afternoon she went with Mother and the preacher said he wished all those who accept Christ to say so. Mother said, "I accept Jesus," and Baby Jean spoke out, "I do." The preacher said "God Bless You." And last Sunday Rob and Margeret thought it would be lovely to take the kids to the children's service in the afternoon. The children sat up in the front seats, and the grown people, lots of them, were back of the children. In the course of his talk, the preacher said, "Now when you obey your Mama and your Papa and are good, you feel so good, but when you are bad the old devil is in you. Did you ever feel like you wanted to cuss, punch everybody in the face, smoke cigarettes . . . ."

"*Dad* did it. *Dad* did it," interrupted Jean, and the preacher had to call the people down ten minutes after for laughing. Jean explained afterward that "Dad smoked a cigarette," but of course most people were left to wonder *what* DAD DID? Later Jean was telling me about going to the altar and kneeling down, and I asked her what she did it for, and she said, "To pray to God and I knelt like a horse." 'Tis said she almost laid down on her stomach and doing one prayer she got her head fastened under the bench in front of her.

The other day at the table she kept asking for something, and no one paid any attention to her, so finally she said "*Dad*, don't you want to make your kid happy?" Recently she told Sue Herndon that "Mother always makes herself happy before she makes her kids happy." But enough of Baby Jean. Rob was terribly embarrassed in church and says he is going to leave that kid at home until she gets older.

We had Crowe for supper one evening and enjoyed his visit. He is a very interesting man with lots of "experiences" to relate, some of which beat anything I have ever seen at Mt. Calvary Temple Church at the river. About people falling in a faint on the floor and one mother came up wringing her hands saying, "Oh, Bro. Crowe, I'm afraid Mary is dying," and he said, "Sister, I wish you were dying just like her, just let her alone, unloosen her collar and put up the window," and Mary was some Christian when she "come thu." One man fell down right in the road and could not get up for crying, and numerous times he himself has been struck dumb with emotion or the Holy Spirit. He paints me mighty bad.

ಶ ಶ ಶ ಶ ಶ

Mother was going to church this morning and was losing her petticoat as she was going in. She rushed into a fence she did not see trying to get over to a house next door, knocked on the front door and when nobody came, she went around this house and ran onto the man of the house. She said, "Can't you let me into your house for a minute, I am losing some of my paraphernalia," and the man who did not know her, was a scandal-fearing married man, and, says he, "My wife is not at home," so Mother went on around back of the house and fixed her skirt. Well, I told Mother I was awfully sorry she did not tell the man her skirt was coming off, for it will be reported all over town that it was drawers. And she said she wished she had too.

Lilburn and his mother, Alice, on the porch dressed for church

PIETY

Going to meeting is just as hard on the system as doing society, yet nobody gets censored for attending church seven nights out of the week. I have missed two evenings this week, but hope to make good the rest of the time. I am getting all bench-backed. Last week, Rev. Crowe said he wasn't going to keep us sitting still so long, but he hasn't made us feel the difference. He keeps saying that of all the places he has been, we are the worst, when it comes to back-sliding and indifference, so I just feel like heading my letter "Sodom and Gomorrah." I have just heard that Sister Allison, the local minister's wife, heard Anna Rose talking in C.C.'s store last Monday and put in, "Are you going away?" Anna Rose said, "Yes, to Columbia to a big tango ball." Mrs. A. told her she ought to be ashamed, and Minnie Lee told Margaret she thought it a shame for A.R. to say what she did to Sister Allison. Oh! You ever-bubbling pot. I scolded A.R. for being *plain [speaking truthfully]* to Sister Allison. There was no use sticking a thorn in her flesh. Bro. Allison hasn't been in to see me since he found me gone Tuesday. I fear he has classed me with the wolves. He used to run in every day or two. But I am here to tell him, I only chaperoned Anna Rose and never *no more than looked* on at the ball. He need not know I wanted to do more, which puts me in the sinner class just the same as if I had dipped my legs in twain, if tango *is* the sin they call it.

ಶ ಶ ಶ ಶ ಶ

I am getting in the habit of dropping in Herndons on my way home from German class and playing casino with Sue and Em. They are sure jolly. Now I am backsliding to cards, but cards aren't any worse than anything else I do, and I do feel like I'd love to know the Turkey Trot. I am getting so I don't care for the higher plane since Clara Woodson has admitted she used to *drink cocktails* now and then!!! It's a happy-go-lucky world we're living in, and it's astonishing how little thought some of us give to what would happen if the end should come and bring judgment upon us. I'm honest when I say I'd be skeered into too weak a shape to ever ask any kind of favor of St. Peter, and I know *where* I'd go. If the Big Gates were to get rusty and would creak on their hinges, it would be the closest thing to Heavenly music I'd hear, being outside. You'd be inside playing a gold pianner [piano], apt as not having too good a time to remember me.... Well, I must get busy and try to be good enough to get in, even if I have to crawl under the side of the tent. I would be satisfied if I'd get a jews-harp to musicalize.

Early Fall A BIG MESS

The Cooperative Revival Meeting in Boonville broke up in a big mess Sunday night, and I wish I had time to tell you all about it. The Christian minister got up and made a talk on the uselessness of union meetings and said the devil smiles every time they hold one and [that] there was nothing in his Bible to uphold any such meetings. I'll tell you about it anyhow! The meeting was a "love feast" and a number of ministers and laymen had made short talks on the blessings of Christian Unity. Weldon, the Christian, had been out of town all summer and the German minister, seeing him in the crowd, asked Bro. Smith, the Methodist, to ask Weldon to make a few remarks. Then followed Weldon's "insult." While Weldon was speaking, Bro. Smith arose and said the congregation would receive the benediction. The Presbyterian minister made a beautiful prayer and following that the German minister made a public apology to Bro. Smith for having informed him Weldon was in the meeting. Weldon said he would like to finish his remarks and Smith said, "We would be glad to hear you, if you were a gentleman." This talking back happened just after Smith called for the dismissal. Now ain't that some church Christianity?

"A LITTLE MISUNDERSTANDING"

I went to the nigger camp meeting that night so missed the racket. The nigger minister said, "To be a Christian, the sensational nerve has got to awaken," and "Though your sins be black as scarlet, they shall be white as snow," and announced they would now sing "Nero my God to Thee." The singing was good. Then the call for sinners to stand up was given. There were only five.

September 25 SIZING UP THE NEW PASTOR

Well, amid much silent expectation and some not so silent, on the part of our Methodist members, our new pastor arrived yesterday. It is a great occasion, the arrival of a new minister and his family. We are going to give them some apples right on the start and be awful nice to them!! But I am not going to hear him preach his first sermon unless I change my mind before Sunday. I like his looks and he talks good. He told me he thought he would like to live here and he could get along all right with the parsonage. Mrs. Duke is shuffling around from house to house. I wish she would come in the bank and report. She has everybody's ideas.

NIECES AND NEPHEWS

[With three married brothers with children living close by, their "doin's" were frequently written about.]

"TIELET"

Alice V. likes to use the toilet at home which she calls "tielet." Margaret was out on the porch yesterday overseeing Alice and Jean before starting home. I heard Alice V. say, "Mama, I want to sit on the tielet." Margaret said, "Oh, wait until we get home now." Alice V. replied, "I spec I'll be out of the notion by then." Permission granted.

Alice Virginia and Warren Kingsbury enjoying breakfast at Fairview

Early Summer   "MIGHTY POOR FISHERMEN"

I have been wondering how "pert" you feel this morning. I hope you are on your front porch watching the breezes go by. I wanted to come up to see you Sunday and was *coming* anyway till Mother said she needed me to get the "lettuces" and to rush the ice cream can, so we could have something for Billie, Julia and three of their kids and Ernest, Hazel, Carl and Lillian to eat. We had a real good time together. William and Warren are spending a few days with us getting tired of the country, and Father is enjoying them. All three of them are mighty poor fishermen, for in spite of their time and bait wasted, we have not even had a fish tail to eat. They are great boys. Warren is building himself a boat out of barrel staves and nails, mostly nails. Father says, "I think he is going to discover the bottom of the pond when he sails in it." These kids save me lots of steps and seem to love to do chasing that I just despise to do. It is such a pleasure to get waited on. No wonder married people want children. Children just wait on them and make their lives so easy.

KID DOINGS

Alice V., and Jean and Carl Jr. are putting a nursery aspect on our home tonight, and I may add the train is running fast in one room; Jean is playing dentist in another, and Carl Jr. is quieting down for the evening in yet another. Yesterday morning Margeret (who eats Limburger cheese for indigestion) ate a bun, and it stuck in her swallow-pipe, so she ate some pickle to push the cheese down. Whether it was the pickle or the poison from the tinsel around the cheese, she doesn't know, but last night in the still hours, she nigh "shut off," the stomach pains put such a crimp into her. She has been awful sick all day and we had to have a doctor!!! So the kids are over to Mama Kingsbury's.

Alice Virginia, Jean and Carl Jr. are still holding forth here at the nursery. The two little girls have what you call spells and are badder than ever.

Yesterday, everybody was doin' it—spanking A.V. into a nervous wreck. When Rob had finished, she said: "That was mighty little to get spanked so hard for—you hurt worse than Uncle Carl." She is incorrigible, but I love her hide, tooth and toenail except when I am working on her hindquarters myself. I think too much licking makes A.V. worse. It strings her little nerves up, so she just vibrates when discords strike her.

Ernest was over today and gave us little Julia's latest. She was pouting and her Grandfather Taylor said something to her and she told him to go away, *clear* away, and he said, "All right, I will go clear off," and went down town. When he got back, Julia was sweet as sugar and was plum lovin' to him and he said, "Julia, what made you scold grandfather Taylor? You made me feel so bad. You scolded me terribly." To which Julia responded, " I did it for your own good."

Early Fall

Alice V. started school Monday and Rob and Margeret are keeping busy taking her and coming for her. Alice said, "Miss Jones asks more questions than anyone I ever heard of."

STREET FAIR

June 7

That merry-go-round music is beautiful to me today. I could just die listening to it. It plays "Casey Jones" the sweetest ever!!! I spent an hour or two in town last night. Soph Richardson was hanging around the "Japanese Ware" booth, taking chances and she won a spittoon-looking vase that she hugged around the rest of the evening. All this ware was brought right over from Japan. The duty on it makes it cost so much in New Franklin!!! There are other things just as remarkable here on the streets. I never saw so many little babies in my life as were brought out last night. Every other woman had one. Wayland Carpenter was sporting his Huber woman, and in the ice cream parlor I observed a diamond sparkling on her "engagement finger." Can't say where she got it.

O! this is the sweetest music out here in the street. I have to get out where I can hear it good.

June 9

Lillie Shea is just riding a little hoss to death on the merry-go-round, and the six pieces the automatic band plays are distracting at times until I wish I had no sense of time, but when I remember it's music and *music is art,* I just want to send out and have a single piece played over seven times instead of six—one paroxysm.

"Rosie, the Strange Girl," it is reported, is a calico-coated male, but the mayor hasn't appointed a committee yet to investigate. Rosie growls and plays with snakes, and is one of the worst of fakes.

I couldn't get up courage to ride that kiddish hobby horse until Friday night. It is a great thing to take a person off his dignity, and I think all elderly people should patronize it if they want to keep young.

The Ferris Wheel was grand too. From the top, I could see the Boonville water tower.

June 11

There is no more "Casey Jones" and the street looks very sad. But I love the pathos of it all. It was a serious thing though, to go out of town Saturday night with everything in a whirl and come back the next morning and find the street cold in desertion. One night Lillian and I were seated in the Negro minstrel show and Miss Annie Hart came in and sat in front of us. Both of us had to get up and move before we could see anything to the front of us and she did get so tickled at the jokes, she would just sway back and forth and say to Mrs. Hart, "Ain't that a shame?" She was a better show than what was on stage and between both performances I felt like saying "Ain't that a shame?" myself. I saw Miss Boggs riding in the merry-go-round sleigh and need I tell you, she occupied it alone. The niggers had such a time. And so did old lady Dr. Wayland who never knows a well day. She was down town every night prowling around, weaving her presence into the shuttling crowd. I couldn't help wishing she was throwing confetti or blowing a tin horn, so she could get all that was to be got out of the occasion. I persuaded Cousin Annie Boggs to ride the hosses of the M.G.R. with me, and we had a fine before-breakfast gallop through the streets. Sophie and Bob Robertson just stayed around the Jap-ware booth all the time, but they never did win as much as the Birkheimers did. Mrs. Birk won the prettiest set of cups and saucers on display and a pitcher and spittoon vase. Lutie won a poodle dog for herself and for all her friends who had her take chances. She was the prize poodle-dog puller. They got some buckets and packed their china and dogs in them and looked like the street-fair going out of town themselves.

ANNA ROSE

[Cissa, a young seamstress had been hired to come live at Fairview while she made clothes for Lilburn's Mother and Anna Rose.]

We had a little "drayma" at our house last night. Anna Rose had such a good time in Fayette, she could not get unhooked up there until yesterday afternoon, and Cissa had wanted her all day. A.R. brought a girl home with her and they drove down town and stayed until dusk, and Cissa had given them permission to go if they would come right back and not get out of the buggy. They stayed until dark, and Cissa's face got plum forbodin' looking. The wind did not get up until after supper though, when Cissa told the parents and me that she could not fit to do any good at night and went upstairs. Soon she came in to me and said, "You go in yonder on the piano and entertain that girl while I take the little pest upstairs and see what I can do for her. I never have been treated this way by anybody I ever sewed for," and the lump in her throat riz with the excitement until the tears flowed out in great streamlets. I was touched and I said, "O come on Cissa and sit down," and she draymatized as follows, "No sir, when I take a job of sewin' I want to finish it, but I have feelin's." (Exit Cissa) Mother sent unsuspecting Anna Rose upstairs to Cissa who was watering the sewing machine with her tears and A.R. begged her pardon which worked, and soon I heard the old time clatter starting. Cissa's hat has come and it comes too far down over her head. I told her she would have to get some little legs to prop it up on top of her hair, and she 'lowed there's already two legs under it and ran up the steps laughing fit to kill. Wasn't that keen?

A NEW BEAU

Anna Rose had a gay holiday. She caught a new beau just in time to get things worked up to a "rose-heat" by Easter, and she is full of "Van Studiford this and that," and carries his picture around with her. Truly Coonie Hammet is "of the past." She had Lorene Dalton with her at home this time, a girl from New Madrid. She is very pretty; her hair is frizzy and she is so teeny. Just 17. I am sorry I am at an age where I use "just" to mean it seems awfully young to me.

OFF IN A CLOUD OF EXCITEMENT

[A visit to a Howard Payne schoolmate whose home was in Jackson, Missouri. This was the two girls' first trip of a distance away from home and they were given an in depth briefing on proper behavior and how to react to approaches by strangers.]

Well, Mam, we sent Anna Rose off yesterday in a cloud of excitement. She and Cousin Xena had been coached "wrong-side-hind part fore" what to do in case Emergency assaulted them. They "wove" [waved] off the hind end of the Limited [observation railroad car] until they faded out and ain't been seen since, but I have heard tell of them.

Homer Wade was to meet them at Union Station and take them to their hotel and put them on their train this morning. That was so unexciting, I told A.R. to tell him I would let him take them out to Delmar Garden if he would let them pay their way. Homer is a dream, but so tight. I knew it wouldn't make him feel bad to have my message. Homer is about as close as I am. I called up Homer a while ago and demanded that he give an account of himself and he deposed and says, he met them and took them to the Marquette Hotel and they ran into John Clark, Jr., a son of our "grocery-man" Clark. Homer knew him very well and asked him to go over to the Y.M.C.A. to supper with them. He had had supper but said he would join them after they dined and go with them to Forest Park Highlands [an amusement park]. Homer and the girls went along, anticipating a thrilling street car ride to the summer garden, but they were doomed to have *that* golden pleasure *snatched from them.*

The above mentioned John Clark led them out into the street to a seven passenger touring car, helped them and himself in, and had the chauffeur drive out through Forest Park, on to Clayton, around by Forsythe Junction to F.P. Highlands where they took the scenic and other things before driving back to the Hotel. I have one crow to pick with Homer. He left our little "babies" to be put on the train by John C. at 7:40 a.m., and he was a somewhat stranger no matter if Taylor and Horace have been buying groceries from his father for fifteen years. I am anxious to hear who made the killing that brought on all that ride. Guess it was good old Homer. *[A facetious suggestion that John's interest was in Homer rather than in the attractive young girls from the country.]* He said the girls had such a good time, and don't you know our "Maude Mullers" did? Homer said he had an awful good time, too. By this time our girls should be safely in the Bird Cage *[the family visited was named Bird]* in Jackson and we are anxious to hear that John C. put them on the right train.

August 6 WONDERFUL EXPERIENCES

A.R. is home with an array of "Arabian Nights Tales" of her own. They had such wonderful Missouri experiences such as "settin' on drummers." Had no end of chances to flirt with the strange group. At the Marquette they left word to call them the next morning but never dreamed the call would come by phone, and they palavered until the box rang nearly off before they decided they had a right to see what was doing. And such a time as they had ordering from the "breakfast program" when John Clark took them to eat. They sampled every dining car they could and generally took clam soup and ice cream. A man having beer with his dinner was the strangest sight to them. They stayed with Cousin Ida from Tuesday p.m. until Saturday. They went out in the machine every night, and once they saw a man arrested! And run in!

"SCHOOL MARMS," TRIMMMERS, AND YOUNG WOMEN

Sunday, Cousin Helen Smith, and I went to Uncle Billie's to pay a party call and stayed until about eight o'clock that night. We had more fun talking about the new school marms, Dorsey and Biddle. Ab and I made the girls tell all about Dorsey staying all night down there on Thanksgiving. I thought to myself maybe those girls would be complimented if they knew we talked about them so much, *if* they did not know all that was being said.

Lilburn and Helen Smith off for a visit

WHAT MAKES HER TREAT ME SO MEAN?

Next day I was counting strong on going to see "Custer's Last Fight" at the picture show and was full of anticipation when I went to the Post Office and got a card from our preacher saying to please come to the Steward's meeting at 7:15. The bottom fell out of everything, and I decided to just hang around town until the hour came, but I spied Biddle and got her to go walking with me until six o'clock. Had a dandy walk, and I told her how I had wanted to take her to the show that night and couldn't, which was the gospel truth, but she said it did not suit her to go anyway. Then we got on to Dorsey, and I told Biddle to ask her what makes her treat me so mean, cut corners, turn in stores and turn her head when she sees me coming, that I certainly did admire Dorsey's back but thought her face side was prettier. Yesterday afternoon, Biddle and I went walking again, and I got my answer. Dorsey said if I did not know why she did it I was so dense I needed to have it beat into my head and that as I was the same as a little pebble she would pass on the street, she deemed it unnecessary to pay me any attention. Well, Biddle said she bet Dorsey would get mad at her for walking around with me, but I got her to walk with me, and we went right by the Lee's house where Dorsey boarded and I *beat* on my *head* with my fist and my newspaper as we passed the front and the side, feeling sure my queer actions would be "saw."

Well, I shall have to answer them strong messages, and one will be that "it is pretty hard to hurt a little stone by stepping on it but, golly! don't a stone bruise hurt?" Then I am going to phone Helen to please hunt up a little hammer to which I shall tie the inscription *"You beat it in,"* and a little hand mirror to which I shall attach a message for her to use to see herself as others see her in the back. I might refer her to, is it the 1st or 2nd Samuel, 17-47, for information as to what a little pebble can do to a good-sized person. Biddle said Dorsey passed a compliment on me the other night and told me the first part of it, that I had such beautiful manners—but then Biddle refused absolutely to tell me the *but,* because it was so unattractive. I'd rather have heard the bad than the good because I know perfectly well that if I ever had any good manners toward Dorsey, they have rotted off and gangrene has set in.

It is powerful exciting, because I never know now whether Dorsey is going to shoot me on the street when I see her, and my heart gets up in my throat, and Biddle said, when I came in the store where she and Dorsey were, Dorsey said, "Oh! my heart. Somebody catch it before it falls out on the floor and breaks." Biddle says she is sorry to tell me but Dorsey *sure dislikes me.*

"A SOCIAL SWELLING"

I hear the Settles are going to have a social swelling on Friday night, in Boggs Hall so they can dance. Edgar said the Hartwig orchestra would play. There are several children and the old man. The children play the piano, horns, and stringed instruments, and the old man plays the devil when he gets hard cider diluted with whisky inside him.

"THE GIRLS DONE IT"

I'm sorry for Clara Woodson too. My lovin' ways are so poor. My, I get so serious when I start thinking about Clara, I just pop. I'll get her yet, if she don't watch out.

ON WRITING LETTERS

The swill-pot of my mind needs emptying and I'll just pour the mess into your front yard. I hate you for not writing to me, but I love you for your natural ways.

I don't have the same emotions two days in succession and if I had two or three more ladies to think about, I'm sure I'd get me some cyanide and leave a note: "Goodby, Mama, the girls done it." I can't keep out of the rapids to save my heart and some of these mornings I'm going to wake up in the bridal chamber.

Of course you know my brunette friend with those awful brown eyes and *exciting ways* is to get off the Limited here Saturday at 3 p.m. to go as my date to Helen's party. I got a postcard 'bout every morning about it, and I'm working up toward the meeting nicely. If things go along well, I am asked to go to Moberly by Mrs. Owen's invite to visit Myrtle while she's there. I aim to go. Am so anxious to see the dear girl and her glad rags. She is pluming herself in St. Louis now. I've molted some myself and "growed" some new feathers at the reduction sale at Albert Meyer's *[men's store in Boonville]* on her account.

I am so glad you can see my jokes. I wrote to Aunt Minnie that I was afraid there would be talk about me setting out so soon after losing Etta the second time, and she wrote two pages of condolence and uncomplimentary things she had heard about the departed (?), and mixed it in with the things she thinks about me. It was just grand.

Mam, Clara didn't forget me and when she wrote, she stopped in the middle of the most exciting case she has had since the trip began. She was sailing around the islands and was soon due at Zamboanga. Clara's letter was disturbing. A nice villain was pursuing her. I wish I could go to New York to meet her, but you know I have no business going unless I am able to kill the villain. You know I am not able to put a woman on good rations, and I'd be a lot less able if I should go, and I might want to when the ship docks. Oh! for several hundred dollars of joy money!!!! It takes that Mam, to make my marrying mare go. If Clara comes back in the possession of that man, Williams, I am going to turn *Lady-hater*. She is due back a month from today.

The new scarf pin is getting like a gold brick to me since everybody who sees it gives me a chance to tell where it was born and how it come across the water to bless my life. And, when Clara was in Nagasaki, Japan, she picked out some tortoise shells, had them polished and monogrammed and put on as backs of military brushes, for old stinkin *me*. Wasn't that sweet of Clara to think of me, when Dr. James was along distracting her mind? Never was no girl as nice to me as Clara. This is such a lovely world when something is coming in, and it all ain't going out.

"COCOMAZING INFLUENCE"

Well, honey, I decided not to wake up in the bridal chamber with Etta. A lot of things helped me decide on the matter!! She helped me a good deal and then a friend of mine, Dr. Alden, brought his influence to bear on the situation. Dr. Alden is a great-great-great-grandson of John and Priscilla Alden, and the strain has about run out, judging from his size. (But he got there just the same, unless something happens.) I think I'll be born again and grow up little. But really, it can't be that the size of a human being counts. It's the human's "cocomazing" influence. Whoever has the most, takes Birdie home. Etta said to Sue, she wondered if I would come to the wedding. Well, I aim to go unless nervously prevented and to sit up front on the mourners' bench, all during the process. Do you know any reason I should not go, if I'm asked?

Paul White said he didn't see how Etta could marry another man, said there must be a lot of money there. I told him he shouldn't think of such things and he replied, "Well, I always look for the motive in all criminal cases." I just love to hear him talk like that.

Kate Leslie is down here to be with Etta during the last hours before the wedding. I went to the Herndon's yesterday and Mrs. Hughes was down, and she looked as full of "they say talk" as our yard is of those measely little "Star of Bethlehem" bulb plants. Well, she asked me who was the woman who made Beth McCullough's underclothes when she married, as if I would know. It never had occurred to me whether Beth had any or not, but Mrs. H. was wanting to explain to me *whom* she had heard Mrs. McC. was being "put off on" by one bunch of match-makers. And she said part of the Harry Dales are out on the farm and what was I to get out of that remark except that Beth ain't got no husband. She said Beth said, "When I marry again, I'm going to get a man who is one of a very large family and the Black Sheep of it so he won't be anybody's but mine." Now if I haven't given you a juicy gob of gossip, I hope to die. There is going to be a special train for the Estill leaving, don't that sound elevating? No wonder she didn't take me. There's nothing special about me. I suppose it's one more chance to go in city clothes to a country wedding, but I still remember how I felt out in McCollough's barn lot with evening clothes on, and what happens once could happen twice, and I'm going to wear solid comfort this time, so I can unhitch my horse with immunity if necessary.

"A LAST LOOK AT ETTA"

I went over to take a last look at Etta yesterday evening and cast my eyes on some magnificent silver plates, candlesticks, table weapons, bowls and pitchers. She has a beautiful display, but you can't tell where they came from as all the cards are removed as soon as Kate records them in the little record book. And I wish you could have seen all that embroidered underwear on display. You could have appreciated it a lot more than I, but even I knew it was time to just take on over it. They were folded up for display so you couldn't tell if they were shimmies or shamies, but I don't think there were any shamies. Aunt Notie came last Friday night, and Mr. Estill has been such a bridegroom they say. Mrs. E. has a lot of interesting things to show and say, and when she showed me how Panama hats are sent in bamboo cases, I never let on that Clara done showed me that and that my hat was getting its block on now. She 'lowed she had something to give me, and she had these two hats twirling them around at me, and I thought my time had come, but ain't nothing materialized yet. I wish she would give me one for I'm crazy to be able to Sunday in one and slouch in the other. I will be in suspense until after the wedding, for Miss Notie is already going so fast she can't slow down. The groom came this morning with his best man. Think of having him in the way for four days.

❧ ❧ ❧ ❧ ❧

"THAT WAS SOME WEDDING"

I have moved all the dust in the bank and am open, ready for biz, but the town went to the graduation last night and did not arise with the sun. This was the sweetest morning out home. The honey locusts are in full bloom and our little world was as smelly as the wedding Myrtle told you about. That was some wedding, The groom came in so fast nobody got a good look at him until he got to the locust bower and right-about faced. And then we watched him for about ten minutes before the first maid appeared. Dr. Allen is a cunning little man and acted so crazy about his bride. In making his promises he kept turning his head to say them right in her face, and I was convinced he had a ball-bearing movement at the base of his skull or he could not have done it so slick. I never saw anybody make love to his woman right during the ceremony, but ask Myrtle if Dr. Alden didn't? There was some of the most dressed-upedness there that it has been my pleasure to behold for some time. Miss May Jennings had on a "dream" with a little slit in front that exposed a most beautiful little ankle and pump when she walked. I saw Gentry Estill kiss her in a crowd but did not know what ground he did it on. His wife wasn't there in the room though. She is a good looking blond *for sure.* Aunt Cliff and Aunt Ella La Force were both there and I had not met them since I got out of kilts. Aunt Ella is the prettiest but Aunt Cliff has more "human interest" in things around here; the former rushed home that night like she was afraid Kansas City would wake up and find her gone. Florence Estill was about the best looking and the best dressed woman there. I never saw her look so well. She came perilously near being pretty. Kate Leslie came in breathing hard. I could see her blow, and afterwards I remarked to Mary Estill that I could just see Kate's bosom heave, and Mary 'lowed, "I didn't know she had any." I might have said it myself, but thought it would not sound well in me remarking that Kate's breast-bone was rising and falling, so I *padded* my remark. We had a little dance at the tail end of the evening, a few waltzes, and Eleanor Doozier of St. Louis and Dan Estill of Kentucky got to doing the "turkey trot," and everybody had a good amusement in watching them. It is so funny and it has the "real name," for our big old gobbler does that step all the time. Then there was a Virginia Reel and Mr. Wallace and Mrs. Notie took part in it, and I want to tell you when he backed around his pardner, he looked very much as if he was draggin' his stomach. Miss Notie was so supple for her age. There were some good looking Estill young men, all tooted out in dress clothes, and I heard some of the other members of the clan braggin' on what a fine bunch of young kin they had. They did look clean cut.

And listen to this which dislocated my whole new reconstruction!!! Florence came over to see Mother yesterday afternoon and 'lowed to her that the bride had said she wished to goodness, "Lilburn could see my underclothes." All I got to say is, "I'm sorry I didn't have the price." I guess the underclothes were better looking on her than they were all folded up on the bed when she did let me look at 'em. Some brides have said such nice things about me I feel like I ain't lived in vain. Mag Edwards told Fred she would be better satisfied if she could take me to Bagdad; and now Etta said she wished *that* wish. I hope Clara Woodson will be kind. I had a card this morning from Clara in Portland, and she said she would kiss her family this morning in Richmond.

June 12 MMMMMEOWING

Oh! I *wish* you could hear Whitefoot [*the family cat*] knocking on the window and mmmmeowin'. Father has been out to inspect his "catch," a big fat ground mouse. These cats bring their "spoils" in and cry outside until Father goes out to see what they have. After he sees, they "proceed to make a meal." Great cats, ours are!

"THOUGHTS OF BEING A DRUMMER'S WIFE"
[A drummer is a salesman who travelled around "drumming up business."]

Agnes Alsop married last night and just as they commenced the wedding march, the poor papa began to scream the awfulest—and they had to take him out and the more they tried to pacify him, the wilder he got. It seems they have to speak very harsh to him when they want him to do something he don't want to do, so one of the neighbor men ran over and ordered him to quiet down and Mr. Alsop said, "Yes, yes, I can hush," and did. He can't talk so anybody can understand him except his immediate family. Isn't that sad? Well, I guess Agnes is getting to travel up to Des Moines. I told Cissa and she said, "Agnes was marrying Mr. Bohs because she wanted to travel but I have known several drummers' wives who didn't get to travel and land in the third storey of some lodging home."

August 18 GAY TIMES ACOMIN'

My sweet Mary Dimmit is to be married on the 12th of September and I certainly would be grieving if I thought it would do any good.

I hope everybody is feeling like "they-selves" and able to go on with the white man's burden. We are all feeling plum good, but it is so quiet at our house that it is uncomfortable, and I have them "seek a female friend" spells right along. A little later I am going to have a little gay time because Clara W. has as good as promised me she would come down and see me at my house for a week maybe.

My tortoise brushes deserve honorable mention. They are beautiful and I shall bring them up to your house on my next trip so you can admire them and call Clara blessed. Every time company comes to my house I get my "militarys" and comb right before them. The monogram is carved exquisitely. I could kiss Clara.

JOY RIDING

Since I wrote you last. I have had a mighty good time with the Billie Smiths. They asked me to spend Saturday night and Sunday, so I met Albert and Ethel down town, and we were to meet some Sedalia girls who didn't come Saturday night because of a wreck ahead of their train. So we picture-showed and lemonaded and then joy-rode home in the Cadillac. Sunday a.m., Ab and I met the Sedalia women, one Beaulah Mumm and one Josephine Franklin. Ab loves short, fat girls so he "Kept Mumm" and I went to "Franklin." Jesse Rose came down for dinner and we had a good one. In the afternoon we crowded the Cadillac, and after supper we rode some more. Albert and I put the girls on their homecoming train, then we went up to church to see whom we could take away. And whom do you reckon we ripped? Law me! You oughta seen Ab and the new milliner, Miss Fulton, scooting along with the likes of *me* and *Sadi Davis* on the back seat with Sadi telling me, "Miss Fulton will be here just a short time, only about three months, and I do hope you boys will show her a good time." Three months!!! Ma, Miss Fulton is C.C.'s new milliner. And anybody like that always gives the men the rubberneck. Of course, we have a native milliner, but she is a long, stringy pullet, not without honor except in her own country, who goes elsewhere to scatter feathers and flowers on people's pathways. Of course, we never "pay no tention" to her. Miss F. ain't exactly pretty. C.C. introduced her and her wares to the public. He had the store decorated with strips of colored tissue crepe paper and a Boonville orchestra. It was just grand. Sallie K. and Mrs. Alsop helped the milliner, and people who looked said to each other, "The hats are right pretty, but I'm going to wait for the Boonville openings before I buy." Or, "I always wait to see what Mr. Cohn has in Fayette." The engine out here in the street ran in competition to the orchestra, so we get more pump noise than music here at the bank.

September   TEACHERS ARE BACK

The teachers are back. Dorsey didn't bring no "hoss-whip" for me back with her. One day she "wove" at me across the street, and yesterday as I passed her house I saw her sitting in her window and I wasn't even going to look at her, and she hollered at me that she had two or three "sorry" things to tell me some time. I think I am anxious to hear them. She has shed that extra fat she had when the last season closed and as soon as cold weather sets in she will be the same old "bluebird." I always will like her for being mean to me. Biddle looks better than ever, and my women folks like her better than Dorsey. D. is not exactly popular with the girls it seems to me. If she were ugly as sin, she would be more popular with them. I have met Bertha Roberts, the trimmer. *[A trimmer is a woman hired by a local store to come to town to trim hats for the ladies of the town.]* She walks around so still-like, nothing moving but her feet, so that if she were water, I'd say she "runs deep." Miss Hershberg, I haven't seen face to face, but she adorns herself with niftiness. Sudie Powers, the teacher grass widow *["grass widow" is a colloquial for divorced woman]*, whom the board didn't know was in court getting a divorce when they elected her under the Miss name, is here sporting her maiden name. There is a Miss Grigsby, too, but I am not acquainted with her yet.

SOCIAL LIFE—"I'VE BEEN TO A WONDERFUL PARTY"

[The young men and women of Lilburn's generation had a very active social life. The time it took to get places by horse and buggy encouraged weekend house parties. Just how sleeping accommodations were handled is not made clear, but it can be assumed, that when beds were not available for all, there was some sleeping on palettes on the floor. Parents of the host or hostess seemed hospitable, tolerant, and cooperative, and Lilburn's letters telling of some of the house parties he attended indicate the party-goers found plenty to do, and as he noted, a "'larrapin' good time was held by all."]

Letter undated, probably late March   AT SUNNYSIDE

These week-end parties have a way of making me feel like I haven't got no sense. It is noon and my face has not been washed. I have had a solitary breakfast, a cross-country sprint to the Junction, a train

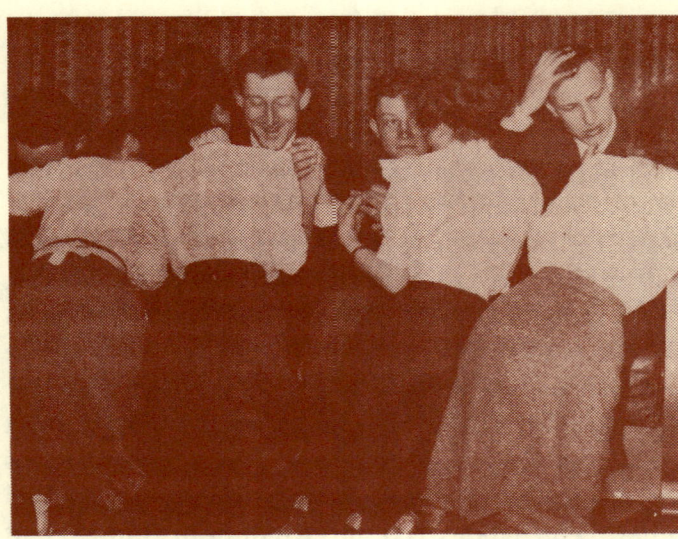

"Wonderful Party"

ride and everybody's work here to do. If the old man ever has happy feelings mixed with the ones we usually think he has then I *do* feel like *him*. But it was worth it. I had such a *good time* and I hated to pull out at seven this morning, leaving all the others piled up snug in bed with another day of good times in store for them.

As I expected, "Moitle" came off the Limited looking all peacocky and pretty and was certainly a nifty package, done up in light brown broadcloth and tied with mink furs. I walked mighty proud down that cinder path by the train and tried to hold my coat so my baggy trousers would not show. There were scads of folks down there, and they looked like they wondered where I got her.

We had Agnes Lewis to amuse Taylor, then Anna Rose, Coonie Hammet, and Fuzzie Woodson came too. It was one slightly gay *[excited and exuberant]* bunch. We had such a good supper when we got out there and after Uncle Charley would not "loan" us his mules, we spent an interesting evening at home. I was glad we did not go back to town for the roads were bordering on bad. We tried the turkey-trot, the grizzly-bear, the walrus-waggle, and all the up-to-date dances, with the two step and waltzin' mixed in. About thirteen o'clock, Uncle Charley recommended through Helen, *beds*, and we dassen't stay down stairs much longer, but it must have been fourteen o'clock before any of us calmed down.

Sunday morning, after a late breakfast, we all took our dishes out to the kitchen and helped do them up in less than no time. (The cook did not come.) Then all of us boys went for a cross country wade and called on Xena *[a first cousin living about a mile distant]* for a little bunch of minutes. We were to meet the ladies at Clark's Chapel but we had so much mud on us when we got there at 11:30, and the ladies had not yet arrived, so we went down the ridge to home. The ladies got to church though and got sore at us temporarily for doing such a muddy trick. I was ashamed but was so sleepy I was glad for a chance to get a short snooze before church let out.

The girls played mad when they came in and acted like we were not there, although we lined up in the hall by the front door to receive them. They just stayed upstairs an age and we played and sung all the lovely lonesome songs we could think of, and they were singing sassy songs back to us. Finally they did come down and took possession of one corner of the parlor, giving us four backs, so we gave them the whole room and went upstairs. Then they played and sung *"Teasing"* and *"Come, My Hero"* until we just could not resist sliding down the bannisters to get forgiven, and we lived happy *ever after*. Brother Stouffer *[the Methodist minister]* was there and I wonder what he thought of so much ragged racket, and at dinner time while the preacher was with us at table, we put on the soft pedal some, and he remarked, "I wonder where is the gay bunch that was upstairs a while back?" We never saw him again for he left almost immediately after dinner and got as far as Manny Lee's where the sleet drove him in. But he had Manny phone back to see if we were going out to my house to stay all night, or going to stay at Sunnyside again? I don't understand why he wanted to know.

[Lilburn enjoyed playing around with words, using and coining new colloquialisms.]

Of course, I worked all week getting grub together, for Margeret to ingredientiate into good things for my party Sunday night, all to get knocked out by the cold rainstorm. We were to journey to my house and Margeret and Susannah were to see that we were helped to some of this and that. We had ham sandwiches, chicken salad on lettuce, creamed oysters (in chafing dishes), ice cream with nuts and cherries on it and some of Mag's good cakes and celery. Then I wanted Moitle to see my new house and home and my folks to look at her. We could not go, so we just ate Aunt Lil out of house and home and went on the same as if we hadn't. About six o'clock Anna Rose and Myrtle slipped upstairs and when they came down they were the best looking pink and white "spectres" I ever gazed at that day. They had rigged out in evening dresses, unbeknownst to Helen and Agnes, so when the latter came in and saw, they went out too. They got Aunt Lil to rig them up in the tackiest riggin' you ever didn't saw and Harris and I got on to what was up, so we slipped upstairs and fixed ourselves to match the female "tacks." We all appeared in the parlor at the same time and made the muchly dressed up girls have a funny feeling. But the comicosity of the situation cleared the smoke away and Taylor and Brickey disappeared all sudden like, as if in a cloud. They came back transfigured, the most femalian looking men you ever saw, and then we boys just gave them a grand rush. They looked like humdingers and we just had a gob of fun in these costumes, until we were so hot we just stewed out of those extra clothes. It was fourteen o'clock again before we went to bed. Everybody was dead for sleep.

I wish you could see the embroidered evening dress which Myrtle wore, which she made herself, and also a white linen suit which she had on one day. She has become a wonder in that line, and then I wish you could see her hair. I made her give an exhibition and it is the beatin'est bunch I ever heard of in this day and age. The hair people tell her that all her extra strength goes into her hair, and it makes her skinny. She has so much it looks like she wears four switches and one main track, and she just wishes she didn't have so much.

Clara is sick and off duty and when I got to the bank this morning, Cousin Will was groaning with a toothache, a cold, and kidney pains. He said any one was bad enough, but together it was _____. He scringes whenever his kidney turns over, and I hope it isn't as bad as it is. So, I'm doing triple duty and being sympathetic besides.

❧ ❧ ❧ ❧ ❧

"EASIER TO PLAN A HOME"

[The following reference to a "shady song service" is to a Negro Camp (religious revival) Meeting. Some of the spirituals were sung in rounds, usually by three groups of three. For example, with the one Lilburn writes about in the following excerpt, those on the left would start with "Where's your mother?"

Then those in the center would sing out, "Where's your Mother?" followed by those on the right. The entire congregation would then sing out "Where's your mother?"

On the response, the groups would reverse the order, all joining in on the final "She's in Glory!"

"Golden Lamb" was another favorite Negro spiritual of the Boonslick Negroes.]

Helen has gone home to get old Aunt Jane to learn her the words of "Golden Lamb" so we can practice it for the Woodson house party. Helen heard it sung at a shady *[Negro]* song service in Fayette and guarantees it to be a reviver. We have been doing:

"Whar's your Mother?"

"Whar's your Mother?"

"Whar's your Mother?"

"O! My Soul !"

"O! My Soul !"

"O! My Soul !"

"She's in glory"

"She's in glory"

"She's in glory"

"O! My Soul!," and on down the family tree about the papa, brother, and sister, but "Golden Lamb" is more of a brazen success.

I am all time registering seismic disturbances of the house party plan. I think sometimes it must be easier to plan a home than a house party.

ﾞ ﾞ ﾞ ﾞ ﾞ

HOUSE PARTY

We were so lonesome at our long eat table *[dining table]* last night, Mother and I squoze it up right after breakfast this morning, so she and Father and Lewis and I can sit snug. First I squoze it to two squares and Mother said, "Put in another leaf; somebody will come before night." So we have room for six. After eight rackety persons get away it does seem kind of still, and Mother said they could come again before school is out, at least she "'lowed" it to me. Mother is a good Indian. Our hospitality came very near not coming through. Mr. Stout *[President of the college]* said the girls might come if no Fayette boys came down, and A.R. told him that the boys were invited and had accepted and Dr. Stout said "under those circumstances, the girls cannot go with you." That was Thursday. I think A.R. tracked him around all day Friday begging him to come across with the "Let 'em" but he had a concrete mind. So she slipped out an S.O.S. to me that night, and I got it on Saturday morning mail. I turned right out of my course to save them children.

A.R. and Grace came down that afternoon, and when they said Dr. Stout was still holding his breath regardless, I mailed my special delivery on the northbound train. I got down on my knees when I wrote it and told him he should have mercy on me who am not used to so many girls as he is. I called his attention to the cooking and cleaning and nut-picking and anticipation that would *go to waste* if he still said "No" and suggested to him the eight sad persons who would be scattered on Sunday by his ruthless hand if he still held out, not to mention *Mother and the cook*. I spread my appeal over four sheets like this and put in a bouquet for him that must have smelled good to him. Carney May came that night but Dr. Stout had not received my letter when she left, and she brought no glad tidings, so we all went up to the phone office to call up our enemy. May Carney, the preacher's daughter, said, "Now while you talk, we will stand outside and have a moment of silent prayer." And Dr. Stout said "Yes," and 'lowed he had something to explain to me. I must say I came within an inch of getting hugged when I told the three girls their prayer was answered, and each one had to call up her man to say, "You can come," and incidentally five minutes more of other slush. I wished I was talking some of it though to Myrtle.

Sunday morning I drove and led all of our buggies to Estill to meet the "young hopefuls" and my Myrtle but the train was three hours late, and I had time to go back home, turn out the horses, eat breakfast, and turn the ice cream freezer before the hours were ticked off. I was cranking up the cream can and the girls were climbing in and out of the wagon, so they could do it before the boys without getting their dresses too high, when the train whistled at Estill. Well, as soon as I could change into my Sunday pants, we bumpty-bumped up the road and met Myrtle with George van Studdiford, Charlie Dawson, and Louis Means headed our way. They filled up the remaining four chairs in the wagon, and everyone enjoyed the novelty of the joy-ride. The train riders were hollow inside, and they took time to fill up before we jolted in to church. We had a real good dinner and everyone did what he wanted afterwards. Did you ever know a Sunday like it? Everybody was glad Dr. Stout "give in."

When time came to go leave for the train, nobody wanted to go to it, and Anna Rose was calculating to put Myrtle and herself to sleep on the floor to make room for all. But I never was to let Myrtle to sleep on the floor!! And besides I felt under obligation to get the boys back on the train, else I would have explaining to do to Dr. Stout. The whole bunch waited on me at the table, being lovely, and when Mom and Dad started to leave for church and came in to tell them goodbye, the boys went through every way of sayin' thanks to be found in the etiquette book.

"SHE WASN'T NO SMALL SIGHT"

Well, it seems the girls, one or more, have been snoozing in my bed every morning after I go to town. Yesterday it was raining, and I was awful late leaving home. A fly was pestercatin' Mayme's carcass in her room so she waited long enough to think of my abode where "no fly ain't bit me yet." I had just put on and buttoned up my union suit when I looked around and couldn't believe my eyes were honest when they told me "there's Mayme coming in in night gown and crimpers." She wasn't no small sight, if she ain't no large woman. She looked so funny with knots all over her head that after she said "Oh! my Lord" and run over a chair and a sewing machine, I collapsed on the bed and laughed three minutes before I could get up and put on my pants. Suppose that had happened here in town!!! It would surely have furnished a *scandal*.

April 3 GOINGS ON

I feel all right around Cissa except when she gets to talking about people who "are nice to your face and talking about you to your back." Yesterday she was late to breakfast and in explaining the incident said, "I over-slept myself. I don't know when I over-slept myself so perfect." Louis stabbed my sense of humor with a spear-like twinkle cast from his eye, and the laugh ran out of my system under my skin until I was as full and cozy as a cream puff. Mam, wouldn't it be funny if I was to fall in love with Cissa? She has been telling me of "a remarkable woman near Fayette, who is lots taller than I am and larger and can sing so loud you can hear her above everybody else in the church." And oh yes—be sure and plant your sweet peas three feet deep. I recommend it upon her good authority. I am enjoying all this new information and me and Cissa are having a good time. She told the McKenzies over the phone, "I just feel at home here."

May 9 PUTTING IT ON THICK

Mam, I don't believe Edna did anything except act a little foolish over Duke—and who is to blame I don't know. But there have certainly been some *unkind* things said of both, and especially of Edna. Her fair name has certainly been tarred and feathered in New Franklin and I don't know where they ever put it on any thicker than here. I have heard more wild reports—one was that Anna Rose and Xena ran off from college to a dance and had been suspended, and Anna Rose was at home and Father wouldn't let her come to town (the punishment) and that was why she was so seldom seen on our streets. If it's so, my parents are keeping it from me. Then again, I heard that Anna Rose and Boulton Settle are to marry as soon as school is out!!! We just hate gossip about our own folks, it don't "set near as good to us," and it smells bad when left at our door. We want to sprinkle lime on it and carbolic acid on the one who raved it. I'm glad I don't feel that way about things I see on other folks' front and back porches. Why, I don't even turn up my nose then.

For instance, Wayland Carpenter's wife had been dead nigh onto six months now, and the way he is *dressin up* and whispering to Miss Huber in Albert Meyer's store excites Howard County's suspicions. We can't help but suspect. Old Pat Burton bawled out Carpenter to me and said, "As the feller says, he was sure talkin to her and she was keepin' right up talkin' back." Wayland must have felt an attack of hot face.

June 10 HIGH-NOON WEDDING

Mattie Lou Knaus marries at high noon tomorrow, and I expect to shut up the bank at noon and see a midday plighting. And Webb Alsop is going to marry a girl to get her to come and take care of his mother. That is what some folks say about it, but he surely must be lookin' out for himself too. The wedding is to be this month and the girl lives in Sedalia. And Miss Lula, who keeps house for W. W. Carpenter, got mad at him for entertaining them Huberites during the fair, and one night she was so mad she went home, and W. W. had to go down and apologize before she would come back to grub and bed-make for him. Crim Carpenter said that and Crim says some wonderful things on other people as well as her own folks. I always feel a real criminal when I repeat gossip like that, but you will think I must be feeling like a convict by now, having the feeling so often.

June 18 SHE DEVILS

This Dave Imber is a character, he knows all about everybody. About how Mrs. Chris Hacker once "fit" with Chris and went home to her papa. How the Papa wouldn't let her stay, saying, "You burnt the blister, now you can go back and sit on it." Dave says that is why Hattie came back.

I heard Jesse Rose say something at Uncle Billie's about finding a crazy woman in the road the night before, but other than that, all you told me was news about the "maddening of Naomi Hull." Wouldn't that make a grand title for a novel? That is mighty bad about Mrs. Hull. Folks say she is a devil, but I have seen her have lots of flowers in her yard, and I find I can't think of anybody who loves flowers as being cloven-footed.

Speaking of she devils—there is one in town, Mr. John Clark's wife, "Louie." They live at Mrs. McKinley's and the neighborhood hears her frequently "trying out" some new rage on him, and one time a chair came out of the front door after him, and another time he came out "holding his back," and another time while they were sitting on the front porch reading, she snatched his newspaper from him, wadded it up and threw it out in the yard. He went after it, smoothed it out, and read it some more. Some months ago, when she was here, she beat him up good, and he went to the osteopath. And one day Clara Landrum 'lowed to Dr. Burrus that Louie had been giving Mr. Clark treatments, and Dr. looked all through the Kirksville Medical School catalogue to find out when Louie graduated, and I thought it was strange that she was practicing when her name was not on the list of osteopathic graduates. Some women like Louie are born osteopaths and from all I can hear she is a prodigy in that line. But after the storm there is such a loving, they say, that all the world is touched. She never stays here long at a time; just comes back to beat up Mr. John three or four times a year. Yesterday when I went for a bucket of water at Doyle's next to McKinleys, Louie was a-sittin on her back porch with her hair stringing around her shoulders, just stringing beans fit to kill, but she evidently wanted to look at me as much as I wanted to see her for every time I raised my eyes to sneak a look without seeming to stare, she had me fixed, and I had to let on I never knew she was there.

🙵 🙵 🙵 🙵 🙵

I hadn't ever hoped to hear one of the John B. [vs.] Louie Clark prize fights? But I did, and I *never* hope to *ever* hear another. I was coming from the train, having put Anna Rose on it to return to college, and as I passed Mrs. McKinley's, Louie let off one big scream and followed it with weepy little ones mingled with words, the only ones of which I understood being, "just killing me. Oh, Oh, Killing me!" I could hear John's voice doing recitative work to her soprano and, Mam!, Madame Schuman-Heink's *"Cry of Rachel"* didn' have *nothing* on this and my hair stood on end one second and kinked up tight the next. Neighbors were sitting out on their porches looking skeered and old Billy Smith (who is claiming lately that he never took a drink or cussed in his life) called across the street to me, "What's the matter, Kingsbury?" and I called back, "You can't prove it by me—I ain't never been married!"

Old Mrs. "Loud" Evans was sitting quiet (for a wonder) on her porch as I said it and looked a hole in me for saying anything—like I shouldn't have disturbed the pin-dropping silence while Louie was giving her cry. She kept her ear-piercing cries up some time, Mr. Smith told me afterwards.

🙵 🙵 🙵 🙵 🙵

July 12 PARTY LINE TALK

Today Lillian was a-listenin' over the phone and heard Dimple Dodson whine, "I met Dr. Fleet and Dr. Gentle both down here by the railroad crossing—do you know anybody sick?" Old Mrs. Wilcox said, "No, I don't unless they was agoin' to Mrs. John Herndon's—she's expectin'—she was here not long ago and looked like it wouldn't be long. I been settin in the yard all evening and they never come back."

Law me! Think of them hangin on to the receivers all the time and not knowing that Gideon Paul Herndon's arrival caused his mother to quit expecting *weeks* ago. Mrs. Herndon has even had time to have sinkin' spells and to come to town since then.

July 25 SCANDAL DOESN'T VACATION

Lillian went down town with her baby. People said to her in surprise, "Why what are you doing in town? Your baby is not a month old." Lillian said it made her feel as if she was doing something that wasn't nice to disregard the unwritten law about not appearing in public for a month, but I told her to "pay no 'tention," being she was running ahead of schedule this season.

The scandal germ is not off on a vacation. Mrs. Louie made a scene Sunday. She came out with a Bible in her hand and started out the front gate, but changed her mind and went in the house just hollerin' and screamin'. This she continued to do for some minutes while Mr. C sat quiet in the yard as if his wife was keeping the Sabbath quietly. Finally, Louie hushed up, came out with her Bible and went on to Sunday School. The reason she hollered and cried the day I heard her, one neighbor told me, is because Mr. C told her to stay away from the store. She had been taking her sewing over there and just "sitting." The other Mr. C hates her like "pizen." Father was in one of the stores getting some bread and outside by the door is a chewing gum case. The Clarks and their little boy were going by the store when the kid said he wanted to spend his money. Mrs. C. urged him not to but Mr. C. urged the other way. So Louie held him up and let him slide his penny into the slot. Then she said to Mr. John, "Let him turn the crank," but Mr. John snatched the crank and turned it hisself in less than no time. Louie said, "Now look at you, you have spoiled all his pleasure." and pierced him with a hat-pin look. So they resumed their walk up the street. Married folks who are rough are a wonder to me. They dent in each others' feelings, but the dents seem to come out in time. Wonder if they don't just seem to disappear? I'd hate to marry someone and then smack her all mad-like.

September 1 "A CASE OF NERVOUS PROSTITUTION"

What is the old saying about coming events casting their shadows before them? Well, I 'low the Gentle affair was just a shadow, for the recentest event sure lays the others in the shade. *[Apparently, a recent scandal must have occurred in the Gentle family.]*

Of course, you'll think I'm alludin' to Mrs. Jim Edwards running off with Franklin's Marshall, Jim Rouse, last night, but that ain't the real sensation, though it did create quite a ripple.

Tom Black and Oland Jones and two little girls, aged 12 and 13, are the "dramatis personae," The gentlemen have been running the ice wagon and use Andy Rawlin's barn for the team, and when they were hitching and unhitching, they coaxed these motherless little girls out with candy and beer. One day the washerwoman, heard a crying racket out there and run out and what she saw or thought she saw and what she stated has caused Tom to skip the country. Olie never did nothing but hug and kiss the little one—he says, and she says, so Oland ain't run yet, but Andy do say he is going to prosecute them as soon as the County Attorney gets back. Why somebody doesn't shoot Tom is beyond me. Mrs. Tom Black told Tom some time ago he had better stop those little children from coming over to the barn, else there would be talk, and Tom let loose and smacked that Margeret Little Black a zinger! She *had reflected* on her husband's *honor*(?). I really don't think Tom ought to have run off when this is a perfectly safe town to live in, do you? Lawsee. I wonder what will happen next? The town seems to have a case of nervous "prostitution."

SUNDAY SCHOOL PICNIC

The Sunday School picnic was in Cousin John Kingsbury's pasture, and they all had an eventful time. Mrs. Biggie Burrows rode Simpich's pony what won't carry double and when "Duck" laid her hand behind her back on the pony's back, the pony bucked Duck off. Cousin Bea and Palmer came to the spread and "brought some green plums" and that was *all* they brought. But of course they furnished pasture for the herd. But speaking of plums, I *plum* forgot to tell you Lillie Bonham came home from Helen's party and stayed until train time. Alice fried ham and fixed a good meal and assembled it, but Lillie said she couldn't eat a bite, she had just eaten so much, so she just came in and sat out the meal. The rest of us got away with a little lunch that surprised her. She said, "This morning when I got to New Franklin, Aunt Annie Boggs *would* have me eat a little breakfast and when I went over to Burrus's I ate a plum ('pum' she said), then Helen had refreshments so really I'm not hungry." Between you and me, I'd rather be a buzzard than a canary bird. I really would for I get a world of pleasure *just satisfying* my overgrown appetite.

PRICE: ONE NIGHT GOWN

Mrs. Dora Mills made me a night-gown and gave it to me for taking a little old acknowledgement *[drawing up and witnessing a bill of sale]* for her when she sold her farm. I used to charge $.50 but now my price is one night-gown with beautiful blue trimming on it and fancy little catches to hook myself in it by. Please take note of changes in rates. She claimed she hated to be under obligation to me but with a clear conscience, she put me a sight further under obligation to her.

HAY RIDE

Saturday night Helen and Taylor Smith gave a hayride for Xena and her company and asked Lillian and me and several other town fixtures. After a long ride, we went to Aunt Lill's at eleven and she was up with an ice-cream freezer and two good cakes to fill us up. Helen and I cut up, and I came near losing my month's wages. Just before we got out of the wagon at Helen's house, I "reached over" and pulled the tail of her shirt-waist out. She came back by pulling all the front of my shirt out of its usual confines, and as I ran to get over the side of the wagon, she grabbed the back of my shirt to raise it, and while chasing me, stepped through the boards of the wagon and fell. Some of the boys caught her and kept her from falling over far enough to break her leg. I feel mighty thankful she did not crack that shin clear in twain as it would have taken all my money to fix it. Her leg swelled up where it was bruised until it was fatter than it ever has been. We rolled the rugs up in the parlor and danced until midnight.

WRITER'S BLOCK

I've been pulling the teats of my brain for an hour, trying to get it to give down something to write about, until I've got cramps in my "pullers." My brain is the poorest kind of "strips" today, for if it should let down a little news directly, I feel like it is going to be old, thin, watery news and not the pure creamy kind I would like to send you.

WOMAN'S WORK

The "Woman of the House" is a *wonderful* being to do so much and say so little about it. I don't expect we realize how tired Mother and other Mothers get, going almost every minute from 5 a.m. until 8 p.m. Not many of the men do that, and it seems to me if I were a woman, I'd rather enjoy a lazy reputation than to dig at housework 13 hours. And house work is hard work, I say. Well, Mother gets along beautifully and Lillian is able to help lots now. Next week Louis will be away at dinner time and nobody will be here for that meal except Dad, Mom, and Lillian, unless company comes. Mam, we love the "comers" and we often say, "it is no use living if folks don't drop in."

We have a coon cook, Miss Evy Rollins of Sedalia and Boonville. She's got that tortoise shuffle on her but *cooks well*. I am so glad Mother can have all her spare time to play with the baby.

ODDS AND ENDS

Our house appears so much more spacious since the Sewing Siren [Cissa] left us last Saturday. Heck! but it was still, with no greeting to me when I got out there that evening. But the Auto-Smiths came out *[The Charles Smith family. Grandmother Kingsbury's two other brothers living in the area were not yet automobile owners.]*, and I begged Helen *[Smith—five years younger]* to stay and help fill up the hole Narcissa made when she moved out of our lives. Helen filled up the space of about one Cissa leg, but of course it helped.

CELLULOID HORROR

We went to the picture show in town that night. We came out of the "Star Theater" all horror-struck. We saw one woman fall over a precipice and spatter on the rocks below, saw her "come to" and crawl home (it must have been a mile) dragging a dislocated hip and fainting ever so often; saw her *laying dead* by the baby when the faithless husband returned from running off with the "pretty little Italian girl." At least we supposed she was dead, but she must have just swooned for we asked Louis who went to the second show and he said she did all that over again while he was there. Some women can stand a lot.

Sunday morning Helen and I polished our shoes and I shaved to go to church, but Mother made me stay away. It was the day we thought Bro. Swann was going to try to "raise a debt" and as Dad and I were not going to give anything, Mother said, "If you aren't going to give something, don't go to give off any influence against the project" or something like that, and of course I "wouldn't a-went after that." But Father came home and said the Swann song was nothing like we had anticipated, so we could have gone with impunity. We went that night to catch up with our once-a-day Sunday habit.

ᔕ ᔕ ᔕ ᔕ ᔕ

Lillian and baby were over here several days last week and we enjoyed them very much. The youngster had the doodle-doo ache at times, but the rest of the hours he was a joy. (I should have told you that Evy speaks of her stomach as her "doodle-doo"). The babe is growing up fast and holds up his head like he was proud of his mother. He loved the cook better than anybody because she would "snook" in while we were eating if he whimpered, and take him on her big fat doodledoo and trot him like a trooper.

ᔕ ᔕ ᔕ ᔕ ᔕ

OF SICKNESS, DEATH, AND BURIAL

[In rural areas of the Boonslick Country most illness was treated at home. Mothers taught their daughters the home remedies their mothers had used to treat them, such things as mustard plasters for the chest, castor oil, turpentine liniment, and herbal tea. "Patent Medicines," showcased on drug store shelves, were relied upon by many. One, still very popular in Boonslick Country at this time, was "Grandmother Schermer's Health Restorer," manufactured in Bunceton. It was made from leaves, bark, roots, flowers and seeds according to a German family recipe. According to the label it "prepared the body for resistance to disease, purified the blood, promoted digestion, regulated the bowels, acted upon the kidneys, induced healthy respiration, quieted the nerves, and induced sound, restful sleep." It sold for $1 a bottle or 6 bottles for $5.

Doctors made house calls by horse and buggy on those occasions when patients did not respond to their own home remedies or patent medicines and left drugs from their pill boxes to be administered by the family. Hospitals outside Kansas City and St. Louis were small and poorly equipped. Hospital treatment was avoided whenever possible. There was a general belief that "People go to the hospital only to die."

When a member of a family was seriously ill, relatives and close friends were frequently called upon to come and sit-up with the sick person. This enabled family members to get needed rest to be able to resume their household duties the following morning as well as look after the sick person's daytime needs. Lilburn's "Mam Letters" frequently included information about illnesses, deaths and funerals of persons he felt she would be interested in hearing about.]

Early January FAMILY SICK VISIT

Last night Father had to go visit Uncle Leonard *[Kingsbury]* who is quite ill. They have called Father to stay all night twice in the last week. Poor old man is so feeble and is unconscious part of the time. Aunt Katherine, too, is sick in bed and was so glad to see Dad, she kissed him although she used to say to our Robert that he and Joe Mcgraw were the only ones she ever kissed.

January 18 LAST WORDS

Well, you are so worked up over Doke's last words, I am afraid my revelation will be a disappointment. On Monday morning he said, "Dad, I had a mighty bad night didn't I?," and Dad 'lowed affirmatively. Doke said "Dad, I'm going to die and everything looks so dark." He dozed off and later in the day he roused up and said, "Dad, everything is light now."

STRONG WORDS REQUIRING MENTHOLATUM

But Uncle Leonard's words were better still. He sat up and said so loud that even Noah, who is awful deaf, could hear him, "Children, I am going to leave you. I am so happy! So happy!" and went off into his last nap. Then when the funeral day came and he was to be buried at twelve o'clock, it was discovered no grave had been dug and we just whooped up the telephone to tell the family about it before they should leave the house, but we couldn't raise a soul, so we had to send "runners" up the road to meet and hold back the procession. Mother was sick in bed and it did not suit to have a "lying in state" at our house, [about a half-mile from Mount Pleasant Cemetery] so the procession was stopped at Cousin Bee's. (I wondered if she had left home in a hurry that morning, thinking to spread up the covers when she got back?) Well, the chief mourners went in at Cousin John's and some others came on to our house and waited until some negroes, our Louis and Henry Davis, could prepare a grave; then they gave the signal and all went over and finished up the ceremonies about four o'clock. Now did you ever hear anything like that? Cousin John just clean forgot that a grave is essential to a successful burying. Uncle Leonard just stayed in the hearse over at the cemetery while the grave was being dug. I know Mother would kick me till she would have to hand me the Mentholatum bottle if she knew I made that remark. Uncle Leonard's last words impressed me. I hope I'll say something like that when I shut off. It leaves such a good taste in your mouth when you repeat them.

February 27   ## "EVERYTHING WRONG THAT A WOMAN COULD HAVE"

Mr. George Cox has "newmony" in one lung and "Uncle Judge" at Fayette has paralysis and Mrs. Theo Todd who went to Oklahoma and had herself opened up is mighty poorly. Mother got a letter from Mrs. T's sister saying things that were all new to me. I don't think they left anything inside of Mrs. Todd but her stomach and a few little intestines. Really it was almost that bad, and she had everything wrong that a woman could have and we did not think the letter sounded very encouraging, but maybe the poor lady will recover. I hope she will if she wants to.

"SOWED HIS LAST OATS"

Mam dear: This morning just put a crimp in me. I was so surprised to find it frozen up and snowish. People with fruit buds, though, can't help enjoying these cold snaps. But there are numbers of people who come in here, wishing it would turn warm and bloom out the orchards so they can sew oats. Speaking of sowing oats, poor Mr. Olie Cox sowed his last this morning by planting some lead in his body and now his work is done. I guess he was a good illustration of "He died as he had lived." He raised some very nice children among the oats, and I have always felt sorry for them. They surely can't be sorry he has gone, though his tragic end must have been a shock. He just got up out of bed this morning and shot himself.

Some say (particulars are beginning to come in the bank) that Mr. Cox told his wife he was going out to shoot a dog, and they do not know whether the death wound in the face, at the eye, was accidental in his having a fall, or premeditated. Somebody said the man, who sold him the "stuff" [liquor] regularly here, ought to go blow his own brains out now.

Mr. Cox has not been put away yet. His son in Arizona "messaged" he would come home but to go on with the "fun'l" but the family decided to wait, and the service is to be at the house at 11 o'clock this morning. The Masons are to have charge of the service and thereby hangs talk, talk, talk. Mr. Cox hasn't paid the order any mind since he championed Dr. Fleet through his scrape, except to pay his dues. Dr. Fleet, as it happens is the Master and he will lead the procession. It is creepy to think of the mockery it is to go through with such a service in a case like this. But it doubtless will be a comfort to the poor widow and the children. I am going to take part in the funeral, I guess. When I die, I want the preacher to be awful careful about what he says about me. The less said of a personal nature about a person, the better, I think. Those who are most interested know, and those who are not interested are just curious and go off and talk about it.

ᛉ ᛉ ᛉ ᛉ ᛉ

Mrs. Knaus' death was quite a shock to her family and her friends. She was writing to Mattie Lou when stricken by paralysis, and passed away a few hours later. Talk, talk, talk, about how each one "took it" and who broke the news and how Rachel must feel for having run off to marry and then not telling her mother goodbye when Mrs. K left the next morning for California, how Morris must feel for having told his mother to stay in Calif. when she was so dissatisfied, and Walker Todd said of his wife, "Oh Becky is up home having one fit right after another."

"WHITE FOLKS ARE JUST LIKE NIGGERS"

I have heard it *all* and much speculating on *how comes*. White folks are just like niggers, I do believe when it comes to morbid curiosity. I will listen every time but am disgusted with myself and anyone else like me for listening so much. There are so many "wireless stations" here in town that all that goes on gets caught somewhere. They do not expect to have Mrs. K's funeral before Sunday afternoon. She was Sonny McCauley's sister and had a spell just like him, the populace has decided. Mrs. Lee Agnew is so sick they are not going to tell her at all, and the Dr. would not let "Aunt Tish" Long be told until all her children had gathered for fear she would go like Sonny did.

April 9   MOTHER'S ATTACK

Mother had heart trouble or acute gastritis Friday night and called me down about 11:00. Father was not at home and I supposed it was time to get up and make a kitchen fire, until she called the second time and said she was sick. Such a running around to get external and internal remedies!!! The turpentine went right to the spot and so did the soda water, for the knife that seemed to be sticking in her heart was withdrawn in a few minutes, but the miseries in her below-knee leg began to do bow-knots and it was necessary to do a lot of "smoothening" to rub them out. I don't believe I ever woke up until morning came in spite of the excitement. Mother got up late in the a.m. and has been all right ever since.

ᛉ ᛉ ᛉ ᛉ ᛉ

April 30   MILLIE GOTT'S FUNERAL

I thought if Rev. Lindsey's remarks had been sifted something beautiful might have remained in the sieve, but Sue Herndon thought all of it was a mess and so did a lot of other people. Well he said it over and over and got everybody either to crying or feeling disgusted, and then the casket was opened. It was one of the prettiest I ever saw, and the flowers were just banked around the chancel and on the casket. They were lovely. Well, I don't believe in viewing the dead in public, but somehow I wanted to take a look, and when I did I said I bet I never would again. I wish I had stayed in my seat and had stuck to my set idea that I always wanted to remember people as I saw them last alive. I think that is by far better. Millie's face was just coated with a white powder; the flesh must have been very dark. It was just like an old time funeral. Even the family went up and there was the usual trying ordeal for them. Well when the service was ended, the funeral procession of Ara Dodson Smith had been sitting outside the church for 40 minutes waiting to begin their service. Lindsey preached that one too and palavered as much at that one as he did at the first. Millie died of pneumonia in both lungs. Dr. Ravenswaay did not come one time when called by the Gotts, and they got sore at him and would not call him in any more until the day Millie died, and he told them it was too late that she had only a few hours to live and he could do nothing. I haven't time to tell you all about how Millie took cold holding the lamp, standing in her night-gown in the door, so Will could fix something outside after night and so on, but there are details by the dozen.

~ ~ ~ ~ ~

Cecile Alsop has peritonitis and appendicitis since Sunday and is in a precarious condition. To quote C.C.:

"She's just been a sufferin' terrible. You could hear her holler all over the neighborhood. She rested well last night under the influence of morphine."

"DRIP, DRIP, DRIP OF SASSIETY"

The drip. drip, drip of Sassiety is wearing me away so fast I feel I am not much of a rock. Girls are getting to be an affliction sent upon me but I, like everyone else so afflicted, just love it. I never get to go see the same woman twice.

Annie Rose came down from Howard Payne Friday afternoon and brought Lois Snarr home with her. I went with her to Arbuckle's party. Lois is beautiful at times but you wouldn't recognize her that way at other times. She looks like she might have two faces. She sings like a "burud" when she wants to and plays a lot and dances and skates. She is a jolly wad, built on the well-fed toothpick style and has dark brown hair and eyes and some freckles, but the freckles don't show at all at night. We got in, shook hands and sat in a circle, until Miss Mary Arbuckle said to play "My Ship's Gone to Sea Loaded with _____." (I'll learn you how to play, if you don't know how.) Then we played Gossip and got to singing some and playing some and the others had the privilege of dancing a little while I was at the piano stool. I got real hungry about half after ten and when they lighted the lamp in the dining room, my appetite fairly leaped and bounded. I have always heard what good cake they have over there. I just kept waiting and hoping until half after eleven, and once Rightie went out and I heard spoons rattling and Lois and I could see something being carried in on plates, but Rightie came back with some cord string and started playing "Ring on the String." I could have chewed the string in twain and I kept breaking it in two so somebody would say it was time to go home. I broke it three times myself and it wore to a thread in places before Myrtle A. said lets play "Pass the Nickel." It was after midnight and I would have given a dime to pass toward home. I got to telling Lois to say "We must beat it," but I finally said it myself just as Rose mentioned the time. I could have stayed all night doing kindergarten work and have enjoyed it but every day isn't Sunday for me. I really did expect something to et. I told Lois Snarr not to think I was paying her no compliment because I made the horse go home on "high." I just merely had to get home in time to change my clothes and get off to the bank. Virginia Cole is from Pittsburgh. I never had seen anyone from that place and I looked at her good. Lois and I disagreed in our opinions of her "beauty." Lois didn't care for her but I thought she was nifty looking. Well, I liked V's figure and she had lovely skin and quite blonde hair which Lois said was drugged. I contended hair like that was possible. It goes with a skin like Cole's and it is always light if she keeps it washed. Virginia Cole's eyes are bright and blue. She was kinda giggley.

~ ~ ~ ~ ~

SPITE PARTIES

Helen and I have planned a "cook out" party for this week at my house, but I have hesitated giving it for fear somebody will give birth in their minds to the thought it is a spite party. Mrs. Jim Evans had a spite party last night to spite Blanche Brooks who had a little "come in" and did not ask Mrs. Evan's guest. I was not invited, so was therefore spited, too. I would ask the horsey Dorsey but fear she would spit in my eye again so I couldn't see to stir the rarebit for the others, so I guess I'll ask Grace Jasper, Dorsey's roommate. The Bible says, "one shall be taken and the other left," don't it? If Jasper will come, Helen and I will call it "Grace's Coming Out Party," and I guess we will have it about Thursday night. I would have asked Blanche Brooks for Ab but on Ash Wednesday she has to quit dancing, picture-showing, and skating, and such "show your stockin' turkey trottin'" things. So it's got to be Jasper to make six. Will have a Valentine flavor to our party. I certainly hope nobody will think I am "throwing a spiteball" at any one.

"COMING OUT"

One of the fashionablest audiences that has assembled this season convened last night to witness "the coming out" of the last of the winter's debutantes, Miss Grace Jasper, who certainly out-favored herself as she made her bow to the Cousinous Society. Never did a debutante put such a shine on herself as did Miss Jasper on this celebrated occasion. The host had two gas jets burning in the reception room which was profusely decorated with flowers. One was on the piano, the other on the music cabinet, while all of the "eats" except the melting kind were displayed on a small table "to one side" of the room. The smell of cheese and olives permeated the atmosphere and served as a grindstone to whet the appetites of all present. After the formal bow, the sextet composed of Smith, Smith, Smith, Biddle, Jasper and Kingsbury rendered a number of vocal selections, one being *"Row, Row, Row—Way up the River He Would Row."* First he'd kiss her then, she would tell him when, he'd fool around and then they'd kiss again. And then he'd row, row, row way up the river he would row, then he'd put down his oars and take a few encores and then, he'd row, row, row."

Miss Biddle was singing loud and strong and her eyes failed her, I guess, or her tongue slipped, anyway, instead of singing "fool around," she said "feel around!!!" I'd have put her out if it hadn't been such a cold night. As it was, I bust my sides and in spite of my trying to go on with the chorus, I'd break down and nearly die laughing. Biddle was that flushed. She might nigh broke up the singing as far as the playing went, but I couldn't have resisted laughing if my life had depended on me keeping my dignity. My ear was the only one that caught the mistake, I think, because the others all said, "Well, what are you laughing about?"

At the appointed time, Helen and Jasper presided over the rarebit and it cooked up full of taste. We ate all of it and afterwards had some *Man-Made* sherbert which was larupin even to the *second saucerful* most of us availed ourselves of. Margeret made a cream filling and put vanilla wafers together with it and they were just flawless to our palates.

The debutante was interesting in blue silk with lace with pink on it. I like her real well and have a date with her for the next Lyceum number, on the 25th.

Biddle had informed me she didn't think "Jap" would come out of respect for Dorsey. I told her to feel around and find out and the next information was that "Jap" would go up with *Taylor* if I called her and asked her to! Guess I can't even light in Lee's rented rooms. Well, I aim to yet if I don't get cut down in my prime. I did the calling and everything was lovely. Mother said she told Miss Biddle to tell Dorsey she wanted Dorsey and me to quit this cutting up and forgive if she never associated with me again; that she was so sorry she (D) was not with us and I perked up and 'lowed "I really would have enjoyed having Miss D, really wanted to ask her but felt like my tongue was tied by her unkindness in refusing my apology." Biddle 'lowed she too thought I was tongue-tied and so did Mother. Having the three girls gave me 3/4 full happiness but I wish it might have been 4/4 joy which it would have been if I hadn't been forced to have it without the blonde. She came in the bank untended at noon yesterday for a check book, but I was attended by Cousin Will and couldn't grab her and spank her like I want to. She tells Biddle such different things from what she served to Clara L. But Biddle claims her mouth is buttoned up and won't tell much. Sometimes it comes unbuttoned a tiny bit. I want to say *this school year has been a very inter-*

esting one. The coming out party broke up with "a little hop" then we "rowed" home. But I am no good at oars like Johnny Jones of the song.

SHE NEEDED A BATH

Anna Rose has a girl home with her over Sunday, a real sweet little thing, but she needed a bath and I was all the time throwing toilet water on her. I never did believe in such methods though, they only complicate smells. Well she was the dancingest little thing and all those new fantangle doin's was what she liked best. She has taught Anna Rose all she knows, a lot of which I could not get onto, and then she has A.R. crazy in the noodle about cards. I don't mind A.R. learning all these tricks but I am afraid she neglects her school work for a game of "pitch" or something else equally important.

March 13   DORSEY'S SKATING RINK FALL

This surely is a simple Lenten life I am leading now. I haven't seen many of the scandal-seekers to collect from but I must tell you about Miss Dorsey hurting herself on the skating rink. She was keeping the fall quiet in town, but through Biddle found out I knew it and I "herd" she said she'd give a whole lot to know how L.K. knew about it!! The fall was awful and they wanted her to have a doctor to look and see if any of her hip joints were unhooked but for some reason she wouldn't do it. 'Spose she had broken her hip and I had been the only doctor for miles around so I'd have had to fix it for her! Wouldn't I have had revenge for the way she mangled my pride? On the strength of the possibility of such a thing, me and Ab and Johnny Cox are all going to study medicine, maybe, if the same teachers come back next year. But if I was an M.D., I'd be more considerate of them than Dr. Duke was. They say he was death on seeing everything and after he'd been to see a woman once, if she called him again, she knew it wasn't no use to put weights in her skirts, or get under the bed clothes, and she just might as well become resigned the minute he stepped on the front porch. This is what the apple tree trimmers told Louis and Louis told me, but I'd heard it before. Those trimmers don't trim the tales they tell, any. Louis taught me "Pitch" and "Seven-up" last night, and I am going right on to 500. Mother says I won't have that calm, peaceful feeling if I do. Mother is an angel. I told her she gave me that calm, peaceful feeling, she and a good happy home.

I really didn't finish telling you about Dorsey. She was hurt so bad she cried when she tried to get up to walk and suffered death for a day or so. When D. taught school the kids all wondered why she cried at times. After three days her haunches were normal.

Saturday night, after Albert and Fulton and Biddle and I sat around in the restaurant and gabbed an hour after the picture show, Dorsey had no beau. She was a clerk at the fire sale that day and drew thousands of men so C.C. sold half out in one day.   . . .While I was at Cousin Nell's playing and looking across toward Lee's, Dorsey came out and emptied a slop jar. I sure felt thankful I was out of *sight and reach*.

Sunday morning I massaged the piano keyboard at church and Blue-bird D. was sitting back in the hind part of the church with a stew-pan hat on, with a clear vision between her and me. Bein' in the choir, I was face to face with her. I regulated my nerve and gazed intently in the Blue-eyed Baby's face, and it melted into a *old time smile*. The next time I did it, she looked out the window. The next time she smole. The next time she smole. The next time she smole. Then she smole on the street. It was just bait she was giving me. She's been sharpening her stinger all this year and now she is ready to kill me dead. She keeps on getting fatter.

June 28

[When school ended in May, the non-resident teachers left for the summer. That Lilburn and Lenore Dorsey had not closed the breach in their relationship is indicated by the following letter.]

DORSEY'S LETTER

I nearly died of surprise yesterday when I received a letter postmarked Williston, S. Dakota, and wondered if someone out there had seen my ad in the Matrimonial Gazette, but found "Lenore Dorsey" signed at the end of an apology. I just gasped over and over "of all things, of all things!!!" She said I hurt her feelings but she acted the chump and was sorry, wanted to tell me before she left but couldn't screw up the nerve, was in the midst of gay stuff, but couldn't enjoy herself until she got square with the world. Well, I took a ruler and balanced my account with her by hunting up and sending her the apology I sent her in February, which she returned, you remember. I added a little more—two or three pages—to it, but I thought the February sentiment was good enough to do now. I told her I was today pulling up all the weeds she had caused to grow around my heart so the memory flowers of her blue eyes, her winter complexion, her smile and her crazy little giggle could grow the better. I told her of all the pretty little talk I could think of and retain in my hot mind long enough to put it in writing, and doubtless she will think I have relapsed and feel like she will have to jerk me around and let me sit on a cake of ice. Well, she can make the ice all right. I was really awfully pleased to have her bow down. I have been wanting her to, and wanting to bow myself, for a long time, though I had long since ceased to expect anything of the kind and had forgotten just what I used to think about wanting to make up. I tell you it is a wonder I ever got over that shock yesterday.

Somebody came in a little while ago and asked me what I had on my mind. I told him "Nothing! It is so hot it is going naked today."

SUCH FUNNY SIGHTS ON THE TRAIN

I was on the train the other night wearing my Panama which I think brought the rain, and as it was in the cool of the evening, one man felt the need of warmth and got up and put on a fur coat. Another man in the car was in his shirt sleeves. Some men in the rear of the car got to remarking about how funny the fur coat, the summer hat, and the coatless men "conglomorated." I thought I would take my hat off and fan myself when the man put on the fur coat. And whooping cough was in the same car, and some poor little kid just whooped a round one every time. One sees such funny sights on trains. One nigger wench got off at the Junction *[with MK&T R.R. branch line north]* and as she went out the door she looked back and said to one like herself, "Goodbye, now be good," and the polite reply was "Thank You." I never knew what to say when told to be good until then.

One green-horn was on the train and sitting by me. All of a sudden he said to me: "Law, I've come off wearing her watch and chain." I asked him all about *her* and he said, "She sure is fond of flowers," and in his hand he had a big bouquet of lilacs and bridal wreath which she gave him at parting. He looked to be about 18 years old. He finally asked me if I had been to see my girl and I told him my mission was one of business and he said, "Oh! Sunday business! You must be a preacher." Then he told me what his name was and asked what mine was. I told him and he replied, "Well, I'm awful glad to meet you. It's an awful night to meet you but people will meet sometimes." The last I saw of him he was getting out of the car with his bouquet in his hand, one in his coat, and a sprig of bridal wreath sticking in his hat. Now all this is gospel truth. He had evidently been out in the rain, he looked so green, like all the other thirst quenched vegetation, since these grand showers.

CLARA WOODSON

Henry and Jo Tindall "come on us unexpectedly" Friday, and of course they raised their ears when I said I had to go meet Clara, and they didn't let them down until they drove out of sight Sunday afternoon.

I was glad for Clara to meet Henry. He's a curiosity she'll never forget. He went all through Clara's clothes hanging up in the closet and she asked him if he didn't look in her suitcase too. He didn't say. He liked her clothes. He told me his shoes were highly shined and wouldn't I hitch up his horse—had Jo tell me rather. And everything Clara said she had or did, "Sister Jo had it two years ago, or else had it now." When he left, he said Clara was jolly, that he met her at breakfast and by ten o'clock he was discussing underwear with her!!! He sat by her at the table sometimes and she said he would reach over and give her a little pat on the leg now and then. Oh! Mam, if I'd known it, I would have moved right in between them.

And over the dishpan, Josie told Clara that if she ever came here to live, to influence "Cousin Alice to hang the mirror over the mantle." Clara 'lowed it wasn't recorded she would ever come and if she *should*, Cousin Alice could "hang the mirror wherever it suited her best."

Clara is still here. Mother has asked her to stay all summer and I am using my influence, but I seem to feel like she isn't going to stay for she is leaving next Sunday morning. She and Louis and Helen and Father have been having a celebration in honor of my absence every day, and Louis is quite "took." Clara makes cornbread that Father eats three cakes of and she is doing Mother's sewing, and society with me from 4:30 p.m. to 10:30 a.m. She is getting such a "holt" on the family that they will be mobbing me if she gets out of my reach and takes the soldier man. She's got a terrible weakness for him.

[A first cousin of mine whose parents, Robert and Margeret Kingsbury, lived just down the road from Fairview, told me that Clara Woodson and Lilburn became engaged during her visit that summer, and that the wedding was to take place in the fall.

One evening, several weeks after Clara returned to Richmond, Lilburn was at the Robert Kingsbury's. He was playing the piano and Margeret was in the swing on the porch. Suddenly the music entered into a surging, rising crescendo culminating in a loud bang. Lilburn came out on the porch, his face flushed.

"I can't do it! I just can't go through with it!" he muttered, shaking his head.

"Do what?" his sister-in-law asked.

"Marry Clara!" he replied. "I simply can't do it. I don't love her."

"Then why did you ask her to marry you?"

"The Woodsons have lots of money. I thought I could find a way to love her, but there's no way. I can't go through with it!"

It would be surprising if Lilburn didn't write some of his feelings about this to Mam, but if there was such a letter and it was returned to him, he did not save it. How he managed to disengage himself, is not known, but a later letter reveals that when Clara married, his name was stricken from the invitation list by Clara's father.]

DREAMING OF SWEET HALLIE

[It was the practice in Boonslick Country, when a family had a female visitor of "dating age" to extend invitations to eligible young bachelors to call upon her. Lilburn's annoyance at not being extended that courtesy is voiced in several following letters.]

You remember Hallie Ogle who's visiting the Settles? I have never been asked to call and the only luck I have had is in the ice cream parlor or on the street when I can get a little look out of her eyes. But Hallie was in today to cash a check and I got so mad at everybody who came in just at that time, and finally we had to give the window to a staying customer and she had to go on out. I was enjoying myself and her so much. She asked me if it was not customary up here for the hostess and host to ask the boys to call, and I assured her that I was that kind. She said that was how it was done in Texas. And Boulton Settle is going camping and leaving her unguarded for two or three days and she said she hated to have to amuse herself. And we said a lot more which you would think plumb foolish if I would tell you, so I won't, but on account of the lack of "callers," I think Hallie is not having the good time she is accustomed to. Mam, I can't help to like to look at her because she wears so many different clothes and hats and she is something to wear them on—but excuse me, if you were not prepared for such a remark from me.

I am sorely tempted to "but *[sic]* in" on the privacy of the Settle home, now that Hallie has said she wishes I would, but I don't see how I can do it. I wish to goodness Hallie was visiting somebody else. Me, for instance. But I always did think what was out of my reach was the best old peach on the tree.

🌿 🌿 🌿 🌿 🌿

Now Mam I am going through a new experience. Never before have I had my passport *through* any man's yard held up. I sure feel strong for what anyone tries to prop up out of my reach, but I am too old to be rash and lose my balance. Between you and me, I'm telling you all this, so don't you squeal on me how I'm getting a lemon handed to me, though I can't feel or taste the sourness because I've got my eyes on the peach.

September 12   THE TEACHERS ARE BACK

Tomorrow the teachers come in once more. Talk about being glad when the birds come in the spring. Give me fall with its bringings. We were all looking forward to the coming of the *[hat]* trimmer whom C.C. got in St. Louis. She came Sunday. I have seen her. To me her personal appearance is positively thrillless. I didn't care to look back after looking forward and meeting her on the street. C.C. says she is "mighty sweet," that she is from Tenn., and a promising trimmer. She and Sadie Davis are thickening up. I haven't the least idea what Miss Dorsey thinks of me and in regard to her I feel as apprehensive as a dog with firecrackers tied to his tail. I know not what the morrow holds for me. If Dorsey horsewhips me on the street, I'd be ashamed, and shocked but not surprised. She looks the part all right.

The trimmer told A.R., Dorsey told her "Mr. Kingsbury wrote me such a sweet letter this summer and I just neglected to answer it." A.R. put a different light on the remark by telling the trimmer how it really came about. The remark from Dorsey wiggled the dagger already in my heart so Monday night when several of us went from the picture show to Moser's to play and dance a little, and Dorsey came down, having gotten up after retiring for the night, I just couldn't see her look pretty at all, though she doubtless did to others. But I was sorry when she got up and went back up stairs.

🌿 🌿 🌿 🌿 🌿

THE HITCH-RACK WAS BARE

Friday night Susanne had Bobbie McGavock to play with and she let me bring Estelle Biddle for mine. We played "Rummy," a new game to me, in which one used the sinful cards, until we got appetites and enjoyed some fruit sherbert and good cake. It began to rain, so she asked Biddle to stay and sleep at her house instead of going back to town in a no-top hack with me. I hated it, but consented as well as I could to the arrangement. Bob and I started to the front gate, but when we got there, the hitch-rack was bare, and so the poor kiddies walked home. Bob's buggy and harness we discovered in the place where I had hitched our old Fluty. Fluty was plum gone with my buggy and the hitch post. Bob's nag was home by then I guess. I figure that Bob's horse got loose and ran over my hitchpost, my horse and buggy slipped off her harness and skedaddled. When we had walked up home, we found Fluty waiting at the shed with the buggy and the hitchpost and no bridle. Nothing was hurt but that one garment, whereas Rob's mare arrived at his home safely, perfectly naked, except she had the bridle on. We were not broke up enough to wish Susanna had not given the party.

When you don't get the news reported on time, remember I am thinking it to you, and if we were living in a world a few years older, I spec I could think it right up to your front porch.

September 12   **SHE PIRATES**

You ought to know how it makes our janitor feel to have the dust settled. It borders on good. I am thankful the Lord put hairs in my nose, else I would have real estate on the lung. I got caught in the rain last night, and when I got home, I felt like I had been immersed in spots, but my clothes dried out by the kitchen fire this morning, and I am not the worse for wear only the pant creases are washed out. The country is so infested with she-pirates that I never spend an evening at home anymore, and I can't keep enough biled shirts and linen collars to keep myself dressed up it seems. Last Friday night Cousin Bee's Palmer had a "Moonlight" with a slick platform and Japanese lanterns for decorations, and about sixty boys and girls trimmed the landscape. I began to dance as soon as the wax was shaved onto the floor and quit with the "*Home Sweet Home*," and just wore myself to a frazzledy feeling two-steppin' and waltzin' my happy self to death. The nigger string music was excellent and Hallie was there. You know I haven't had a word with Hallie since she cashed her checks and I have been wanting some of those looky looks given on the street interpreted. I just hogged every dance I could with the gray messalin pretty neck child. Once three of us were claiming a dance, and I just had to take things in my own arms and lead her off with me. Hallie was most of that party to me. She can't understand the situation like I do and she just "beat my face" so to speak because I did not "pay her no mind" like I intimated I was going to do when she cashed the check. I just felt like a dog and to prove I did want to come I "dated" for Monday night, knowing full well I would probably get scalped by her "consort," Boulton.

Saturday night was full of Biddle, and we ate at Wilkinson's ice-cream-cold-cream joint at a table with Dorsey and Hirshberg. Dorsey and I have the hatchet out of sight but it wouldn't take much scratching to unearth it. I fear I buried mine like a dog does a bone, with a resurrection in view.

Tuesday night A.R. and I went to the picture show from force of habit. I wanted to see the girls and she wanted to see the boys.

TEACHER RESTRICTIONS

The teachers can't dance at all and can't go to the picture show or have company on school nights, but they can go to out-of-doors rollerskating rinks. I guess I must learn to roll. The rink is to be opened about Friday night. The trimmer for whom I have had the pleasure of buying a hunk of orange ice, since I last bared my heart to you. can do anything she wants to. I really think she will be a credit to the city limits. Girls are plentiful here. One afternoon I looked into C.C.'s store and a great wave of timidity swept over me when I realized I was the only man there with Helen, Frances McCutcheon, Dorsey, Sallie Davis,

Anna Rose, Ruth Berkheimer and an inanimate suit form. I went out to Helen's last night and tonight A.R. and I are asked out there for supper. I haven't seen my Mother for a long time it seems to me, except at the breakfast and supper times.

"A PROTRACTED VISIT"

Up at the Palmer waltz, Cousin Katie Cox trounced up to me and said she wanted me to dance with her dear friend, Mrs. Heck. I learned Sister Heck was Constant Continual Performance Blessing Smith, brought to the hall by one Biswell youth of her neighborhood. A.R. asked her if she was home on a visit, and she replied affirmatively and added, "a protracted visit." On further investigation, I learned Mr. Heck only "used to was" and "cannot is" now. I never had heard of the dismemberment of relations, had you? Palmer just adores rags and the dog-walk and she was all time doing them. Cousin Bee says she thinks "rags are downright cute," but I told A.R. the other night I didn't believe they were originated for any Heavenly purpose and what conscience I have left tells me I am not going to play for any more raggers. Let 'em two step and waltz. If I didn't have my kid sister, I wouldn't feel so keen about it perhaps, but I just can't stand to see my Sis raggin' and dog-walkin' promiscuously, cute or no cute. But everybody's doing it!.

SKATING RINK

Saturday night everyone was at the skating rink. A.R. just mopped up the floor about three times, but it only bruised her knee. Albert Smith was talking about the fallen and he said there were a whole lot of them who fell at the end of the rink where we were and he asked some girls, "I wonder if anybody fell on the other end?" I just couldn't control myself then. The truth is they just fell on all ends and sides and I believe I will continue to watch others instead of producing my own downfall. After the rink was closed about twenty of us went over to "Fred's" and drank and ate. Helen and Taylor and Fannie McCutcheon and Ethel, Albert and me and my girls and the school teachers and the trimmer. After that was over, the teachers all went home and the rest of us janeyed in town until Ab and Ethel came from the train with Josephine Franklin, Genevieve Imhoff, and Margeret O'Connell of Sedalia. Then we all went into Fred's again and took on some more drinks and don't you know the teachers all came back to get something to drink before we left and their comin' in was the signal for Ab and Taylor and Me to set right up to the strange girls and we were the devotedest things until the educational bureau left. These girls had the drapings and the slits on their suits and the stick-up on their lips at the proper angles to make them mighty good looking and Imhoff was the prettiest. She has beautiful hair and eyes, desirable eye lashes, though a particular person like Lois would say, "She is a little stout." O'Connell was thin as a race horse and has run a good race I judge. Her Dad wouldn't let her come until Ethel promised to get her out to Catholic mass Sunday morning, but when the Cadillac got to the church the mass had all been gone an hour. O'Connell danced like a feather but don't ask me how I know. She has lines in her face and I don't know whether she is young or old, but I liked her and "Genny" best.

All these children could play and sing some. I was down to Albert's most every day. Sunday, Lois and Anna Rose were there too, and so were Taylor and Bettie Arbuckle, and Frances Long spent a few minutes. The girls were going back to Sedalia at 2:00 a.m., and I thought of sitting up but decided if I didn't get a little sleep somebody will be sitting up with my embalmed corpse. I am so tired and sleepy but my mind is active enough to imagine A.R. and Lois on the skating rink tonight with me looking on from the side, hoping someone will come down with a bump so I can be jarred awake.

ea ea ea ea ea

Skating rink is just like Chautauqua to me. I hate to miss a number but I never get to go in the day time. The programs are always interesting, and somebody new is always falling all over himself. Helen and I went down sprawling on last Tuesday night two times, but neither of us has been distinguished that way since. Saturday there was just one mob of humans on the rink and it seemed dangerous, but nobody got any bones snapped and times *were* good. I may have told you last week that I wasn't going to skate. I put on the rollers last Monday night and have missed only one night since then. Anna Rose never wants to quit. We go home tired as dogs, ravenously hungry, and eat an eleven o'clock supper and can hardly get to bed before we drop off and forget everything. Lois Snarr stayed until last Friday and she just got sweeter all the time. It is just as well for me she went, as I was thinking she would make me a good wife if I could get her.

Hallie is going home and she came by this morning to tell me so. She says if I wait for her to write to me she will never do it. Now it seems to me girls are mighty impudent these days. The idea of the boy writing first. She must be an old-fashioned girl. Well, I expect to see her hand-write maybe.

Nearly every night some of the teachers or the trimmer asks a bunch to come up to Moser's after the rink closes, to dance and sing and play. I think A.R. and I have been four times since last Thursday, but as I have just naturally beat all of the sound out of "B-natural and C-flat" keys, I am going to stop playing for without these important sounds, I will ruin my little reputation as a rag producer. I would think Mrs. Moser would get sick of such doings every night as she gets up at 5:30 every morning and she can't sleep through all the racket we keep up. I get right mad at Bobbie Roberts for making fun of me for wanting to go home at a decent hour and if she don't quit, I am going to tell her something embarrassing. She tells me I will never do anything if I find she wants me to do it. Maybe it is the lack of sleep that has put the crows-feet in her face.

"GIVE ME WHAT I MARRIED YOU FOR"

John Tinsley has rode off into the night and Estherline is making a still hunt. He rode away Saturday night after telling his hired hand enough work ahead for a week. John and Estherline had a rukus Saturday morning. Not long ago a lot of men were working around the barn up there and she came to the door and called, "John! John!" And when he didn't answer, she approached closer and called louder, "John! John Tinsley! You come in here to the house and give me what I married you for." That was the time he went in and beat her all up to thunder. She had been better ever since until Saturday. I stopped here and burned one of the Egyptian deodorizers over my letter.

February 11   **AIN'T LOVE GRAND?**

You don't know these people but several months ago Jim Rouse ran off with Mrs. Edwards (not Miss Sallie) and created such a stir in Junction society. Poor old Mrs. Rouse is awful deaf and carries one of those black snakes with a funnel on the tail for people to talk through. She still loves Jim and womanlike wants him back. She goes to a fortune teller—some coffee ground nigger, I imagine, down there and asks all about Jim—and the fortune teller is slick and says. "He still loves you, Mrs. R.—he and the other woman ain't getting along well at all. He is getting tired of her." And at this point Mrs. R. gabbles out the words: " I hope to God he'll kill her." Now ain't love fearful?

February 17

If I had let myself think so, I would have concluded it was disrespectful to our churches to tango-turkey trot—and so forth on Sunday. I know I didn't have enough brass to ask forgiveness last night for doing it. I knew the Lord wouldn't "pay no mind" as long as I had that "Wasn't it fun?" feeling. Well, if I don't quit a lot of things I'll be associated with old man Tanner *[the town reprobate]* in the next world a lot closer than I am in this.

"GREAT BIG BLUE-EYED BABY"

I dined with the boarders up there [at the Mosers, the boarding house where a number of the teachers lived] last Sunday and had such a nice dinner and I liked Miss Fulton at the table. Then while "Nellada" et and did the dishes, I taught Miss Fulton to sing —

> "Oh you great big blue-eyed baby,
> you're the sweetest thing I know—
> and desire—Oh! Oh! Oh! Oh!
> I just like to betcha,
> if you linger long, I'll getcha!
> You're a great big, blue-eyed baby. I want to pet you
> Like a child of three. But there is one thing I want
> Understood—when you're around me, I can't be good.
> I want to hug and kiss you like your mama would
> Her great big, blue-eyed baby!"

—to some catchy tune, and Fulton has those blue eyes besides. She learned it fast—so I guess she knew something about every word in it.

ta ta ta ta ta

April 3   THE FLIRTATIOUS VIOLET

When Gertrude was down here the last time we were walking through the budding apple trees and we came to one which had beneath it hundreds of violets. No other tree was affected like this and we wondered how the Lord happened to make that one the most favored. Gertie is so nice and sentimental and she couldn't quit thinking about how pretty they looked, and when she got home she wrote a little of her "slop-over" down and mailed it to me. But I took issue with what she said about the modesty of the Violet and claimed that while I thought Violet was a perfect lady, I did not think she was any better than anybody else, for she was a flirt and was one of the very first to parade herself before the public gaze and had even been bold enough to put herself out to attract my attention.

ta ta ta ta ta

I saw Agnes Daisy Kayser who has had her hair done by the new process [permanent wave] which keeps it in curl six months and only gets straight when it is dusty. Well, it must have been dusty at the concert as it had not much more curl than mine.

ta ta ta ta ta

April 21   "IN THE HOLLOW OF HIS HAND"

Did you know while I was having the time of my life with you Glenidaites, my Mam was getting herself most killed? When I got home, I found Lillian's suitcase in the hall and wondered why it hadn't gone to Sedalia until I got into Mother's room and found her all bundled up on the back of her head and neck—the ugliest bruises I have ever seen. Well, my eyes certainly stuck out in astonishment and she and Father related the Sunday's "holdings" to relieve me. They had been to church and had started to Horace's and were going down the Clifton Heights' hill when the "holding back strap" broke and let the buggy run up on old Duke. Old Duke won't stand for anything like that and he nearly jumped out of his breeches and was going lickety split by the time they got down the hill. The horse just went mad, he was so frightened, and Father could not stop him. Mother wanted to roll out but Dad kept telling her to hold her seat as they passed Naomi Hull in her buggy (just shaved by) and headed for the railroad crossing sign and the ditch beyond. Just as they got on the tracks, Mother rolled and fell right on her neck and shoulders, striking on the iron rail, and that was all she did for some minutes. Father stopped the horse a short distance further down the road and hurried back as fast as possible. Mrs. Hull and Stella Snell, who lives up on the hill, were working with Mother by that time and soon restored consciousness, and in a little while Mother was able to go home with Father in Hull's buggy. She was so jarred up that every shake of the buggy hurt her and the bruised spots swelled badly yesterday, but by the time I got home, the swelling had subsided a great deal. Mother was so sore she could hardly move, but felt better this morning though she can't raise up unless we pull her up by the hands. So there is quite a soreness yet. Her body was not bruised anywhere else. She rolled clear of the wheels. We hope she will be able to be up in a few days. They started to phone me but as Mother did not seem to be seriously injured, decided to let me round out my day with you in happiness.

I think the Lord must hold our family in the hollow of his hand whenever any of us drive Duke. This is about the tenth time I've had chances to feel thankful that our family circle is still unbroken.

A NEGRO BAPTISM

There isn't anything going on but a protracted meeting and I am supposed to go every night. I am doing like I am supposed to do and am playing the sinner's marches, but none of them seem to be doing any marching. They sing, but they don't *move out* any. I guess everybody is like Henry Chipley, who was moved at the last River Church Negro meeting. He testified that he had been in the Vineyard a long time, that he had been a child of God for fourteen years, but had always been "skeered" to tell it. I think that is what is the matter with all of the New Franklin Methodist members.

Did I ever tell you that I saw 16 Negroes baptized not long since. There was hardly enough depth in the river to get all of big Alice Boggs under the water, so after trying to get her clear under once and failing, they just pushed her head under and let her bosom get wet as the water ran off her head. It did the same good, doubtless. They put 16 under in 20 minutes, which was saving time as well as coons.

Gathering at the river

WE BELIEVE IN SINS AND GETTING FORGIVEN

Tonight I read Mother a little booklet called *Eddyism*. It was divided into three parts: "Is it Science?" "Is it Christian?" and, "How Long Will it Last?" I had never read much about Christian Science before and really did not know for what it stands. Mam, I thought prayer was used in their treatments but Sister Eddy said, "Prayer is a hindrance." Mother said, "Oh! I'd hate to think of jumping into bed without my prayers. Don't you reckon Sister Minnie ever prays? We had a real sensational time reading the disclosures and neither one of us is going to embrace the C.S. faith. We believe in sins and getting forgiven and we don't think C.S. is the Holy Ghost.

Christmas in Boonville at the Billies'

[Lilburn managed frequently to be with us for at least a portion of our obervations of the Christmas holiday. He was present at our home in Boonville, Christmas 1913. It was one of the warmest Christmases of record. Lilburn undertook to teach my brother William and me to ride the bicycles given us by our Grandfather Taylor. The following summer we crossed the ferry and rode the bikes to Fairview, stopping off in New Franklin for a soda with Lilburn.

[Left to right, William Kingsbury, Lilburn Kingsbury, Jere Kingsbury, W. W. Kingsbury, Mrs. W. W. (Julia) Kingsbury, Ernest Kingsbury, Julia Kingsbury, George Warren Taylor, and Warren Taylor Kingsbury.]

1914

[Absence of the teachers during the Christmas holiday and bitter winter weather cut into Lilburn's social activities, giving him time to read Gene Stratton Porter's best selling **Laddie**. *Of it he wrote to Mam, January 2,]* "I have not read anything so refreshing for a year."

[He continues]

"I finished Hall Caine's *The Woman Thou Gavest Me*, and kept hoping until "The End" that I would get something worthwhile for my eye strain, but I never did. Perhaps I read it too fast. It shows though how people with the Catholic religion soaked into their forms, never get it out of their systems. And the Catholic viewpoint of divorce. It was all right for a woman to have a child by a man other than her husband, at least, the priests closed their eyes to that, but they couldn't hear to this woman getting a divorce from her husband, so she could marry the father of her child and keep it from being what begins with a "B." I know you won't want to take time to read such trash, so I am telling you something of the hang of the story. The lady has consumption and dies of it at a real pretty time and "the world swings round to the sound of the international rag !!!"

TEACHERS

The teachers will be back tomorrow if they live and keep their health. I have been trying to get some extra sleep in anticipation of an all night vigil soon. I think if I resolve anything, it will be to go away from Moser's at 12 p.m. always.

Father got on a tear to do something smart, so he packed a box of apples and sent it by parcel post to Will Chandler at Gilliam. Some rural carrier will give Dad the dickens, for the box weighed 48 pounds, (two pounds under the limit). It cost 52 cents to get it delivered to Willie's mail box.

OIL-WELL PROMOTION

There is a fellow in the country trying to get people worked up on the oil pitch. They say the town is undermined with oil, full of the juice that makes people rich. I hope it is. I am undermined with love for you, Mam, and you have done found it for sure. Your near-chile, Libus.

ta ta ta ta ta

January 6   **DANCING CLASS**

Mam, remember the little card from the Walz girls inviting me to join their dancing class to learn the tango and so forth? I did not think a thing about it then, but A.R. and I were in Boonville Sunday night and after Sister Julia said she and Billie were going, I got right in the notion. A.R. and I haven't announced it to the family yet. I think we could persuade Mom that it is the thing to do, but Dad just 'spises to be persuaded. I hope no one will think I want to do anything besides dance the tango, when they see me learning the strokes tonight.

Of course the teachers are all back and Sunday night, after we came from Boonville, the lights were on and the piano was going at Moser's, so A.R. and I opened the front door and walked in on some dancing and smoking and courting and idling. One of the boarders, Mrs. Chandler, looked like she thought we had blurred our social manners record by not knocking, and I rather felt like it would have been better if we had entered like nice people. Boulton Settle was chinning Miss Dorsey. Biddle was upstairs but came down and chinned with us before we left.

January 15   TANGO-MINDED

The dancing class was postponed from Tuesday night until Friday night of this week, as there was a show in town Tuesday. It seems tomorrow night will never come, but I won't be ready when it really arrives if I don't stay home and press breeches tonight. I have been practicing the new steps faithfully whenever I remember how I want to look like something when I do them. I must have had a clumsy birth, for awkwardness is something I can't seem to overcome. And if you don't get some graceful lines to do the tango on, you're certainly doing wrong, all wrong.

The poor tango reminds me of a woman who had gone wrong in some way. I guess somebody did make the tango go wrong at first, and now when it is trying its best to live its reputation down, everybody is just kicking it into the gutter faster than it can get up. Mother has not only kicked it down, but Father has *spit* on it. All sight unseen too. Well, I am going to quit when I see anything worser than a walz or two-step. The new gyrations are lots of fun and exercise, and you know this close indoor work demands that I should have the latter.

DATING DORSEY

I saw Miss Dorsey and asked her to walk home with me, and she said she would if I would get her back by half past eight. Mother "give" an oyster fry with cold dill pickles, and we asked Dorsey what else she liked and had the supper to her own taste. Mother said Louis looked at Lenore like he thought she was going to bust. I didn't think she ate so very much. I don't care to have company who won't eat a lot. I kept trying to bust her. After supper, with that "half-after-eight" condition in mind, I set about making her forget the time. I picked out a lot of pecans and put them on one side of her, and put a box of fruit chocolates on the other side. I moved her so she had her back to the stove and me and the "Pinochle deck" took the front seat. She is a good teacher and let me beat her several times. After a while the phone rang and somebody was caring to speak with Miss Dorsey. The voice at the other end said, "Don't you know its half-past nine? Boulton Settle has been here 45 minutes waiting to take you skating." Our watch really had stopped and we didn't know it was so late. I am all time crossing Boulton's path unintentionally. But I didn't care and Miss D. said she didn't either, but we went right home, and she got to skate from 10 to 12.

NEGRO SHOOTING

The negro who got a hole shot in him here Sunday night is going to get well. He thought he was going to die and sent for Xena Bly to come and tell him goodbye. Ernest and Mag Chancellor had to go over to the cabin of the Blys and tell the message. Annie said they couldn't go out to town that time of night, but Xena wanted to tell her lover, Maybe Darby, good bye, [and] so had John Bly hitch up and take her to town. And after all that trouble, Maybe is surely going to get well.

Later in January   **ROASTING DORSEY**

I was going to give you four quarters of this morning, Mam, but got to writing a roast of Dorsey. I've been my pleasantest all in vain. Well, I am either going to make her glad or mad. The way she has acted has stiffened my mind, and my ideas have crystallized and I've got a home talent song about her. Last Sunday, Helen, Anna Rose and I sang it so much we might nigh popularized it. I feel just like a "bleeding heart" broken since Dorsey turned me away three nights. Once she was tired; the next, she thought she was going to Fayette; and the next night she knew she would be in Fayette. She did all this throwing away in one phone talk. Haven't seen her to say "howdy" to since her return. I don't know whether she don't like my person or whether I make her mad somehow, it all amounts to the same thing ... but Heaven knows about the Blonde. She is worse than the uncertainties of life. She is Declaration of Independence itself, one I'll never learn. I noted the independence tone of the card myself and it was to say the least, interesting. I don't like 'em too easy. I can forgive 'em for being too hard a sight easier than I can for being too ripe. As "old Dr. Kingsbury" used to say: "The apple that falls without shaking, is a little too ripe for me. They are nearly always mushy."

As for me, I've been cheered up by Biddle this week, and I took her my copy of "Miss Beauty" as she is a Southerner, Tennesseer or Kentuckyrine, one, and I thought she'd "bust her sides" at it.

A SHORT HONEYMOON

John Gray's honeymoon, seems he put on a white shirt, collar and tie, and was married. Then he took his bride home and took off all that white clean clothes. His bride saw how dirty his underclothes were, and she said, "Mr. Gray, if you don't take a bath, I won't sleep with you. I'll sit up all night." Well, John was married to his dirty clothes and would not grant the bride's request and give up his first love, so she sat up all night and went back to her old home the next morning. Dr. Fleet says this is true.

ᖗ ᖗ ᖗ ᖗ ᖗ

A LETTER FROM MAM

[Only a few of Mam's letters to Lilburn were saved. The excerpt from this one, written shortly after the above, expresses Mam's indignation of Dorsey's treatment of Lilburn who had become as dear to Mam as her own children.]

... Honey, I was so indignant at that "Bunch of Vanity" for her treatment of you, I almost "biled" over and if I ever again hear of you extending any courtesies to her, why I'll disown you. I felt a strong aversion to her the day she was here, and couldn't even see that she was beautiful, as Martha did. No indeed. There must be something beautiful in character to illume a face, and hers was the kind that is all on the outside, and a rag doll could be just as attractive and have just as icy a heart and appreciation of life and what is worthwhile. Dorsey impressed me as vain and consummately selfish. Myrtle says she told Mabel she was in love with Boulton Settle. "So mote it be." I'm truly glad it is not you. Her heart will always be at the bottom of something, selfishness perhaps, and B. or any other fellow is likely to have the ice break and be swamped who skates across her heart. I don't advise any such.

January 23

[With teacher Dorsey cold-shouldering him, Lilburn focused his attention upon Nannie Estill of Sedalia, a young and attractive first cousin of his first love, Etta Estill. A weekend at her home where "Nannie and I traded tango steps all afternoon" enabled him to schedule a rendezvous with her in St. Louis the following week. Of this he writes to Mam.]

MEET ME IN ST. LOUIS, NANNIE

I got to Union Station about thirty minutes before Nanny arrived, but as soon as she came we ate breakfast in the Union Station, and everything was so good. I knew all the time I was going to be a proud man to be the "guardeen" that day for the best looking brown eyes I have ever "went with." The eyes wore a taupe brocaded suit, the skirt of cloth and the coat of velvet, and the best-looking lace waist, a cloth of gold hat with fur on it, and the cutest little patent leather shoes. And the best looks. After breakfast, we found a taxi and went out to a tailor shop way out on Olive and parted for the morning. ... I was hunting for some pumps to match A.R.'s dress, but couldn't find anything in yellow, so I got bronze which they are wearing with any kind of evening or street dress, with hose to match. These pumps were very high-heeled, awful looking that way, and laced up in front with ribbons and had six or eight little cut steel buckles on each. I liked them very much. I was to look for a wedding present for the Woodson boys and get Mother a *wrapper* but didn't have time so met Nannie at 12:15 at Scruggs and we had a delicious lunch. The best eats of the day. Then we went to the Columbia and saw a fine bill of vaudeville. Ellen Beach Yaw, a grand opera singer, sang the "*Mad Scene*" from *Lucia* and two of her own compositions. The latter were lovely and enhanced by some scenic effects. Of course there were laughs by the hundreds at foolish things gifted people can do, and we were having a mighty good time. One of the women said, "He is one of these men who is all in front of himself." Meaning old man Pot-gut.

After the matinee, we shopped a little bit more, went to the [Hotel] Jefferson to get the proper atmosphere, and then to McTague's for dinner, where we had music with our meal. We enjoyed every minute of it and stayed until time to go to the Shubert to see *Peg O' My Heart*. This was the real thing we had come to see. We both expected a musical comedy, but there was no music from the stage except a little song to her lover about "Friendship." The orchestra played the popular *"Peg O'My Heart"* song frequently though. Peg was an Irish colleen. Her wit was like a razor and all of her lines had been boiled down until they were the pure essence. Nearly every line made you want to laugh or cry, and yet you always laughed. I never saw such a clean play with such a clear appeal to the good that is in one, and Nannie and I *certainly enjoyed* it. I can't think of anything I ever liked better.

Nannie and I were in a terrible rush for fear we would miss our train out at 11:38, so we rushed out of the theater, got on four rubber tires and were whisked off to the depot in such a hurry that we arrived thirty minutes before the scheduled departure of our train. We had to laugh and Nannie said we ought to have taken a street car. She was exceedingly considerate, and now and then we would almost have an argument on the street about where we would go to eat and how we should go. She acted as if she hadn't been used to flying around, hitting the high places. I knew she was used to it, but nevertheless I appreciated her consideration and would have found pleasure in spending all I had, if it had been necessary. When we got on the pullman, Nannie sat on my new hat and mashed it right flat, but I was positively so full of good times I told her to do it again. And once when I moved over to sit by her, in getting up I bumped my head on the side of the car until the sound made us think something was cracked.

If it had killed me, I was in the state of mind to enjoy it. But of course we couldn't chatter all night when other people wanted to sleep, Nannie being one of them, so the last I seen of her, she went off to her shelf and then after a little while, I sought mine. We both got home all right, and I have been wishing to do it all over again, and to quote from the church discipline, "The Lord being my helper, I will."

February 2   HESITATION WALTZ

Last Tuesday night I went to dancing class and had a right good time like I usually do. We learned to do the "*Hesitation Waltz*," and everybody likes it better than the "tawngo." There was another lesson on Thursday night but the ferry has not been running and I would have had to cross the river in a skiff and besides thinking it would be awful cold to get ducked in case of accident, I felt like I would hate to get drowned on the way to tango class, with my parents so opposed. So I have missed one session. I want to learn the Charmeuse Waltz, and then I think I shall hesitate about going any more.

BEFORE "SHORN TIME"

Peake Vincil came over from Columbia last Sunday to see Anna Rose. He is an Engineering School Senior and wanted to come over before "Shorn-time." To prove their manhood, engineers have to grow beards for a month before first semester finals and he wanted to show his off. Peake is a right good looking fellow but his whiskers ruined him this time. He had side-burns and a goatee that ran from ear to ear under his chin and over and above, there was "misplaced eye-brows" surmounting his mouth. He looked like he was awfully pleased. It was so dark in the room Mother couldn't tell the black fuzz from anything else. Well, I must tell you of the transfiguration of Peake. I don't think Mom and Dad paid him any mind much. They were talking at the supper table and something was said about the Vincils and Dad asked Peake if he was any kin to the Vincil who was such a humdinger in the ministry. Well, when Peake said "He was my grandfather," Mam and Dad just boosted Peake right up nine notches by leaning toward him and saying, "He was!!!" I knew then that with Mother and Dad, Peake's future was assured, for his grandfather was Secretary of the Grand *[Masonic]* Lodge of Missouri for "years and years" (Father says) and Secretary of the Missouri Conference for ages and was "a grand old man."

MOST BEAUTIFUL DAY OF THE WEEK

Friday, the most beautiful day of the week, I went to Boonville to the dancing class. Had to get to the river in a machine and my right cheek was exposed to the wind. When I got to Boonville, the barber didn't have to shave but the left side. The right was cut clean. It was mighty raw out that day. I had a time getting a pardner *[sic]* for the class. A.R., Julia, and Hazel had a beau, a sick baby, and a bad cold respectively, but I prevailed upon Hazel to flirt with pneumonia, and we had a lot of fun. Self-praise is half scandal, but I can't pass up this compliment. Miss Walz walked up to Hazel and me, who were "hesitating" and 'lowed, "Yours is the best I've seen on the floor tonight." That broke the spell, and after that Hazel and I never could do so well.

PARENTAL MISHAPS

Mother was going around the kitchen the other morning singing *"Gathering Home."* She had been cautioned not to go out on the porch because it was coated with ice. She forgot. Singing happily she stepped out the door and was gathered to the floor in a knot. I didn't know how much of her was broken, but when I got her up, she decided to have either a sprained ankle or a broken toe, but we talked and rubbed her out of the notion. She has forgotten she came down. The day of the Estill sale, Father was driving along and on a sharp curve, met an automobile which startled his horse. The nag gave one sharp jump to the side, and Father, and the lap-robe, and his hat all fell clear out of the buggy into the road. Dad was fussed or stunned a little, for he said he didn't know who was driving the car, and it was Bob Wayland. Dad has forgotten how it feels to fall out of a buggy. But he said one cannot imagine how quickly he went out.

BALLOON OF ELOQUENCE

Louis Williams told me all about the sale. Mr. Estill must have been quite nervous. He got up to speechify and specify who were the mamas and papas of the colts. His balloon of eloquence rose gracefully, but his drag rope hung in the family tree of the Kentucky Horse and the fancy names and blue-blooded relationships were as so much tangle-foot for him. He was forced to descend without making much of a flight.

Brother Ginn broke my ear drums at church last night. I sincerely hope he will never preach for us "agin." I was sitting right close to him, and when he would go to howling like a hurt dog, it was almost more than I could stand. He was a little hoarse and if you have ever heard a mad dog growl, you know what I experienced. I felt like the Whitten child did when she asked him not to preach so loud. I had a head-ache last night to begin with. I just feel awful bum now. I wondered if it would be a scene if I should jump up and holler as loud as I could. Bro. Ginn is a good man, though.

"SYMPATHETIC ORCHESTRA"

A.R. is trying to get up a "Sympathetic Orchestra," that is, a lot of ginks [crazies], to play tunes on combs. We practiced last night and there was a spoonful of enthusiasm. For my part, I can play on a comb at home, and I am not looney about coming to town every other night for that purpose. The church is divided. Those who believe comb-playing is fit to be done in church, and those who don't. Nell Blankenbaker was over listening last night, and nobody could have played sweetly enough on a comb with her looking curdled as she did. Practice comes again Thursday night and we will see whether everybody gets tired or not. I am going to play the tea kettle later on.

I went to Sunday School for the third consecutive time. I may go again. Rather enjoy it. The preacher hit me in one remark. He said a man in the church had no business going to Boonville to get a whiskey or a tango. I saw him going to B___ yesterday and whispered my question,"Are you going over for a tango?" He had to laugh and I guess he won't shoot at me any more for a while.

February 27   PRINCESS MOVIE HOUSE

The new "Princess" picture show opened here last night. It is very handsome for so small a city. The grandest feature is the ventilation. It is quite a large picture show. There is a stage, fancy electric lights on ceiling and side walls, and the building has a sporty metal front with a bay window ticket office. For three nights there is to be an orchestra here; one man and five women, and they are really excellent musicians of their kind. Some of them sing well and last night the musical program was worth the price of admission, but the pictures were pore.

March 4   "ONLY ONE RELIGION, THAT OF TODAY"

Sunday I was in Boonville at the Billie's, and that night Billie made an address at the Epworth League at the church and there was a sacred concert. Billie's remarks were very good, but a part of them were intentionally and with malice aforethought (I feared) aimed at the preacher who had been criticizing some of his church members for doing the tango. Billie said that the worst thing about the tango was its name. Just the name sounded like something bad. He read an account of a meeting of the Methodist Conference years ago where one minister made the motion that any Minister of the Methodist creed who should conduct a liquor sales department should be barred from the conference. Five times this motion was put to a vote, and it failed to carry. Billie said, "This would show that things were at least no worse today than they were some years ago, and if the man who made the motion turned his face to the wall and wept, he had more to weep for than you have sometimes, Bro. Smith."

Well, I did not know what was going to take place for Bro. Smith's hands twitched and he brushed his bald head, and Ella Thro Smith, his wife, looked death. Billie kind of shocked me when he said there was one song we sing from which he gets nothing, and it was *"Old Time Religion."* He said there is only one religion, that of today, and today's religion is just as good as the best. He said we must not judge a person without considering his environments. That he had heard people say they wished they had lived at some good time already passed. He cited instances in Science, Business, Politics, and Religion to prove there is no age in the past in which conditions were better than they are now, and said he doubted that anyone who had studied the matter would, if it came to a choice, prefer to, to use a slang expression, *go way back and sit down.* He told the Epworth Leaguers not to get discouraged because they meet with obstacles like those which had caused such an uproar recently (tango! tango! tango!), and challenged them to look into the future for something to go on. And so on and on. I bet Billie would feel scandalized at my synopsis of his talk. I told him I was "proud of him for Mama!"

A PRETTY PACKAGE"

Baby Julia got off a good one. Mr. Jeff Davis's sister-in-law died next door to Billie's and Mr. Davis arranged to have the hearse drive up Billie's auto driveway by the Davis side door, so they could take the body out that way, the front steps being very steep, and the body very heavy. From a window little Julia watched the body carried out and put in the hearse, but she had no comment at the time. When Billie came home and asked at the supper table, as usual, about the day's happenings, Little Julia piped up and said, "Oh! Father. They had the lady done up in the prettiest package with flowers all over it."

I have no girl to rave over this week, and I miss it so.

🙢 🙢 🙢 🙢 🙢

March 16   NURSING AILMENTS

Last week just wasn't for me, I was so out of everything except what I was just pushed into, I wanted to wipe it off the calendar. I didn't have any abscess on my liver, but it needed turning over. Sunday a week ago, I did a very foolish thing. Stayed in and nursed a cold. Wore a hot water bottle on my face and took all the loosening ingredients that everybody could think of. Denied myself three grand sermons during the day and was no better off than if I had cut out around as usual.

Anna Rose has a bad cold and coughed so bad in church last night I said to her on the way home, "You ain't going one step to Columbia with wind like you have and if you don't get busy tonight and tomorrow and mend yourself I won't chaperone you an inch." She took salts and castor oil and a hot lemonade and a scalding footbath as soon as she got home, so I know she wants to go to Columbia with a super-human desire, for she never indulges in salts or so, except on state occasions.

A CUT-UP FORD

Billie took me for a ride in his new Ford the other night. It has electric lights that go out as soon as the engine stops and grow dim or bright according to the speed of the engine. I thought he was going to have an electric starter put on it, but I probably misunderstood for it has a plain old crank. And this Ford has been cutting up about starting, and the other morning I waited a half hour on the thing and then had to walk to town. Beat Billie in by ten minutes. He had to push the car down through the yard and down the little hill before it "give in" and lit out. The man at the Garage in Fayette, filled the tank with water through mistake and Billie and he worked laboriously for a couple of hours before the mistake was discovered. If the Ford does not "look to its laurels better," Billie is not going to keep it. It is practically a new car, but he got it on a trade. He and his family were over in the Winton yesterday, and he said he regained his self-respect riding in it, which he had lost riding in the dinky Ford. Sister Julia said when she got in the Ford and rode, she could close her eyes and imagine she was riding in a tin bath-tub which ain't complimentary to the Ford or road-louse *[another derogatory appellation applied to Fords]*. Did you read about the fellow who had such little sense someone said to him, "I could put all the sense you've got on the back of a louse, and it could lope from here to San Francisco without ever raising a sweat?" I do not want a Ford myself and will never get one if I can raise a few dollars over the $500 mark. I hope more of my kin-folks will buy machines though. I don't care whether they get Packards or Fords as long as they will claim kin with me.

"QUINTESSENCE OF MAGNIFIED SIN"

Well, I have gone to church until I'm calloused. The sermon, I mean *sermons* not services, are from 75 to 110 minutes long. Last night was the longest one and after it was all over, and the people were going out, I just sat there until Bro. Allison came over and I asked him to please help me up. Bro. Crowe went off somewhere Saturday to whet his butcher-knife. Was going to Moberly and got on the wrong train and had to go to Columbia, Centralia and then back to Moberly. I wonder how far it is to Moberly as the "Crowe flies" that way. He "praught" on "Modern Phases of Unbelief" last night and held the "aujience" (as Bro. Dillman would call it because he can't say it right) well. I haven't seen such a mob in an amusement resort since the Princess opened. Crowe really is a splendid preacher, only he has been preaching it is wrong to play *tiddle-de-winks* and do the *cake-walk*. Gospel truth, Mam, he hollered long and loud about the evil of these horrors. Well, you won't catch me sinning in those two ways. As far as tiddle-de-winks and cake-walk go, I am just as good as sanctified. An Oh! how he licks his chops with that word, "tango." That kind of dancing is the quintessence of magnified SIN. But not once has he referred to pinochle or cards of any kind when I have been there, so I have one amusement left, but if I keep on going I know he is going to snatch that away from me. Some of the people told me of a little incident. Anna Rose went to church late one night after the preacher had started on the home stretch. She was going to the choir which sits on a platform at the left of the pulpit. They said that just as A.R. was ready to step up on the platform, the preacher let out something about tango, and A.R. hesitated just an instant and looked at him like she had been electrocuted on the spot, and they said it was right amusing, happening as it did. Maybe you can imagine how A.R. could look without saying, "Well, is that so?"

NEGRO WEDDING

Last Wednesday evening I was starting home and ran into Miss Sallie [Mrs. George Edwards] and Miss Biddle, and Miss Sallie said if I could live on oyster soup alone to come home with her and see Mayme marry Cody Estill. I could have lived on pea-soup to see a coon wedding. After soup, Mayme cleaned up the dishes and at seven prompt, the living room door was thrown open and in came Mayme and Cody, followed by Mr. and Mrs. Palmer Murry. Mayme said she must ask her sister, Lucille (Mrs. Murry) cause if she didn't, Lucille would think she was mad at her for marrying that "no-account" Palmer.

Miss Biddle stayed set down but Miss Sallie, Mr. George and I riz up and Mr. G. sure put in some extra words for Mayme's ceremony. He gave us a chance to object if we wanted to and them a chance to object to each other if they so desired, before he told them to join right hands, and Mayme stuck out her left, and he pronounced them stuck together for life. Mrs. Edwards shooed them back in the kitchen and let them drink grape juice from little thimble glasses and eat cake, and it was all over as soon as Biddle and I stuck our names as witnesses to the wedding certificate. Cody and Mayme looked so happy. Mrs. Edwards was hoping all evening, I think, there would be a slip between cup and lip again, but Cody didn't have no rheumatiz this spring.

St. Pat's Ball   UNIVERSITY OF MISSOURI

Columbia was quite pleasant for me. We got there about half-past nine and we went up to the Athens Hotel and hunted up Mrs. MacFarlane, She is State Regent of the DAR *[Daughters of the American Revolution]*, lives at the hotel, and sits on her dignity. She is between 50 and 60 years old and is large enough to be imposing, and she was all-firin' nice. A.R. didn't seem to need her or me either, but we all ate together at the hotel, and she seemed to enjoy being with us younger people. She talked D.A.R. quite a good deal and advised A.R. to be a Daughter and me to become a Son of Ogun, but we aren't old enough to take up with such yet.

Sister MacFarlane says what she thinks regardless. Peake Vincil had dinner with us, and she laid him out for smoking. He said he didn't know what made him feel so miserable and she 'lowed she could tell him, he smoked too much. She knew by his complexion and then gave a vivid account of how her tobacco-bearded son whom the doctors gave up on as a hopeless victim of tobacco, and she had him quit tobacco and it took 15 months for him to recover. Don't think Peake enjoyed his dinner.

After dinner we went to the parade and the knighting exercises and the demonstrations at the Engineering Building and the vaudeville performance which was held in the Auditorium. By that time it was six o'clock. I send you a picture showing the crowd around the cloth and wood bridge over which the victims, the Senior Engineers, were led, where they kissed the Blarney Stone and while doing it were hit on the back by St. Patrick who made them Knights. I reckon a million germs were left on the Blarney, and I hope they sterilize it. While A.R. and I were standing in the crowd, we noticed right in front of us, two good-looking, well-dressed girls who were gawking at the Senior Engineers and they talked thus, which made A.R. prick up her ears higher than the sticker in her new hat.

"There he is. They are right together." "Who is that fellow with him? I can't remember his name!" —"Vincil—isn't he goodlooking?"—"Uh-hu"—and we all gawked together. As soon as they had subsided, A.R., who was dying of amusement began in tones sufficiently loud to carry to the two females, "Did Peake tell you where to meet him? He said he would be with me just as soon as the "kow-tow was over." I wish you could have seen the two girls gawk at Anna Rose.

Robert Tindall asked me to go out to his staying house with him after supper, and as I was leaving, I heard a clatter coming down the steps and looked around to see A.R. all breathless and haggard-eyed gasping to the clerk, "Oh, I've knocked my flowers out of the window and don't know what direction to go to get them." I knew where her room was, and I chased out and found the posies in the street and restored them to the distressed, a big armful of pink and lavender sweet peas and ferns, and when I saw A.R. at the ball later, she was surely "living happy ever after." The hall was very large and had a lot of elaborate decorations which nothing short of a world of back-aches could produce. The whole top was a lattice of green and white, said lattice work extending half way down the sides of the wall. All the lights were white and green and a huge electric shamrock at one end of the hall winked continuously at the funny dancing ways of the crowd. The men don't wear dress suits to the dances over there any more, for democratic reasons, but the girls haven't quit putting on the evening furs, silks and satins. The music was beautiful and just seemed to pull me in, and if I had known earlier that no dress suits were allowed, I should surely have accepted the invitation to dance as long as the train would wait for me. The programs for the girls were fans, with kid backs and card ribs and on each rib was room for listing two dances and pardners. The end of the ribs and backs was in the shape of a shamrock. A poor description of the best looking program I have ever seen. I got back to N.F. at 2 a.m. and went up to Lillian's where I expected to get to sleep, but I couldn't wake a soul, and knowing them to be sound sleepers, I gave up and walked home, to find all the Edmonstons out there tucked in snugly. I wondered where was an axe!!! But before leaving for the country they had telegraphed to McBaine to tell me they were leaving the key behind the shutter for me. I did not get the message but they "done what they cud," and I'll have to forgive them. A.R. got home in the afternoon.

🙦 🙦 🙦 🙦 🙦

April 2

We hope Mr. Spring is in earnest, wooing our ward, Miss Fruit Tree. He certainly has her going his way, and we hope she won't be fooled. Several times before, you know, she has just "throwed herself away," on him, and it always takes her a year to get over it.

REVIVAL AFTER-EFFECTS

We are almost lost with no meeting to attend. We raised a nice little bit of money, the easiest in the world Sunday, about $150, and sent the gospel spreader on his way rejoicing if money has any effect upon his feelings at all. The Overstreets got the most good out of the meeting: John, two of his sons, two of his sons-in-law, all joined the church. All of them but two had been baptized into the Christian Church, but they decided to change faith. The two, while they went to the Methodists, want to be "put under" and are not going to take advantage of the Methodist exemption of baptism. To me, in my ignorant condition, the only difference between Christian and Methodist Churches is the amount of water.

Sometime in March   ## GRAND MARCH ON SKATES

Mam, we do the Grand March on skates at nine o'clock every night and it really is lots of fun. But listen to the gab. I told you Mrs. Duke was using her legs to advantage on rollers, didn't I? Well, one day, Sister Allison, the preacher's wife, went to look on and she saw Mrs. Dukes doing the modest didoes *[unconventional acts]* and the next day Preacher Allison went to see Sister Duke and told her that Sister Allison cried all night after seeing Sister Duke skate. And Sister Mat Burrus said that they might as well be dancing as to skate like they do here, that she didn't think they ought to hold hands. Mam, this is might nigh too unbelievable to repeat, but Sister Duke's own mouth informed me, Wednesday night at prayer meeting. Brother Allison is said to have stated that he had asked different ones about the rink and one person told him there were three things he had to contend with in Franklin, viz: the skating rink, the pool hall, and the dance hall. Mrs. Duke 'lows she guesses she will have to quit as such a ruckus has been raised about her skating and now she comes and looks on all watery-eyed, and when I pass her, I feel like saying, "Come in, the fallin's fine," but I hesitate. I must say that this skating rink is properly conducted so far as I can see. The Kincaids and Sprinkles who run it are nice-acting people, it gives opportunity for outdoor exercise, is doing me good, socially, and all that goes on is right in view of all the people who crowd the seats every night to look on, and I must say that I do disapprove of church people running it down or thinking that church people should not attend as often as they please. They don't run the rink on Sunday. If it were not so "drip, drip, drippy" on my pocketbook to go regularly, I would like for it to stay all winter which they will do if they keep coining the money. This is just a big picnic every night and such grand hand-squeezing!!!

The Burrus faction are at outs with the the Allisons yet, and the other day Mrs. Burrus asked Lillian why she did not come to the church society. We heard in town through other talkers that Lillian told her she would come to the society when she (Burrus) treated Mrs. Allison right. Mrs. Burrus went home and just cried and Julia Lee wondered what made Lillian talk that way to Mrs. Burrus, and oh! Mam, it is just a sight all this talking and crying of Christianity.

Sometimes I think that all one needs to do right is to listen to his conscience and obey it, but I don't find it satisfying to have a raw conscience. Something is all time bothering, so I guess I will continue to pin my hope to the church with all its unrest.

Early Spring   ## "BUNCH OF VANITY"

Mam, didn't you lay out the "Bunch of Vanity" though! *[The reference is to Lenore Dorsey, one of the teachers he was infatuated with.]*

Well, I'll put a snow-white lily in her hand and say she looks awful nice like you fixed her. And won't grieve none.

The day we were visiting at your place I thought the mesh of her net waist was too coarse to be real pretty, but I didn't think of you seeing through it clean to her soul. It is a good thing I didn't see all you did, else I might have thrown her into that hollow down there, but her teeth, her red lips, and her eyes when worn with dark blue and her "figger" helped her to get by with me. I was not thinking of her *soul.* You know how a child can think so much of a rag doll, and more of the beautiful bisque face? Well, what am I but a little child? Being so simple-like, I didn't think about the inside being of saw dust when I admired "The Bunch" so profusely. Cutting out the soul, I do think she is a good-looking blonde, but of course I admit a man couldn't get much of a soul kiss from saw-dust.

AT THE PEARLY GATE

Bro. Allison took dinner with the folks last night and A.R. asked Mother, before him, if she might go to the dance last night. Poor Mom asked the preacher what he thought about it and it won't be necessary to tell you, knowing he said he thought if a church member did it, St. Peter would "shet de do" in the face of the offender. A.R. took the risk. My ideas of what is right and wrong are getting so clogged up, I don't know one from the other. I just hope I am not so bad when I die, I'll say something awful like evangelists tell about when they describe death-bed scenes to scare the liver out of the congregation. If you and Mother aren't going to get in, I might as well go on and yield to some more temptations instead of trying not to. Be no chance for me.

June ## THE PREACHER IS A HUMDINGER

A tent meeting began over here across the street by Simpich's shoe-shop last Sunday and they say the preacher is a humdinger, and when I don't go to church Father tells me so many funny jokes, it is making me sorry to miss anything. I aim to go right regular. The best one I have heard is about the way the deacons of the church endeavored to suppress shouting. One night at a service, an old lady who was prone to become emotional, got very happy and cried out, "Glory to God." One of the deacons stepped up to her and said, "Sister, you must try to control your feelings better in order to keep from disturbing the meeting." She was quiet until she burst out with another "Hallelujah." Another deacon tried to influence her to be still. Again her happiness overcame her and the third deacon spoke to her but it did no good and so those three called another deacon and they decided to put her out if necessary. So when the old lady began again, they picked her up and carried her down the aisle and she shouted "Hallelujah, Glory to God, I'm following the path of my Jesus. He was carried into Jerusalem on an ass and *four* are carrying me."

RELIGIOUS DISAGREEMENT

I got into a terrible discussion with Mother, Dad, Miss Biddle, Mr. George and Myrtle about religion and also picture shows. Biddle thought I was terribly pessimistic when I said I didn't expect much from the next generation after the influence of a lot of the present picture shows set in on the children and eats like a canker. And then I said that people are so loose in their religion these days that I didn't see how hardly anybody was going to get to Heaven by the rules that have been taught to me. She thought a lot more are going to get saved than I do, and that was where the real difference was in our opinions. I never saw such a lot of criticizing as there has been since this union meeting began and I can't help but do some myself. It looks to me like most people's religious creeds consist of rules that let them do just as they want to, and if they can do that, why that is all the Heaven they need.

Safely through another week
It has been my lot to sneak!

Mother didn't have that good luck though. Last Friday she forgot to get dinner until about 11:30 and had to have some fire in a hurry. The customary thing to do is to get coal-oil, which she did get in a little cup, and was pouring it into the stove from the top, watching where it fell, when all of a sudden there was a flash, and when Mother felt of herself she was sans eye-brows, some eye-lashes, and hair over her forehead until she looks like a high brow. Her face did not show the burn until yesterday, when blisters puckered out, and it hurts her now considerably. If she were not my own dear Mother, I would say she looks like an Irish biddie with her face so red. She is thankful the damage was no worse and that she still has some hair to do up. She sure lost her bangs.

WHY ALBERT!

They are telling a good one on Albert Smith. When Nadine *[his married sister]* was at home she felt the need of a laxative and compounded some figs and senna leaves into a very good looking candy and after using what she wanted, set the remainder on a small table in the dining room. They say Ab is always nosing into things to eat. The family were at dinner at Guy Blankenbaker's and someone said something about Ab meddling, and he spoke up and said, "Well, I found something this morning that you thought you had hid and I just helped myself." They asked him "What?" and he told them "Candy." They said what kind and where and he told them it was in the dining room and was fig candy. The light dawned on Nadine and she threw up her hands and said, "Why Albert! Why Albert!" as the horror dawned on her, knowing as she did it was *only a matter of time* and he had an engagement to take some H.P.C. girls riding that evening.

❧ ❧ ❧ ❧

July 17   SCRATCHIN'S GOOD FOR CHARACTER

I will try mighty hard to keep from getting hurt, Mam, but I would rather have what comes with getting hurt than to sit off and "stand idly by." I think I can stand any thing that comes up. Nothing ever scratched deep yet. They say scratchings when they are deep are good for the character. I guess I need a few to improve mine. Maybe Nannie has not done any plighting with *anybody*. I don't know. I am just skeered to death she has. But then I worried months about a fraternity pin that turned out to be her brother's. I hardly have time to give to love any more, but if I did have, I would certainly get nuts in my head about Nannie. She is the nicest girl I have ever known.

Later in the Summer   FIZZLY AND GURGLY

I am so full of pleasures I am all fizzy and gurgly like a soda water fountain. I feel like I broke my good time record. Nannie promised to go with the Billies and me to Arrow Rock on the 11th and 12th. All last week, we was prayin' and hopin' for pretty weather on them dates and I did little besides read weather reports and run out and look at the sky every time a cloud floated over. When Saturday came, I stewed all day to be gone. I couldn't be in Boonville to meet Nannie, but Billie and Julia did it better than I could have, and at 5:30, after staying here at the bank until 4:40 and then running around to Lillian and Carl's and shaving my face and dressing, I was met at the ferry by B.& J. and Nannie in Col. Winton, who was sporting four new shoes. We drove up to Wagner's Ice Cream Parlor and cooled off with some ice cream and immediately afterward "hit the trail." We were way out toward Arrow Rock, when there was an explosion by the right hind shoe, and Nannie and I looked at each other in horrible alarm, for we felt a blow-out so soon was an ill omen. To our surprise Billie kept going and Julia kept composed like she liked to hear the tires blow up the first trip out. N. and I who were occupying the five back seats held council and decided Billie was trying to reach Arrow Rock before stopping, but we knew the casing would be cut to shreds. To our dismay, there was another report on the same wheel, so I leaned over to see how it looked if two inner tubes had been in it, and Julia looked around and saw me leaning out and just laughed because the reports weren't no blow-outs, but only back-fires from the engine, which occur when the driver cuts off and then turns on the gasoline some times. Nannie and I had the thrill of a blow-out just the same.

Arrow Rock Tavern

This tavern was a popular stop-over point for those traveling the Santa Fe Trail. Arrow Rock is now a National Historic Site and one of Missouri's most interesting state parks. Friends of Arrow Rock carry on an active program of building restoration and history-oriented events.

About seven o'clock we sat down to a dinner at the Tavern and had fried chicken, fried potatoes, hot biscuit, good butter, stewed fruit, pickle, strawberry preserves, etc., and a jolly good time. We climbed up on Mr. Winton's stomach and rode on to Marshall where we went to a picture show. Afterwards we found some good drinks to quench our dry throats. After loading up on candy, we drove back to the Tavern and were shown upstairs to our rooms. We explored the whole thing and the thing that impressed us most was the numerous stairways. Nannie had the D.A.R. room with the big old canopied bed and the bell rope running up through it to the ding-dong on the roof. On three sides of this room there are stairways and on the other, the street with a door opening to it so you could walk out in your sleep and break your neck without ever knowing it. We all got some sleep but the Laclede Hotel in St. Louis is a quiet spot compared to the hostelry in Arrow Rock. Automobiles whirled by and puffed up that hill every little bit, and Sister said she had to jerk her feet up every fifteen minutes or so to keep them from being run over by those cars which whirled by her window.

Breakfast was so good to us and as soon as we could get the machine fed up, we rode down to the river and then out another road some distance before we decided what we were going to do. When Billie said how would Lexington as a destination suit us, I thought he was kidding, but we went back to the Tavern, loaded in our luggage, told the landlord to look for us back for supper at six p.m. and turned our radiator to the west. On to Marshall, Malta Bend, Grand Pass, Waverly and Dover, we rode, over some bad roads, but mostly good, until we got within six miles of Lexington where we struck the beautiful new rock road and literally set them rocks afire, goin' some. We were having dinner at Mrs. Nickell's Home at one o'clock, and everything was so good. We planned to start back about two and were getting ready to depart when Billie noticed water leaking from the radiator and discovered a little tube which carries water from radiator to engine had burst. A lucky find, too, for we might have burnt up the engine on those rock roads and been setting out there yet. We waited for repairs to the pipe, and Billie found the mechanic could do some work he thought he would have to take the car to Kansas City to get done, so it was four-thirty before we hit the country grit. We went right through to Boonville with only a stop at Malta Bend for water, at Marshall for sandwiches and two rounds of lemonade, at Arrow Rock to tell the cook we couldn't get there, and arrived at Boonville about 9:30. It is 81 miles to Lexington, and we had the ride between

Arrow Rock and Marshall twice, so our straight out riding totalled 190 miles, besides the over town and through by-ways janeys *[colloquial for journeys]*.

Nannie and I went to Sedalia, leaving Boonville at 10:15 and had a ride in that little Ford taxi out to her house, and after all day in a heavy machine, we nearly had our teeth shaken out, rattling over Sedalia's rough streets. I caught the Flyer back home, got to bed by 3 a.m. and haven't felt responsible all day, for we whirled so much my head has kept it up.

The Billies and Nanny Estill

Billie and Julia and I all like Nannie so much. She did herself proud as to her way of lookin', being prettier than ever, and we just had one continual performance, until our enthusiasm got so high, Sister said she would make a motion that I invite them all to go again this fall when fire will feel good in the old fireplaces at the Tavern. I could hardly wait until the motion was seconded and carried before saying, "With all my heart, if Col. Winton accedes." Julia and Billie spoke for him and said he did, so we are planning already to have another grand time when the leaves get gay. Nannie agreed not to get married, so if we live and keep our health, we will get to Kansas City the next time. Billie liked Nannie because she didn't squeal when we almost collided with another car going as rapidly as we were and when we almost ran into a horse and buggy.

August 20

[From time to time Lilburn passed on stories that he picked up in town.]

Did you hear about the Negro preacher who said, "I'se gwine preach a powful discourse today. First I's gwine define the indifinable. Second, I'se gwine explain the unexplainable; third, unscrew the unscrutable."

There was a woman who swallowed a spoon and got all stirred up about it.

One day a motorist had a break-down and asked a farmer if he knew where he (the motorist) could get a spark plug. Old whiskers said "I don't know whether he is any good for that or not but I've got one of the highest steppin' hosses in the country."

Once there was a blind man who could tell what kind of machine it was by hearing the motor. One day he was being put to the test, and at the garage various machines were being run in and out, and the blind man was naming their make very accurately. "That's a Chandler, that's a Cadillac, that's a Cole." Just at that time someone flushed the toilet nearby and they asked him what that was and he said, "That's a Ford." This is the latest I've heard on the Ford.

GOSSIP

Mrs. Hughes Slee and daughter, Lillie, were in here late Saturday afternoon when I had time to stand at the window and "gass" with them. I never saw Lillie look so nice, just like if someone would sprinkle some lime and social fertilizer on her she would put out shoots of personality and positively bloom. She is remarkable as she is, having been produced from the same "hard-pan" soil as her mother. It is too late to use plain fertilizer on the the latter, but if she could be snowed under with strong manure, maybe in the course of time the riches and beauties of gentlewomanliness could grow on her. I give herewith a sample of the conversation.

"The Clarkes's been makin' quite a fuss over that Hollan's girl's gettin' married. We heard them talkin' over the phone a good deal, all soft like: you know they talk like they wuz afraid if they strain their voices they will go into consumption. (Mirth) I think Mr. Bob wanted that girl, but he waited a little too late, just a little too late. He talked up mighty loud (for him) to her at first but as the time come closer, he kinda slowed down."

I said I thought Mr. Rob was a mighty nice man and she replied, " Yes, but he's so queer. All of 'em is, and you have to go clean to the back of his head to find his eyes. I reckon the Hollan girl done well from all I hear, but the man she married musta had right slim chances."

Lillie interposed: "I have seen her ever so many times when she would be visitin' the Clarkes, and she would come to church and I never did think she was pretty."

I told them that for years I had been trying to catch Minnie looking pretty but never could do it. (More mirth) Then she jumped over the neighborhood as follows: "Why do you reckon Flora Rose don't set to Rob Clarke? Looks like she would work on that case. You know Flora's chances *never were* anything,"

Maybe you haven't heard that there is another Edmonston baby, a boy who did his first wail at 4:50 Tuesday morning. I inspected him this morning and he was an American Beauty in tints all right. From reports he was pretty yesterday afternoon, but it wore off during the night and Lillian said he was so ugly she guessed she would have to name him Lilburn. Trouble with that name is you can't "nick" it so it sounds like anything.

August 27

[This letter reports on another "machine" trip made with the Billie Kingsburys and Nannie Estill. This was to take "Mr. Winton Six to the hospital in Kansas City to have his bowels gone over." A heavy rain threatened the trip but ended in time for Nannie to catch the train down from Sedalia.]

OFF TO KANSAS CITY

I went over on the South Limited and soon we were heading towards the land of the setting sun. The only car to have been out on the road before us was Dr. Van Ravenswaay's and he was going to Marshall to see a patient and Bettie and the kids were going along for the trip. But he hadn't gone far when we took up with him having a broken engine, and Dr. asked to go on with us which we allowed. It was hard travelling over the soft road and the water in the engine of Pete just boiled so often we had to stop every three or four miles and go in a farm place to get water to cool it with. We let Ravenswaay do the work and we laughed at him. Sometimes it was a milk bucket he borrowed; sometimes the top off a cistern; and sometimes a coal bucket, and he was all time saying "Huh? Huh? Huh?" Once we came up on a gunny-sack in the road which seemed alive with its twisting and squirming. Someone cried out "Chickens ahead!" and Ravenswaay got out to see. About the time he got to the sack, it began to roll over and over and he wouldn't touch it. Billie got out and cut the string holding the bag closed and five cats all sizes and colors sprang into the air and took off in all directions. It took us four hours to get to Marshall, and inquiring about the road further on, we learned that it would never do to try and go on to Lexington that night. We stopped at the Ruff Hotel, had dinner, went to a picture show and to bed early as it was raining, and we thought we had better leave old Pete and use the high-powered Chicago and Alton cars for the balance of the trip.

We left Marshall at half after five Tuesday morning and arrived in Kansas City three hours later, had breakfast at Townsend's, and then while the women shopped, Billie and I went out to see about the new fixtures for the new Farmers' Bank *[in Boonville]* and then met the women at Morton's, quite a confection cafe, and stayed there a little while before going out to call on Pete Winton's kinfolks. They were lovely to us and took us out in a 1915 model sporty red car, all over the east side, by Lula Long's and around the Cliff Drive, back over the boulevards to Troost Park, out by Electric Park, over to the West Side to Penn Valley Park, out Coleman's Drive, back over Gilham Road past Lee Crabb's to the Union Station and on up to town. It was the blissfulest time of the day. The drives in Kansas City are ten times as pretty as those in St. Louis and Mam, you couldn't be dragged away if you would get up there. The views from Cliff Drive are perfectly magnificent. The boulevard system is just perfect. I went crazy over it. We next had lunch at Emery, Bird, and Thayer's. where every thing tasted so good. And then we went to Jenkin's Music House to hear some Victrola records and at five p.m., me and my friend pulled out for Sedalia, leaving the other couple to start for Marshall at 6 p.m. I was afraid if I went to Marshall, I would not get back to New Franklin for the next day, as we thought the roads would be muddy. But Billie and Julia had a fine run home. I got home at ten p.m. tired and happy and after eating a lot of peaches, I went to bed and tried to sleep, but I was thinking a lot about that good time.

September 10 LEARNING TO DRIVE

[Lilburn's Father bought a Reo. automobile] People would fuss about the rain a lot more if they were not afraid they would get struck dead after all they said about wasting water all summer. But hasn't there been a great multitude of water? As fast as the roads look like something, they are made to look like nothing, as far as running an automobile is concerned. The Kardells *[kinfolks in St. Louis who had the Reo agency]* stayed six days and Henry labored valiantly with Father, Anna Rose and me, teaching us to drive. For the present Mr. Reo has his rear wheels blocked up off the floor so we can all get in and run the engine and shift gears to a finish, but where do we get? Nowheres! We solved the garage problem easily. We just cut a door through the front room of the house out in the yard. It is right in line with the road from the gate, and the car fits easily. As soon as we get a door on and the approach built we will be heading right. But there is a locust tree and a fence on one side, and a persimmon tree on the other, and I hope I can back between them.

One day while Henry was still here, he, Father, Mother, and Lillian were coming from Fayette and were over-took by rain. Henry ran like thunder to get out of it and forgot that new culvert up near McCullough's and eased over it like the dickens and Mother and Lillian and the little baby raked the rib of the top with their noses. Lillian's glasses were smashed, while Mother's were driven down into her nose.

When we looked, there were still skins sticking to the rib, our ladies had been so skunt. Mother's eye is still black and Lillian is just getting to look normal. It came very near being serious.

Late October

[Under Missouri's Local Option Liquor Law, Howard County was dry while Boonville permitted the operation of saloons. The Boonville Anti-Saloon League was conducting a vigorous campaign to vote saloons out in the November election. This excerpt describes the Parade staged as part of this campaign. It was witnessed by many Howard Countians.]

PROHIBITION PARADE

The ferry ran to accommodate the Howard County people who wanted to see the dry parade, and a party of us went over. It was over a mile long. First, came the automobiles. Heading the parade was Pete Winton, dressed in white with a huge electric cross pinned over his bosom and Mrs. Billie pressing on the electric horn every step of the way until it sounded like a parade of whistles. Following the automobiles came the band and every cadet in Kemper *[Military Academy]*. The wet ones remonstrated in vain and the boys looked very military. Then came the women and children by the hundreds, walking two abreast, and all dressed in pillow cases and sheet costumes. Then there was the water wagon and after it more women and children. There was an immense dray loaded with dozens of young girls singing "*Where Is My Wandering Boy Tonight?*" Then there came the horse-backers riding impressively, two abreast. And after it passed up and down the street, there came a big automobile loaded with men and little boys carrying "VOTE WET" banners. It was all very exciting and as much fun as any St. Louis Veiled Prophet Parade for we couldn't be in that with our automobile even if we had wanted to.

Three hundred women went in a body to call on W.F. Johnson to ask him to decline to accept $5000 said to have been offered him by brewers to lead their campaign. He gave the women no satisfaction. Mrs. Judge Williams and Mrs. Will Trigg led the procession, and she read the petition and Mrs. Williams made some fittin' remarks. Sister Julia said she was lucky enough to get in the office, so many could get no nearer than to stand on the steps, and she said it was all very impressive with Mrs. Trigg's soft, sweet voice and several of the women crying audibly. The women were to call on Judge Cosgrove and Whit Draffen but they got news of it, and both got in a machine and left for the country. Before the election, the women divided into groups of fifteen and every thirty minutes one day, fifteen women would call upon each wet merchant and ask him in the name of morals, their mothers, and a clean town, to vote dry. Herman Zuzack [owner of the Five and Ten Cent Store] got to looking like an article worth less than ten cents before the day was over. Things were interesting over there. I nearly fell dead to hear Sister Julia tell of getting up to go to a five a.m. prayer-meeting, way before daylight at this time of year, and Billie patrolling the streets at night to keep down devilment.

Mid-November   A MONDAY MORNING

[Excerpts from a letter to Mam reporting on a trip taken to Sedalia with Frank Brickey, (one of Anna Rose's current beaux), and Anna Rose to Sedalia to visit the Estills. Frank drove a Moon automobile which they called the "Old Fool" to distinguish it from "Old Spirits," his "loud-mouthed" Ford. Automobiles in 1914 were still a novelty, few people owning one. It was quite the thing and considered adventurous to take pleasure and sight-seeing trips out into the country or to nearby towns.]

We had such a lovely trip I must tell you about it before the glow of the good times fade the least bit. Frank and A.R. and the "Old Fool" were here at the bank at 2:30 Saturday afternoon to pick me up and off we went to Sedalia. We had a splendid ride and the roads were good, and I rattled around proper in the back seat alone, for we could not all sit in the front seat on account of a kind of saddle partition between the cushions. We got to Sedalia at ten of six and snook down town to the florist and got flowers for the ladies. We had a lovely supper, served in three courses. Just after supper, Robert and Anne and Gentry and Mary [Estill] blew in on their way home to Howard County from Kansas City in the Cadillac. About 8:30 Mr. Wade came down on the train from K.C. to smile at Mary Estill, the single. All the married people went riding in the Cadillac while we six hopefuls got in the Brickey car and went Mooning out to Lamont, 14 miles and back. We slept late Sunday morning, had breakfast about 9:30 and took a ride before dinner that nearly froze our faces and forms, the wind was so cold. All of us Howard County folk were supposed to be back in Boonville for the last ferry boat at 5:15 p.m., so dinner was hurried up on our account. It was a big turkey affair that you could not enjoy in a rush. Every one was talking all the time about leaving and racing back to Boonville until there was only two hours left for the race when we finally had our coffee. Mary Estill, the married, felt she must get home to her children, and Frank had to be in Fayette this morning and I was keen for the ride, but Nannie said she wouldn't come back with us so I was going to stay over until the night train. A.R. and Brickey said they would go back by way of Glasgow, but I thought I'll be durned if they do it without me, for I hadn't been that way, so I began to beg them to stay over until evening and then drive to Boonville and get the ten o'clock train across to Howard County. Gentry was telling Mary he saw no use in going to Boonville yet if they were going to miss the boat, and Mary said she wanted to try and make it, and I was pouting because Nannie wouldn't freeze her new fur tails off in the wind, and to our hostess it must have looked as if the whole push was just dying to get away. It got positively embarrassing.

Finally, I had a happy thought that we should all go home by way of Glasgoww and take the Nannie Estills all with us, and they could go back to Sedalia on the ten o'clock train. Mrs. Nannie said I better not ask her if I did not mean it, so there was a wild scampering upstairs to put on more clothes but at last, at 4 p.m. Robert, Anne, Gentry, his wife, Mrs. Nannie, in the Cadillac left going North to Marshall, with Frank, A.R., Mary, Nannie and me following them like mad. Oh! but the wind was sharp and we shivered but snuggled up as well as we could, and in an hour and forty minutes we were at the Hotel Huff at Marshall for supper. All ten of us were seated at the same table and I have never seen ten rosier faces in my life than we were. It was a very gay bunch and the other diners must have wished they were one of our bunch for it was fun from the start to finish. The menu was typewritten and of course it made us all hungry to find a dainty listed as "Broiled Steank". The supper really was fine and we all fell to. After we left Marshall, Frank led the way and we beat the others to Slater by ten or fifteen minutes, driving the 16 miles in forty-five minutes. From there on to the boat landing at Glasgow we had splendid riding and of course the crossing in that old tub was exciting at night with these two 4500 pounds each machines both on at once rocking the thing like a cradle.

We did our fastest running from Glascow to Fayette where we waited at Frank's garage a long time before the others caught up with us. We missed the 10 o'clock train so of course the Sedalia people decided to go home on the Flyer at 2 a.m. and under great protest from our guests we brought them home with us and built a big fire in the fire place. Mother and Father got up and dressed at midnight and we had a nice party until train time. Frank, A.R. and I saw them off at about two-thirty in New Franklin. We were up at 7 this morning and you can guess how I feel. But the trip was lovely and I never enjoyed a 70 mile ride more than the one with Mary on one side of me and Nanny on the other, laughing fit to kill at what Mary would say.

❧ ❧ ❧ ❧ ❧

The "Old Fool," Frank's Moon, was all wrent up after the Sedalia trip. Three of the springs were broken, and in going back to Fayette that Monday morning, the hood blew off and blew through the windshield and Frank escaped with a little cut on his face. But it will be all right again in a few days, and we hope by Wednesday to be "sittin' purty" once more.

Eleanor Clark got her face so cut up in an accident at Boonville that they had to take twenty stitches in it to close the wounds. Her brother, John, was driving the machine and to keep from running over a child he ran the car into a tree and shattered the windshield. If I was a mean man, I might say that the Dr. knew Eleanor and thought it would be a great chance to stitch up her talking mouth a little, or there would have been less stitches.

*****

November 11th

[A report on attending two vaudeville shows in St. Louis.]

I heard a parody on "Toreador" which run, "Tore down the door, when the bull began to roar" which was fine. Trixie Frigansa said every time she swallowed a spoonful of soup, it stuck out on her somewheres. She is quite large and concerning a skinny man, she said: "Well, if it wasn't for his Adam's Apple he wouldn't have any shape at all. One fellow said he used a drug store's phone one time and the druggist demanded pay. The phoner was calling for car-fare and told the druggist he would have to wait. The druggist was so insistent that the man said, "Well, if my face isn't good for ten cents, you will have to collect from the other end." And he said the druggist did with both feet.

One man said he inherited his slowness from his father, that his Mother told him, "You would be two years older if your father hadn't been so slow proposing."

In Early December

[From time to time Lilburn reported on Anna Rose's suitors. This letter discusses two of her current ones.]

Bill Darneal is mighty nice and so is Charlie Watkins, and if I were Anna Rose I never would choose neither until one of them forces a choice upon me. They do know where to get the best candies, and Charlie has asked me to bring A.R. to Kansas City the last of this month so we can go to a show or two and eat at the Muehlbach *[then Kansas City's premier hotel]*. That's mighty nice of him, but I never like to be a chaperone in this day when they are not necessary, and I always hated anyone who went with me in that capacity. I don't want Bill or Charlie to hate me. If either one of them would just think to get tickets to the Russian Ballet early in February, I surely would go, but I know of nothing else that would be the plaster to bring me out. I am glad I am not bald like Will. Why I might as well be dead as not have a pompadour pate this day and age.

VICTROLA-ING

I took time one day to count up the value of my Victrola records and the result was a halt in future purchases. You can soak the greenbacks there mighty fast. I had a thought recently that the people we meet in the world are a lot like records. Some we think we want to know, but after we come in touch with them, we thank God they were sent to us merely on approval and that we can get rid of them. Did you ever meet a person who can be compared to that kind of record? And then there are double-faced records, and sometimes they don't give nearly as much pleasure as just a simple inexpensive kind. So it is with records. There are a few records which we like to hear as often as possible, but if we are not awfully careful how we handle them, there will appear little scratches that get on our nerves. Haven't you seen loved ones like that? Most of the people we meet, we like somewhat, make a fuss over them for a while, and then other people absorb our interest until we just get pleasure from the old friend now and then? Is that what happened when you were getting Victrola records? This is the process by which a girl's lovers are filed away. And sometimes they get filed permanently, don't they?

One night I was watching a record spin around and I had another thought. I have had two lately. The second is that the years we live are very much like the little grooves on the records. At the beginning the first years seem long, long ones and they just seem to last forever, but later on they just whirl by until life is just like one Christmas after another. They say the years are all the same length. On a record, the outer revolutions are made as quickly as the inner ones, although your eyes would lie to you about it.

I am beginning to look to see if I can find a grey hair on my head, A thought like that must have a grey hair for a papa. You would think I was going down the decline of living.

WINTER WONDERLAND

The thermometer let the mercury do a spiral glide down to 16 below zero one night and down to zero a time or two, and we just shivered and shook and shivered so!!! We had a big sleet storm that made the earth look like a wonderland. Wednesday, everything was on display in crystal that sparked like cut glass in the sun. Early in the morning, just as the sun was coming up, I would be on my way to town and things were lovely to the slideling lights of the Big Hot Ball in the East. But at night, Mam, was when we all went crazy. The sky was the coldest blue you can imagine and made a perfect backdrop for the trees which looked like silver, all draped over so gracefully under the weight of the ice. Telephone lines looked like long festoons of tinsel glittering in the moonlight and all the shrubs and grasses were as if studded with diamonds. When I walked across a corn-field and struck an ice-crusted stalk, the ice would fly and rattle on the ground until I played like I was a bull in a china shop. At night we would look over toward the cemetery and Lula McGraw's tombstone was reflected in the moonlight like a ball of fire. Pretty spooky!

"Winter Wonderland"—Fairview

1915

February 27

I don't believe I thanked you for your Valentine post card. But, don't you know, Mam, you dangerously arouse the curiosity of one or two others before I get to see the mail? Yessum! And I have seen curiosity so stirred up that I never feel tempted any more to say anything on a post card. Much less rave. But if you can think of any way I can improve on the situation short of "cave man methods," I'll experiment.

Frank Brickey has sold his garage and is planning to locate in Louisiana. That is the way it goes a lot of times. Just about the time you make a friend, you lose him some way. I will be sorry when Frank is gone for good. He is such a whole-hearted soul, and even if he has gotten careless since I have known him, and rattles the spoon in his coffee, when he sips it at the table, and his soup too, I can't help liking him even if he does say things like, "Mr. Sam Brown hasn't aten breakfast for 35 years." It is boarding house life that is death on table manners, and it is chauffeur talk that is death to English. I sure hate to see him go.

Palmer Kingsbury stayed with us one night and I think I have missed a lot by not knowing her better. So it is with a lot of people we just barely rub elbows with at church or some other place like that. There is so much we could learn from them.

ta ta ta ta ta

March 11   **MARYLAND HOTEL, ST. LOUIS**

[Anna Rose accompanied Lilburn to St. Louis. He was having his eyes treated and the two of them between appointments with the "eye doctor" shopped, went to the theatre, and went sight-seeing for several days.]

THE PLAY'S THE THING

After dinner at a soup saloon we hurried to the matinee to see Marie Dove, a darling in her role in *Diplomacy* (by Sardou—I call it sour dough, not knowing for sure). William Gillette, the man star, was splendid. I just hung forward all four acts to get every word.

But in this, like most other plays in which things happen, effects on my feelings are spoiled by the actors responding to encores with bowing and scraping. Last night in the climax of the third act, Marie Dove "riz" to heights, and after crying out her love for her departing husband and finally falling in a faint with a splashing drop on the floor, instead of letting us go on thinking she was lying there yet, the curtain was lifted in response to the clapping and she showed herself all smiling like she got over the other awful quick. As soon as *Diplomacy* was over, we went to the Hippodrome and stayed until eight and then chased to the Columbia and stayed until eleven. We had about seven hours of spotlights and today my eyes took a different story to Dr. Post.

MAGNIFICENT CATHEDRAL

This afternoon we went to see the Catholic Cathedral and I was impressed. From the outside, it appears finished, but stone cutters are at work on it yet. I was amazed when we got in to see such a huge unfinished hulk. The pews are in and the furniture such as confessionals, temporary altars and such. One notices great canvasses stretched up. Behind these the workmen are cutting and hammering out things of beauty.

Anna Rose and I were just plum ignorant of Catholicism, and we sat down in Foster Jr. Wade's pew to watch the worshippers come up the aisle and do strange little crossings and bows and then kneel and say their prayers. One woman was near us, and when she got up, I remarked what a wonderful building we were in, and she said, "You must see the Chapel of the Holy Virgin," so she asked us to follow her. I was close behind her and nearly collided with her when she stopped an instant to kinda cross her feet and bow to something. The Chapel of the Holy Virgin is nearing completion. Though it is large, it is a mere corner of the church proper. All of the ceiling and walls are mosaics in the loveliest colors, and I was able to understand why it will be years and years before it is completed. The whole thing inside is to be of mosaic work. The main dome rises to the height of a six story building. The woman explained so many things to us. In the Chapel of the Holy Virgin, there were little stands with lots and lots of little cups which contain blessed oil and a wick. It seems if you want something, you come in and ask Mary to intercede for you with her son to grant it to you, and then you get up off the little prayer rack and slip an offering in a little box. Then you get a tapir and light one of the red lights and beat it out. The light will burn all day. This woman says that it stands to reason that a person can't pray all day, so the red light represents you and your prayer all day long in getting Mary's intercession. Then we saw St. Anthony to whom if you pray every day for nine days (a novena) you stand a chance to get what you want. Whenever you pray to him though, you've got to sneak a little money into his box to buy bread for the poor. Then we got to talking about Confessions and she told us how she confessed and what the Priest was supposed to do. And then she showed us the little doll houses [confessionals] of which there were several.

In each one a Priest sits in the middle compartment with an ear to a lattice work hole on either side. If there is someone confessing on his left side, he shuts up the hole on the right. I asked the woman if she didn't have to tell all the details of her sins and she said, "No." It seems you say, "I am guilty of a sin of rash judgment," or "I am guilty of immodest thoughts." To the last the Father would say; "Aren't there enough beautiful things in the world of which to think?" I always thought you had to do more than that. For instance, if Louis Williams was a Catholic, he'd have to tell the priest that he noted so and so had a pretty leg. The priests never look around to see who is talking. No wonder, if he never hears any particulars!!! No priest has ever been known to tell what anybody confesses. They are "given grace to keep from it."

We got the views on marriage and divorce next. And there are thirteen disciples. The new one is Judas. We saw a little girl go all around the church and say prayers in thirteen different places. The expressions of the faces of different worshipers are interesting. Most always it was unhappy, possibly that of a person who is so full of his religion and the love of Christ, he feels unworthy to bow before HIM to ask anything. One woman had a mere baby kiss the feet of a large image of Christ. Our conductor, Mrs. Finn, told us a lot and if ever I saw a person on fire with her faith, it was she. She seemed to feel it all over. A.R. was so interested in the Holy Water dip at the door. She asked Mrs. Finn what it was and was told that Catholics do that on entering the House of God, just as they do all they can on entering the house of a friend to show honor to their host. It was a nice time we had at the Cathedral. The germ of Catholocism is truly in the blood of Catholics, and there is no Protestant anti-toxin for it.

April 5   **PASSION PLAY**

Mam, the Tent Show play Saturday night was something. I can't seem to realize that I have really seen it. I didn't get all of the lines, but perhaps you haven't heard a few I retain in my mind, so I shall repeat one to prove whoever wrote the play did make it up-to-date in one spot. I know she must have got it from some modern book. In one act, young George Washington thinks he is madly in love with Mary and is declaring his love, saying he is consumed or burning up with passion. They are at a tea table and tea has been served very hot. Mary, to divert George's mind, says, "George, drink your tea." He replies, "It is too hot!" Mary smiles and says, "Drink it George, it will cool you off." This was all I got from the play for my twenty-five cents, but Billie said he thought them few words were worth it.

April 9   **WISHED YOU WERE WITH US**

The sunshine today just cuddles right up against me clean through my clothes, and I just love its touch. The trip to Arrow Rock was ideal. We couldn't have had a balmier evening and Winton behaved like a good soldier. When we got close to our destination, we looked back across the river to Howard County and saw your snow white fence nestling against the hills at Glenida, and all wished you were with us. We had a real good country supper, and we ate so many biscuits the hired help just leaned against the wall to keep from going down in astonishment. The biscuits were good and hot, and so was everything else.

UNCHRISTIAN TALK

I heard our preacher said he never saw people help out one another and then turn around and talk about each other like the people of New Franklin. Mrs. Duke said she wondered why they did it, and I came so near to saying something about her looking at herself, but remembered what the the preacher said.

Mother has been feeling good since she has been getting out in the fresh air. I was amused at a letter she wrote to Aunt Minnie saying, "Uncle Brown tells me you are too proud to use a cane, and I am surprised at you. Get you a cane and be thankful it helps you get about better." I just know that is not the way to talk to a Christian Science woman.

RAVELING *[A Lilburn effusive-complimentary remark]*

Last night I had occasion to look up some "history" in my old letters to you and I was shocked and surprised how many different girls I have "raved over." I know it has been a "shameful and shocking" proceeding to you. But, I do not intend to quit raveling to you as long as there is a raveling left of me.

This is such a funny world. It is now you have something to tell, now you haven't. But it is certainly an awful darn interesting one for anyone who hasn't seen or lived much of it, like myself.

A SUSPICIOUS CHARACTER

One night when I was returning from visiting Nannie in Sedalia and got off the Flyer at some unearthly hour, one of the trainmen said to Mr. Conductor Lee Mudd, when the train had started on, "Did you notice that tall fellow that got off back there?" Mudd said "Yes." "Well did you notice how queer he acted? I tell you there is something crooked about that fellow. He will bear watching!" Mr. Mudd replied, "Maybe so. He's cashier of the bank up town."

This fellow must have thought I was trying to hide from somebody. I usually stroll up and down the platform until the train starts in order to get fresh air for the Flyer always smells like a pot of stewed garlic, and perhaps he thought I was restless. And then I am always so anxious to get off over here, I may have seemed over-anxious to the trainman. Of all hot cars, the chair-car on the Flyer seems to me "the Melting Pot." People are sleeping all over themselves, some snorin', and little babies turned upside down almost, and all of them apparently enjoying the air.

June 6   JOYOUS SUNNYSIDE WEDDING

A good deal has happened since my last, but of course Helen Smith's wedding was the cream of events. When Wednesday came it was as clear a sky as a marriage bell ever rung under, and the birds all got religion and shouted, and the air was right kissy. I went to Sunnyside with Henry Harris in his Cadillac. The people were collecting in little groups about the fence and the steps, and it didn't look very cheerful to me so I went up on the porch and glad-handed around there and then mixed with the insiders. The three Brickey boys soon began to play and they play well. Nearly everything they played had love in it. By this time I had gone up to the third floor and had seen the wedding presents, but still I wasn't satisfied, so I just butted right in to see the bride. Margeret Boggs was Lady of the Bridal Chamber, but she let me sit up with Helen until the last and let me tantalize the groom who was walking the floor outside in the hall, prancing to get in. But Margeret wouldn't let him in. People kept coming up to the door, begging to even kiss the bride through the key-hole. It was real funny what people would say when they laid eyes on the bride. Some nearly forgot to say anything and some snook out feeling worse than they did before they got in. Some were all damp-eyed. Just as the hour was fast approaching, Helen had to have a drink to float her vows, and I had a terrible time getting it from down stairs. I had to have it passed up the steps over the heads of numerous guests, and Uncle Charley had to know who wanted it and what I was going to do with it.

Sunnyside

William Jefferson Smith, Lilburn's maternal grandfather, originally settled in the Missouri river bottom. Floods led him to build Sunnyside in 1857. Bricks for the building were burned near the site and the timber for the woodwork was cut from the farm and kiln-dried on the premises. The dwelling is on a hillside which slopes to the north and east and its bright location inspired the second daughter, Taylor's first wife, Sallie, to call the place "Sunnyside." The home became a center for social life in the Boonslick community.

Two songs are too many at a wedding. By the time Lillian sang one, the bridal party was all in line upstairs just bucking to go. And they started to the strains of the second song, but I did get up my reins in time to stop them. Mag Boggs was all shaking in green net and the best man was more than nervous, but old Helen was the calmest pullet I guess that ever flew down off a roost. She just glid down the steps by the bannisters which she had slid down up until the day before, and her train was all rolled up when she got down but nobody could tell it except us who were upstairs leaning over for a good view. While they were getting down into the arena, Henry Harris asked me if I thought I could ever go through with it, and I told him, "I wouldn't with just anybody, but under sufficient pleasant provocation, I guess I would." Helen and Billie *[Duval]* promised each other everything in the Discipline and the ceremony was a coon's age long, but I stood it well, as I had the railing to lean on. Helen pinched Billie just as he had to say, "I will," but of course I did not see the pinch. Uncle Charley blew his nose which was a sign to Aunt Lill that the irrigation project was opened up, and it was quite wet in spots. I think Anna Rose was the chief mourner. But pretty soon Bro. Poague prayed a little bit over the "contracting parties," and the kissing that set in reminded me of the hail storm we had a month ago yesterday. I stood up on the steps and watched the siege. It is a great wonder, after being pestered like she was, that the bride's mouth wasn't all out of shape like Molly Conroe's used to be. Aunt Lill passed around the lips and came up the stairs blindly, and Lavinia did likewise. Taylor was in his room with Forest English, both crying and little C.I. and Anna Rose were using the two beds in the front room for tear mops. I felt awful bad myself, once, but it was too pretty a day to cloud up inside me.

Weddings have something about them that is much like funerals. Somebody said to me, "Yes, she looked so happy," in the tone of voice which would have fit the remark, "She looked so peaceful sleeping there." During the ceremony I couldn't describe my sad feeling except it reminded me of the song Marie Kendrick taught me last week:

"Do you ever think when the hearse goes by,
That one of these days you've got to die,
And your eyes will fall in and your teeth fall out,
And the worms will crawl in and the worms will crawl out."

I think it the saddest song.

While we were eating, the bride and groom had gone into the cook's room, had changed their clothes and skedaddled over the chapel hill to the machine in which they with Taylor, A.R. and the best man, drove to Glasgow and caught a train for St. Louis. It was a Wabash train that went to Salisbury to connect with the main line, and they didn't get to the city until nearly midnight. I think I would have preferred a few riceings *[Rice was considered a symbol of fertility, and friends of newlyweds showered them as they left on their honeymoons]* in order to catch the Limited at New Franklin.

Helen looked like a doll. She sure done herself proud when she put on her wedding dress and wedding face. Savannah Duval was here electioneering for sympathy because she didn't have but one brother and he was gone from her. Helen gave her the wedding bouquet after a lot of us had taken out a lot of roses, and Susannah was awful glad to get it and said, "I wonder if this won't be as much of a bride's bouquet as I'll ever get?" I knew it was "Speak now or never" for me, but I just let the chance slip by, like I have so many other times. As Billie started off with Helen, Aunt Jane *[a Negro servant]* said as she grabbed him by the sleeve, with misery in her voice, "Look here Boy. This is my chile—you be good to her!" And after they left she said, "Law Miss Lillie, Baby's done gone." After the guests left, Alice Boggs, the cook, said "Law Miss Lillie, I's got the funniest feelin'. It ain't nothin' as if Miss Helen had done gone away and was comin' back."

The wedding presents were beautiful and there were so many of them. So much silver. Nearly everything but knives and forks in the Mary Chilton pattern. Got knives and forks in the Mothers' pattern and several other patterns. All of them were pretty. Lots of cut glass, some pretty serving trays, set of sherbert cups with silver deposits and spoons, lots of pretty linens, and scads of things I can't think of. Everybody whom I hear express sentiments on the subject liked the looks of the groom. Helen wrote from St. Louis that he was the best man on earth, so we may consider the question settled.

KISSED IN THE EAR

Mayre Kendrick was with us several days and she taught me that it is terribly ticklish to be kissed in the ear. She would do it regardless of consequences, and Mother looked out and saw the consequences one day, and I guess she thought it beat all she ever saw at the picture show. There is one thing sure. I will not be kissed in the ear with impunity.

BOONVILLE GOSSIP

If I were a newspaper reporter, I would be in Boonville interviewing Freddie Sombart to find out what is the matter that he has a wedding blister *[i.e., that he had the sense that he had been burnt by the wedding]*. Tillie Gott told us that Fred and his wife had separated and that it was too bad to tell over the phone. I shall bend every untiring effort I have to discover what canker was eating on their wedding happiness, and I hope it will not be too bad to relate to you. I hope Fred did not tie up the purse strings too tight at the start. When they married in June and went to the East, Frank Brickey went down to St. Louis on the Limited as they did, and he said that long about six o'clock the porters and waiters in the dining car decided to make a little lunch time and came through the Pullmans calling "Supper." But Fred had no speaking appetite until the last call came, and he said, "Katherine, we can get just as good food at the lunch counter in St. Louis as we can in the diner and a whole lot cheaper." And the last Frank saw of them, they were getting them there too. Now you would *expect me* to say such a thing to my *Katie*, but it was unbecoming to a person who is just mangey with money to talk like that to his bride. Last week I saw the place where the Fred Sombart home was to be built. A dwelling had just been removed from a beautiful lot up on High Street. Katherine was engaged to another fellow just before she married Freddie and maybe she has made a mistake. Well, anyway I hope it is no worse than that.

August 17   XENA KINGSBURY'S CHURCH WEDDING

I want to tell you about "Xena's Big Day."

Sister Minnie and Margeret began on the church on Monday and with Mr. Stammerjohn [the Boonville florist] spent much of that day, Tuesday and Wednesday decorating. I am here to testify I have never seen anything of the kind so pretty since me and Wilkes Booth Lincoln was borned. When it comes to artistic ability, I will put Mag and Min in a contest against anybody, and they will get a result that will make you wish everybody could see it and make you feel sorry it can't be a "permanence."

Every bench had its own foxy satin ribbon ties with smilax *[a tender green twining plant]*. The rear bench had just a rosette and teeny streamers a trifle longer and so on toward the front where the streamers reached almost to the floor. Three benches from the front, there was a pair of white gates with flowers and smilax decorations with tulle put on for good measure, and Alice and Jean stood there and opened them when the relatives were piloted to their seats, only they got tired and sat down and let the ushers do it. On a line with the front seat there were four square columns, about a foot square, one at either side of the church and the others toward the middle with a solid piece across the top of all of them. Those columns were covered with white and had vines entwined about them and on top there were baskets of Wandering Jew just growing there, and lots of pink butterflies had lit around about, and right in the middle was a big white dove just a flyin'. There was another white dove too and there were to be a whole drove of little white ones, but these didn't migrate here in time for the ceremony. All the front of the church beyond these columns was lined with white. The chancel railing was white with vines interwoven and big white and pink hydrangea blossoms were used profusely here. Ferns were on the back of this railing on either side. Back of the pulpit was a lovely piece of work. The design in which the ferns and hydrangeas and white tulle bows were all arranged on the white background stirred up my enthusiasm very much and I just admired it "till the cows came home." To the right of the altar the piano was turned with its back toward the audience, and the way Miss Min had decorated that was just like herself, and you know what she can do when she *does*. Nobody else, I guess, would have put a Battenburg scarf on the piano just as she had it, and there was just enough green to make you so happy you wanted to die on it some of these days. Professor Sauter was clear out of sight at the wedding which did not detract anything from the beauty of it, only I was crazy to see him foam at the mouth as they say he sometimes does when he sets right on the piano stool. I can't begin to make you see how pretty the church was, Mam, but everybody has been remarking about it and you take it from me, and I promise I am honest when I say this, it was just lovely.

About six o'clock the day of the wedding (the Limited was late and after all it did not bring the wedding bouquets) all concerned were wondering what kind of posies they would wear. Stammerjohn at Boonville phoned that he had four roses. It was too late to get anything from Moberly or Sedalia, so everybody got busy in their flower patches, pulling everything that had a blossom on it, but Stammerjohn saved the day with pink and white asters, and sent over some lovely bouquets which did very nicely, and I think the wedding knot was tied quite as tight as if the bride had carried more than the four roses in the asters. We all laughed good at the orange blossoms in the veil which were off Sister's big begonia!!! But "she got by with it." The ushers found seats for everybody, I think. There were just enough to crowd the church to its full capacity.

Rob and I were the last ones to come in before the Father and Mother of the bride. It was "some dress" the bride wore, and she did look lovely. It was pink embroidered stuff with green trimmings. I looked at it after the wedding and the skirt has four layers of thin materials. There was a great big pink hat that got wore too. There wasn't anybody else in Kin-folks Row dressed up at all. We all wore what we had and I put on a coat that evening. When we were all seated, Professor Sauter commenced to raise the devil softly at the piano. I forgot for the time being how he might foam at the mouth, and Sam Lay got up by the piano and sang *"You"* and that old chestnut, *"I Love You Truly."* I have heard that latter so many times, it takes something else to put me in that flowery, dreamy, crazy frame of mind. He and Professor Sauter had practiced together only once so they didn't get along so famously, but they worried along to the *"Here Comes the Bride"* lockstep and the ushers, side by side, broke through the atmosphere to the altar followed by Anna Rose and Adele Mayte; only the groom and best man were in front of them. Then along came Adelaid Broeder, the maid of honor, and then little Adele Blankenbaker who put rose petals in the footprints of the bride. And Xena was quite a picture as she "did the aisle" to reach the side of her waiting husband-to-be. She was a little pale, but at the house before we started she was the prettiest thing to the blonde line I have ever seen. She was a darling. Prof. Sauter put a whole lot of little hysterical runs in the wedding march that he must have learned at San Francisco or when he was bathing in the ripples at the beach. It was a slow "come-in." It took eight minutes for them to get settled so Bro. Poague could read off the wedding service. It always makes Father tired to see a preacher read the vows so Bro. Poague has promised him since then to memorize them for the next time he uses them.

After the wedding everybody stayed around and had a fine visit together, and when we did go back to Horace's, we met Xena and Herman coming this way in his Ford runabout, and we concluded they were off to Moberly. But they returned about mid-night from Fayette and stayed at home until the next afternoon, so nobody had a chance to do them dirt. We would have "shiverreed" maybe if we had known they were up here. They have gone to North Dakota for two or three weeks.

ﻴ ﻴ ﻴ ﻴ ﻴ

August 15 WEDDING POSTSCRIPT

Xena and her God are back but are going to Huntsville soon to live. We had a letter from Xena soon after she got up north and there were six pages of HAPPYGUSH, and when we all read it together, Lillian spoke up and said, "Well, she will soon get over it." In a day or two, we were over to Mr. Estill's and they were telling us of the letter they had just received from Xena, and we told them how Xena had written to us and Mr. E. said, "Well, she will soon get over it." Xena had been married four days, Lillian four years, and Mr. Estill forty and twice at that. When Xena got back, I was tempted to ask her "if she had gotten over it," hoping she would say, "No," so that I could tell those who said she would. I'd hate to think I would get over anything if I were going to cash in my single cussedness for a Promissory Note of Married Happiness. When Ida Kardell came up last week, she was talking about Xena's glowing reports of happiness, and I told her what those others had said about getting over it and she said, "Well, she will, and that gush won't last long!" I guess the glitter of married life just settles down into a serious business proposition like anything else worth while. And like anything else that ties us down, I guess we just wish like the dickens we could get a little vacation once and now and then.

August 15   COMPANY COMETH

We had company by the wholesale last week. In fact, we have had company ever since visiting came into vogue. Adelaide Broeder stayed with us a week after the wedding, and she was a sweet thing and a charming guest whom we were sorry to see leave. Last week Ida and Henry Kardell and their two young brats, Aunt Lena and some incidental guests swarmed on us, and we had quite a gay time visiting and riding over the country. Before they got away Smithy and Aunt Rose arrived. We had Ella Ward and her daughter; Anna Rose came down from Fayette to stay in the kitchen while Mother sat down with the company some, so the eating or feeding proposition was no trouble at all. John Henry Kardell is a humdinger, and I would tell you what a warm number he is, but I fear it would burn up my poor typewriter ribbon. He had Warren come over and one day they went on a plugging expedition in Father's melon patch, and we are still cutting melons that look good on the outside but are soured inside. One good thing about John Henry, although he is a devil, he will not lie. The day Warren was here, they had such a good time. Warren lost his hat, his coat and his underclothes and all he had to wear home on the train was a pair of overalls and a shirt. I guess he has learned that some clothing is absolutely necessary. It has rained at least forty days and nights this summer, and it seems so funny to be gathered around a big wood fire in the fire place the last days of August. I don't remember when it ever happened that way before.

UNIVERSITY OF CHICAGO'S SMITTY

I must tell you a little about Smitty before he and Aunt Rose leave for Chicago next Saturday. He appears to be particularly well-informed on so many subjects for a child of his age. But his views are rather radical to us. He believes nothing which he cannot prove, consequently there is a great deal about heaven, hell, and God which we have "been raised on" which means nothing to him except foolishness. There is no such thing as Charity. He told Mother that her religion could do him no good, that it was out of date, belonging to the middle ages, but said he wouldn't have her changed in her belief for anything. His theory of the beginning of the earth and life hereon is damn foolishness to me but worth hearing him expound. He says that the sooner "etiquette is corrected" so that people will be brought up from infancy without clothing, the better the world will be morally. He claims the very fact that we wear clothes for the purpose of covering up nudeness suggests things to the mind which people would not think about if they had been reared naked. I doubt if etiquette will ever be corrected that way but if it is and we all get the benefit of the correction, I bet I will just laugh myself to death seeing things to get even with people for laughing at my pretty (?) form. It would be a humorous sight wouldn't it? It would seem like Prosperity had come to make things cheerful. I can just picture certain of my customers coming in the bank now. I have told you a few of the things Smitty believes so you can get an idea of what he is picking up at Chicago University.

September 15

It is raining more than ever. We never have to be saving with water out home this season. Everybody can get in and fill the tub up as far as he likes. This season we invite our company to enjoy these family privileges.

CIRCUS TIME

Saturday night we went to the circus at Boonville: Ringling Brothers with their four trains of shows were there and people flocked to town by the hundreds. There was a misunderstanding about the show-ground, so it looked for a while as if the show would not unload at all, but the Commercial Club used their influence and an effort was made. The ground on which the tent was put up was a wheat field and the rains had made the ground so soft the heavy wagons mired very badly so that thirty horses and two elephants had to pull them out. There was no parade and the afternoon show was put off until 4 p.m. But they had so much difficulty with the soft ground they couldn't get ready by 4 p.m. and hundreds of people went home disappointed. But at 7:15 they put on a show that was good but it was not half of their usual program. Not even the horses in the show rings could perform because their feet went down in the mud so badly. The menagerie was not displayed at all much to my disappointment.

Probably September   **AUTOS AND CHANGE**

Machines are really bringing big changes into our lives. They have sure altered our ways of coming to town and going to the country. It used to take us so long to get to Sunnyside or down to Glenida to see you. Only two or three years ago, everything was by the horse and buggy pace of the century past, but today we belong to the up-and-now class with machines spinning along at 25 or 30 miles an hour. The machine has become the new horse. It just eats gasoline while the old one eats corn and hay if he can get it and it gets mighty expensive. The man who owns a team of horses has to put out as much to keep them as it costs to keep a small family. If he has a surplus horse, it's better to sell it at a sacrifice instead of keeping it through the winter, for it will eat its head off. The new has been put on and the old put off, and the lightning rapidity of the age we live in demands we use the instrumentalities that do things quickly so we can keep up with the changes taking place.

We have run our batteries all over at the heel until we had to send them to St. Louis for an operation on their "innards." We always carried a bottle of distilled water in the machine for the purpose but neglected to pour any in the batteries, so the worst happened. However, Arthur Bell took the batteries out of his machine to let us use them until ours get back, and we are about to run them down because of a connection he forgot to make when he put them on our Reo machine. So we have to turn Reo's liver over with a crank whenever we want to go, and it is hard when we have been raised on a self-starter!!! Anna Rose took a sore back with her to bed last night which she attributes to cranking the machine. The first time she was able to crank it she ran out and cackled the news to Father in the garden, and he thought she was giving a fire alarm. "O Papa, I cranked the car, I cranked the car!!" No pullet was ever prouder of her first egg.

MACHINE MEANDERING

Last Sunday there was no church and we talked up a trip to Randolph Springs for lunch. John and Bee Kingsbury, Father and Mother went in John's machine, and Smithy, Palmer, A.R., and I brought up the rear and gathered dust all the way to Huntsville. Before we got to Armstrong, John's Reo had a blowout, and we stopped for rest. Then we went on to Moberly and got John's son, Robert, and his ugly wife and pretty child and headed back to Randolph Springs. We got out of the city a couple of miles and were not pursued so we returned to the city to see if we could find the others. We did at a garage. They had

had the second blow-out and were buying themselves a new casing. Finally we started out again and John's Reo got to cutting out and refusing to pull right, so when we were near Huntsville and they had a third blow-out and we had to take the extra wheel off our machine and give it to them, we just turned into the next pasture and had our lunch, and I never expected that both machines would ever get home without more blow-outs, and we were both on our last legs, no extra casings at all. But we did get back to Fayette all right; only John's Reo got worse and worse, so we went by Randolph Springs and put a lot of that Sulphur Water in it, hoping it would do some good, but it seemed to make the machine weaker so it could hardly get up the hills. Bee just drank and drank of the mineral water, but I am no game sport like that when I am going out on the road where machines meet and pass us just like it was in the city. We had to follow along behind the sick machine all the way to Fayette and got tired of that but we had a "dinner" and just snacked as we cut down the miles. We finally overtook Paul Barton, the mechanic from Horace's garage and Reo was working so badly by then, Bee was distressed and I almost croaked when she leaned out and said, "O! Thank God! We have found you at last." When we arrived at Armstrong she leaned out again and said, "Lilburn, I am *just sick*. Stop and phone Horace Bell to meet us out of Fayette, for we will never on God's green earth get up the Given's Hill." They had to buy two new casings with inner tubes that day, so I bet they will never want to take another trip like it. You know Cousin Bee's stingy hide is so tight it can hold the purse of all the family and still not be under a strain. I thank Heaven it didn't happen to Father, for it takes all we can get to pay for the gas and to get Horace Bell to put this, that, and the other in our car. For instance, our water pump turned out to be busted in four pieces the other day. Rob just rubs it in to us the best he can because we have to pay more for riding in a Reo than he does for parading around in a Ford, but to protect us from his jeers, I tell him we can stand it even if we don't have the corns where Ford people have them.

FINE APPLE HARVEST

We are right in the apple harvest once more and the Jonathans are turning out fine. We had more than 1400 barrels of that variety. Horace had about the same number and expects to have a bumper crop of other varieties. If nothing happens, his apples will sell for between fifteen and twenty thousand dollars this year. Do you think anything can beat apples on those old hills back of his house? We got a good price, and apple men who come through now say it is the best price they have heard of. We will have four or five thousand barrels if the fruit turns out like the Jonathans have. I certainly hope we won't have the hard time harvesting our apple crop that the other people have with their wheat. Some wheat is not threshed yet.

ಶಿ ಶಿ ಶಿ ಶಿ ಶಿ

October 20

I gave myself a Victrola for a birthday present, and I anticipate much musical enjoyment from it this winter when the roads get bad and make town seem miles and miles away in the evenings.

NOT THAT KIND OF WOMAN

I was over to Boonville Sunday evening and had a nice visit with the Billies and Hazel. Arthur and "Nan" Wallace came in and I was so amused at the conversation about the Wheeler Revival meeting that is soon to begin in Boonville in a specially erected tabernacle. Nan said she had been notified there would be a prayer meeting at her house this Thursday and that she was to lead it. You know she is not entirely that kind of woman, although she is a going-to-church once-a-day Christian Methodist. She said they were welcome to her house but she just couldn't lead the meeting.

Paul Prosser and Eva Sue got married Saturday, and so many can't see what Eva is getting. When he went on his lecture course, he borrowed the cash to buy her a half dozen pairs of silk hose and bills swarm around him like flies at the restaurant at Orrick, Mo. This is the juiciest bit of Fayette news tacked on to the tail of the account of the wedding. I guess he wasn't any goose though. He knows stockings are used to hold valuables, and I reckon he wanted to save what Eva Sue put into them worse than he ever wanted to save anything else.

Mid-November   ITCHING

[Apparently Lilburn contracted a skin infection from sharing a bed with me on one of his visits to my parents' home. I had acquired my itch from my seat-mate at school and infected most of the family. The infection was called "the Seven-year Itch" because it took so long for the then available ointments to cure.]

I have to scratch myself so often I don't get this letter written very fast. I have funny red spots on me. Wherever I rub the tickle, a red spot occurs and stays since yesterday morning. I hope it ain't itch or leprosy or poison oak. Over three weeks ago I was at Billie's and the beds out on the sleeping porch looked so inviting I deserted the one in the house given me and crawled in with Warren and slept there. The next day I was amazed to see Warren weeping because he itched so and I wondered if I had been exposed!! Now at this late day my skin is cutting up. They think Warren had shingles but that comes along one's belt. Mine is on my arms, my right hip, and my left leg with a couple of splotches for good measure on my chest. It looks a little like poison oak I had in the summer, but I truly hope it isn't anything.

November 12   VICTROLA-ING

We are having such a good time with the Victrola. It has been cool enough to have a fire in the hole in the wall every night and we have played records after supper until just time enough to get in the machine and get to protracted meeting. Then we have come back and enjoyed it until bed-time. We have such interesting bird records by Charles Kellog, who imitates their voices just perfectly. Then to the accompaniment of *"Humoresque"* he sings like birds very beautifully, and also to *"Amoreuse Waltz"* which is lighter and more spring-like. Then we all like the four "nigger" records by the Tuskeegee Institute singers. *"Live A' Humble"* and *"Good News"* are particularly good and true to real live darky singing, and *"I Want to Be Like Jesus"* takes me right down to the Ugly Bucks of Franklin Church at the river. Red Seal Records are not very numerous at our house yet, but I have some of the things I like best: the *"Caprice"* by Kreisler, Schubert's *"Serenade"* by Elman; and I am almost sorry I didn't get the record of [John] McCormack and Kreisler in its place, although Elman's record is all one could wish. I would like to have McCormack's voice in it though. I don't think I ever heard a prettier record than *"The Rosary"* by Alma Gluck and her husband, Efram Zimbalist, who accompanies her on the violin. It is so beautiful you just get sad when when you have to get up and go shut it off or start it over again. I have become very active by jumping up and down while working the Victrola. There are not many records I like better than *"To a Wild Rose"* by McDowell and I nearly wear it out, and Grieg's *"Morning"* is in the same danger of getting worn. And Mendelssohn's *"Song Without Words"* is fine and the one called *"Sorrows"* is just full of melody, and sometimes I think it the prettiest of all. Mother likes the machine so well she has promised me all eggs the hens lay can be turned into record money, but it seems they have only laid off. As a special inducement one of these Sundays, I may move the Victrola over to the barn and give a concert. We have a couple of real lively dance records, and we have fun watching Mother's Methodist foot pat the floor. One time she said, "I'll declare it's no wonder young people get to dancing." *[Red Seal Records featured the name artists of the day. John McCormack, an Irish tenor, commanded the highest prices of any artist at the concert halls of the country.]*

SHE SHUT OFF EASY

Did you read the obituary about Mrs. John Ivy which said, "The people of the upper bottom lands near Boonsboro were shocked when news was spread that Laura Isabel Ivy had breathed her last." Even living as far away as I do, I knew it was just what they had been looking for her to do for weeks. The way the paper stated it reminded me of the Bushmeyer boy here who, after his mother died, said, "Well, there is one good thing, when she did shut off, she shut off easy."

SCANDALIZING

And that brings me to a nice scandal. Harry Wyatt's Pearl has left home and in this week's *News* he advertises that he will not after this date pay for anything she may buy." And who do you suppose the villain is? Sam Raslee who has worked for Henry this summer and *against* him as well. Pearl has gone to Columbia to stay and get a divorce. Mrs. Billie Long is taking care of the two little boys, and she and Billie are all cut to strips over the way "Pearl done," and every time Harry comes over there, Mrs. L. breaks down and says she can't stand to have him come without Pearl as he always brought her with him before.

Pearl has no complaint to make against Henry; says he has always been awful good to her, but as Harry says, "She has just been persuaded away," which would be plainer put, if he said, "She just doesn't love me." But I guess it would choke most any man to say that and he don't like to admit it to himself. Harry asked me if he ought to have shot Sam, but I told him it would have been a shame to waste the shell and it wouldn't have brought Pearl back anyhow. Harry thinks he will beat Pearl to the divorce as he thinks he could never take her back without suspecting her every time she did anything in which any other man was concerned, and he just might as well get done with the affair and start all over again.

❧ ❧ ❧ ❧ ❧

December 7 IN THE EVENING BY THE FIRELIGHT

Instead of going to the dance with the rest, Mary Hunker and I went out home and lit the fire in the hole-in-the-wall and sat by it and played the Victrola. Music goes to Mary's head, and she said I must excuse her if she didn't say a word, that she was having a lovely time. There are certain records that should never be played except in the firelight alone and they were very effective on this occasion. We had such a nice time, while she was in the quiet humor. I didn't have to talk any either. She was kind enough to write me a note saying she never would forget that evening by the fireplace. I shall always remember it with pleasure myself.

TURKEY DAY DOIN'S

Thanksgiving morning A.R. and Louis Means went to Columbia to attend the Missouri-Kansas football game *[the biggest game of the year, ending the season, was then played on Thanksgiving]*, and the remnants of us went to a grand dinner with the Billie folks in Boonville. Just as we were finishing the bounteous feast, it began to rain, and we had to start home immediately. We went as fast as we could but the rain speeded up too, and by the time we got home, having no curtains with us, I was just as wet on my left side as I would have been all over if I had gone to the ball game in Columbia. I had on all my glad clothes and was sitting in a pool of water, no pleasant situation, I assure you. Mother and Father fared better on the back seat with some robes to protect them. I spent the rest of the day with a hot iron in my hand drying my clothes and re-creasing the things. We just knew they couldn't have the game in Columbia until we got the score late in the afternoon. They played right in the mud and water but all the time we were sorry the people who went to see it would have to stay under shelter and miss the game. Anna Rose got home on the special about 8:30, and I knew as soon as I saw her that she was a ruint looking woman as far as the glad rags are concerned. Her best hat which used to have a flat brim was all caved in and the brim had the rakishest curves to it you ever saw. It looked like the milliner from Cave Creek had made it, and the water squashed in her shoes, and she complained of having been wet to her knees. Louis put his rain coat on her while he got wet to the skin all over. And there they, with ten thousand other people, stood regardless of how much rain was falling. Anna Rose said the spectacle of 10,000 FOOLS was inspiring, and few had the courage to seek shelter. Bird of Paradise flowers, long waving ostrich plumes, handsome suits of velvet, broadcloth, and beautiful fur coats all suffered alike, and A.R. said it was so funny to see the red water streaming off one woman's red hat and down over a snow-white coat, making her look as gory as a stuck hog. After the game there was no place to go where one could take off clothes and dry off, but A.R. and a bunch went down into the furnace room of the Athens Hotel and warmed up until train time.

December 31   CHRISTMAS GIFTING

For Chrismas I got a flat tire, a candy headache and the itch besides lots of nice things. Something has broken out on me, and I've been salving and solutionizing valiantly for a week. Dr. Fleet says it looks like dermatitis. Halloween I piled into bed on the sleeping porch at Billie's with Warren and the next morning he was crying with a breaking out. But I had no trace of it for several weeks and not until the last week has it been awfully interesting to me. William has had it–and so has sister. I try a new ointment every night and as we have a holiday tomorrow, I'll be at home for two full days doctoring.

It has been a very quiet Christmas week. Christmas Eve, Mrs. Edwards's cook was off so she and Margeret had a little "handout" for Sue Herndon, Bob McGavock and me. We had creamed oysters, celery and pickles, chicken salad, coffee, cakes, candy, nuts and such a good time. About 8.30 p.m., Mr. Edwards set up Freddie's Christmas tree and the rest of us decorated it and played with his toys. We even filled the bath-tub and ran his steam boat, and I ran his train miles and miles. We left his tree looking mighty pretty. I then went by Lillian's to see their tree and after I came to the country, spent an hour sitting around the tree at Rob's house. And I went back over there at 6:00 a.m. to hear Alice and Jean say, "Oh," and "Ah," as they found each new present.

Mam, you would like to hear Melba sing Handel's *"Sweet Bird"* and Michelson does warble *"Charming Bird"* beautifully. Then Martinelli sings Mascagus' *"Seranata"* so pretty. These and a double Hawaiian record I bought with money Mother gave me for a Christmas present. I've ordered seven more records I hope will be here tomorrow for my delight on Sunday. Jenkins allows one to keep the records three days and requires one to purchase only one fifth. I order a lot I never expect to buy just to hear them. I gave Father a new light fixture with friction igniter, and we got some to put on our old-fashioned gas fixtures as well, so we have almost done away with matches.

I am so glad to have a two day holiday the same as at Christmas, and next year it will be this way too. I've already looked at the calendar.

With lots of love and many thanks.

1916

January 1   **ON FADS**

A couple of months ago I bought myself a Victrola. It takes the place in winter time of automobile pleasures of summer. I am buying myself poor in records, but I just can't help it. Margeret Edwards says it is just my "latest fad," and I always have one, to which she attributes my good times and sustained kiddishness. It is a fact, there has always been something to interest me: stamp book collection, writing music, trying to write stories, German and Spanish studies and lots and lots of girls. I think I am catching a picture craze now. I think Wallace Nutting pictures, hand colored photographs, are just wonderful. I got me *"The Pergola at Amalfi"* for Christmas.

But to go back to records. I have some beautiful ones and all the singers willingly perform without being begged. I have some lively dance numbers and when all the kids are here at once they all dance about and they nearly walk their Uncle Libby to death. Up until Christmas they were still ignorant of the true identity of Santa Claus. It is too bad children ever find out. I wish I were believing in Santa Claus today.

January 8   **SOME THOUGHTS ON MARRIAGE**

On the train to Fayette the other day, Anna Rose was told by Mrs. Burrus she was going to Moberly to catch a train to Chicago so she could attend her sister's funeral, but our Rosie forgot it by the time the train got to Fayette and as she got off she said, "I hope you have a nice time" and got the answer, "Well, it will be a mighty sad one." Which reminds me that Mrs. Snoddy called up Mrs. Capito and asked for full particulars about Mrs. Jack Calloway's funeral and after being informed said, "Well, Mrs. Capito, I'm mighty proud to know about it." I was proud to hear her say, "I'm feelin' bettern I've been a feelin'" when asked about her state of health.

Rosie has just started the "Perdita" waltz and I can't begin to tell you how lovely it is. If it were not for what people would say, I'd like to leave this world listening to something sweet like it. Rosie and I have little impromptu dances—just us two—about the room at all hours.

I have all the Honolulu records I want. Finally got the sacred Hyka song which is sung in the "Bird of Paradise" as Luana goes up to the crater to throw herself into it as a sacrifice to appease the wrath of Pele to save her people from the volcano. It made a deep impression on me, when I heard it sitting in an inky black theater looking at a mountain of fire—gazing intently lest I should not see the splash she made when she took the last leap.

These waltzes make me feel so good toward everybody, and I am so sorry for the distressed and the ill and so thankful I don't have anything but the vanishing "itch." And Mam, it isn't me to get after the

Lord for not providing me one of those nice things called *"wife."* Maybe I do seem in way of living to be like "the first quarter" of the moon—or like I had been spanked like the moon looks like on the wane—but I can't help it if my life isn't rounded out and full, like the love flowers that have bloomed for you in the summer at the foot of Mount Rainier and now, on the plains of Montana. I have no fuss to pick with married life. It is all right and I love to see it, and I'd like it under certain circumstances—but Mam, I'd have to prescribe the circumstances. It takes a lot of worldly goods to keep a disposition sweet and sunny and to make a girl enjoy being practical—and I haven't that much. Of course I do truly sleep mighty cold some nights—but I don't have to get up and make fires in the mornings—but shucks—what is the use of trying to make my position look pleasant to you married folks when you are just stewed in the syrup of married happiness. Today I am very happy and it is sufficient unto the day. I have just been thinking I haven't a single plan made for the year—outside a determination to get more pleasure out of my work by a closer study of it. And socially, I have no ties or obligations to keep me from drifting into some very flirtatiously interesting waters. I just hope I'll be as fortunate this year as I have been in the past—in taking wonderful cruises that do not put enough barnacles on my bottom to disable me from booking further sailings of my craft. I never will forget my last cruise with Nannie Estill, but as I look at it now—it couldn't have gone on forever—any more than I could be happy now if I were the father of Clara's baby, and living under old man Woodson's wing. But I do appreciate all your good wishes and I'll have lots of fun telling you about how they hatch out and grow.

January 19   WILL OR CHARLEY?

[Anna Rose, who had been courted by a number of boys, had narrowed her choice for a husband down to two residents of Richmond, Missouri. Both men's families were prominent in the community. Will Darneal, the older of the two, had assumed management of the Darneal Mercantile Store, Richmond's largest establishment. Anna Rose sought to get the preferences of her family.]

I must tell you about Charlie Watkins who came down from Friday until Monday. After he had been around a day or two, Anna Rose made a canvass and asked each of us to vote which we liked better, Will Darneal or Charlie Watkins. I had about made up my mind to vote for Charlie but remained neutral. Mother told me that when A.R. asked her to vote she felt like telling her, "Of course I like Charlie Watkins better than Grandpa, but I didn't like to tell her so." Louis Williams said she didn't like much to ask him for he always made fun of which ever one she was talking about. I did not hear what Father said but he and Charlie went to sleep Sunday afternoon when they were entertaining each other in the sitting room, and both had a long nap which gave Mother and A.R. a chance to sleep a little themselves. Lillian voted for Charlie, and I suppose that is because he said more about her two children than Will Darneal did. (I have learned it pays to rave over cubs if you don't want to awaken the bear instinct in a woman.) That is easy for me to do for I like most any brand of kids if they are reasonably clean.

February 4   A CASE OF RECORDITIS

Now isn't it grand that you have the Victrola. You like it yourself, so you will make allowances whenever I seem to have a bad raving case of recorditis. It has newly broke out in the form of two songs by John McCormack. One is *"A Little Bit of Heaven"* which is bound to become a great favorite. The other will not because it is sung in Italian. That makes no difference to me. Of course I like to know what he is singing about but John *never* sings about anything but love, and if you can't understand him, you can just imagine he says whatever is in your mind. I think he has more of the tender emotion in his voice than any singer I have ever heard. The second record is "Carme" and Fritz Kreisler [*the nation's most popular violinist*] plays the accompaniment. I just "give way" beneath its charm and the last thing at night and the last thing I do just as I start to town in the morning, is to massage my spirits musically with the harmony of this record. It is a great thing to have some pretty melody running through one's head. It seems to have an effect on the "physicality" of a person. If I have had a bad, cross day, none of the music has been running through my subconscious mind during that period.

SUNDAY SCHOOL SUPERINTENDENT'S FALL

If I had a wife I might lose her and if that didn't happen, I might have a child and it might die like little Cousin Harris Smith did. But then I think maybe I would be willing to run the risk if there were not so many other perils for married people.

Just listen while I tell you of the fall of Ernest Jenner. He is superintendent of the Methodist Sunday School, a church steward, member of the City Council, a member of the School Board, a member of both the Odd Fellows and the Masonic Lodges and the K.P.s also. He is one of the main singers in the choir, the passer of the collection plate, and the husband of a wife and the father of one child—a little girl—(at least this is all the children we know of) and other prominent positions. He was not satisfied with all those honors, and last Friday night, as he was visiting Mrs. Guy Pettit and trotting her on his knee and talking "baby talk," Guy poked a revolver into his face and made him sign a check for $500 for breaking up his home!!!! I guess the victim didn't have the money to pay the check and (don't laugh) he went to get Dr. Fleet to doctor his case!!! He was so scared the next day he was gray in the face and told a lot of people and made me promise not to tell a soul. I went home with a crowded mind thinking I would not live over Sunday, burdened with such a lot of scandal, and much to my surprise and delight the news had beat me to the home folks. The town just went talking wild, Mam, and there were meetings of the principals involved to arrive at an agreeable settlement and after much palavering the distinguished citizen paid the Wounded Man fifty dollars to let the matter drop. It was the second time he had been caught. The other time he paid $25 on the installment plan!!! Some people talk about the high cost of living, but there is nothing to it, it seems. Several years ago, the man who helped our Sunday School Superintendent out of this scrape, had to pay $3000 for what said Supt. in 1916 paid only $50.00. (Both of these men claim that they "never got value received.")

The Supt. said he had "made a clean breast of it" to his wife but she told Sue Herndon it was a case of black-mail, that her husband was called over to the house, not knowing what was wanted and just as he stepped inside the door, the gun was drawn on him. That he had never been in the house before. It is quite a coincidence that Dr. F. and this man got caught in the same house in the same room. The only difference is that in the recent raid, the man had his clothes on. Guy stuck the revolver inside through the crack of the door, before he ever looked in the room, so he must have been "skeered." Now, "Ain't that nice doin's? Ain't that elegant?"

The Supt. seems to think he has done himself great credit by getting out of the financial part of it so easily. Tells of his experience glibly to his friends. He was warned not to go by two men who were in the store when he got the message to call on Ada Pettit, but he didn't pay them no mind.

MISTAKEN LOVER

Eddie Harris, a negro boy here in town, had a married colored lady for his girl, and one night he went to her house drunk, and hearing the grammophone inside talking, decided Jane was false and entertaining another lover. So, he broke his way through the door. Upon entering he began knocking furniture around and seeing his reflection in a mirror thought it was someone else knocking over things to get at him, made for his reflection and knocked the glass into a thousand pieces. He threw the phonograph out of the door.

POPULAR MAYOR

Hal Callaway was in here and told me he was Mayor of the Junction, and when I seemed surprised, he said, "Yes, I've been Mayor for two terms. I'm very popular, but little thought of."

ta ta ta ta ta

February 10   ## A RESIGNATION

The latest on Mother!! She was telling the merits of aspirin. "I'll tell you it's just fine. My brother Tom once had the back-ache so bad he couldn't straighten up, and he went to Boonville and Mr. Roeschel gave him some aspirin. He took some and went out and *threw up hay* all day and has never had any trouble since.

Ernest Jenner has resigned as Supt. of Sunday School and Steward, and Bessy "Just wept night and day." She had thought her beau was so perfect. I didn't go to the quarterly conference to hear his apologies. Dad said he sure did look agonizing when he made his statement.

ta ta ta ta ta

March 26   ## SORROWS OF A TRAGIC DEATH

When the message of Helen's death came, we felt like we had been hit over the head and were groping around in the dark. We heard just a few minutes after the end. Someone tried to get Anna Rose but she was in Boonville and Rob took the message. They asked him to notify the Smiths and Rob told the man he couldn't go down there with it, and the man said, "Well, somebody will have to do it." He immediately thought Mother would be the person to impart the news, but she was in Boonville, too, and then Rob asked me if I would go with him. All the way out there we talked about what we should say and whom we should tell first, but when we went up the front steps we hadn't a thought as to what we should do and say, only Rob said I would have to do the telling. I was some trembly person when I went in the hall. Uncle Charlie came out in the hall, and I told him. As I said, it seemed to stun each of us until we couldn't realize what had happened. I then learned Aunt Lill was sick in bed, had had high fever all night before, and Taylor thought best to keep the news from her, but Uncle Charlie thought best to tell her and did. As soon as she found it would be necessary to start within an hour if she went at all, she got right out of bed and went to dressing with great composure, telling Charles to get ready. She even curled her hair on a curling iron, and was ready in about thirty minutes. In the meantime Mother, Father, and Anna Rose had come from Boonville.

A.R. was in Piggott's and had just selected the lace for a baby pillow she was making for Helen's little one and was just deciding whether to get pink or blue ribbons for it when someone turned away from the phone and said, "Helen Smith is dead." A.R. hurried up to Billie's where Mother and Father and Mrs. Vaughan and others were at the dinner table and having held in her feelings all the way up the street just bursted as she went in Billie's house and fell on Father's neck, and for a little bit was unable to tell what was the matter, which alarmed everyone there until they nearly had a fit. It was a terrible blow.

A.R., Uncle Charles, and Aunt Lill left on the afternoon train and as Carl was able to get the Wabash man to stop a fast train at Lexington Junction they arrived at Richmond at 9 p.m. We were unable to get any of the details of Helen's death except that the baby was never born. When they got there, they told Billie if he wanted her buried up there, it would be all right, but after they went to bed, it seemed as if they would die of regret if they did not bring her home, and they were so dissatisfied and grieved to "Think, Lillie, we can never take her home with us" that Dr. Buchanan, the doctor who stayed at the house after Helen died, told Billie how the parents felt and he said that although he would love to have her body there near him, that if they wanted to take her home, it would be all right. In the meantime, Aunt Lill called me at 11 p.m. and told me the funeral would be in Richmond and to start with C.I. *[Charles Isaac*

Smith, Jr., Uncle Charles' son] and Lavinia the next morning. I gave the announcement to the public and it was generally known in town by 8:30 the next morning when C.I. called and said to arrange for the funeral down here as they had changed the plans. I had to phone all over the country again.

The Richmond people were lovely and did everything anyone could have done for Billie and the Smiths. A short service was held at the house just before they left Richmond. It commenced to rain before the train got in here, but lulled long enough for us to get out to Sunnyside with the body, and then it rained sheets of water.

Mr. Curtis had charge of the body here and after it was placed in the parlor, he left the house and I saw him drive out toward town without having asked anyone if there was anything desired, not even if they wanted the casket opened. In a few minutes Aunt Lill came out on the porch and grabbed me by the coat lapels and said, "Where is Mr. Curtis? What do you suppose he meant by leaving without opening the casket?" I said it beat all I could figure out and I would get in the car and run him down, which I did but I didn't know but what Hiram Curtis would be getting the best of me for the car skidded over the wet road terribly, and I couldn't get enough speed to overtake him until I got clear to Elmer Amick's in the Junction. Mam, I was so right, I could have talked to a man a lot bigger than me, I was so full of indignation. I told Hiram what we thought of him and he said he could explain the whole thing. "I threw a screw-driver up to Hemp on the hearse and it hit a bottle of whiskey in his pocket and the bottle broke and the whiskey ran all over my clothes and when I rolled the casket into the parlor, I heard your sister remark to someone 'It smells like a beer keg in here,' and knowing the whiskey was on my clothes I thought I had better get away as soon as possible." I assured him it would have been much easier to explain about the whiskey than it would be to explain why he would go away from a home of distressed people without asking if there was anything to be done, and the sooner he got back, the better it would be for his business. He turned around and came back and was pale as a sheet when he came up to the house and apologized to Uncle Charlie and had Uncle smell his coat to prove the story. A.R. says she bet he poured some on his coat after I got after him. Anyway, Uncle Charley couldn't smell any on his breath and said they would drop the matter.

Hiram overdid himself being thoughtful from that hour forward, and conducted himself beautifully at the services. He opened the casket and dear little old Helen looked so sweet, Mam, in a most beautiful gray casket lined with white china silk. The top lid folded back from the front and the side pieces which broke the angle on which the top rested, folded outward and it was just lovely—if you can think that about *a casket.* There was no glass to it at all. It just looked like she was asleep among billows of fluffy silk, with the prettiest little round pillow under her head. She had on her wedding dress, her wedding ring, and a strand of pearl beads about her neck, the latter used to lessen the notice of her neck which seemed just a little swollen. In one hand there was a single white rose.

Mam, I have always thought I did not like to look at a person whose spirit has gone, and I thought I would remember Helen as I saw her last, but A.R. said I must see her as she looked so sweet, and will you believe it, I just felt like I couldn't look at her enough after I saw her the first time. We had all felt so terribly bad when we thought she was to be buried in Richmond, we felt almost happy to have her home again and after the others had gone home, Aunt Lill, Margeret Chancellor, A.R., Carrie Gibson and I sat down on the floor beside the casket and talked about the sweet old thing we loved as Helen. Aunt Lill said, "Oh, I feel so much better since I brought her home. It's all right! It's all right!!," And she showed us a lot of the little baby things she had brought home to cherish as memories of her grandmotherly dreams. Some things Helen had made so beautifully herself, some she hadn't finished (a baby pillow) and some, others had given her. Aunt Lill seemed almost happy as she talked to us and we went over all that had happened to Helen while she was sick, and talked of the good times we had had with the little cut-up. It didn't seem to me like Helen was dead. It seemed like she was just taking a nap and would presently wake up and we would have another one of those cutting up dances around the parlor if we had someone to play for us.

Aunt Lill made us promise we would go to bed when we got tired, but not one of us wanted to sleep. We all felt we wanted to stay with Helen every minute we could, and a part of the time we had a nice time in the parlor by the side of the dear little girl, and the rest of the time in the sitting room or down stairs. When Carrie and I were snooping around down-stairs in the kitchen hunting almost in vain for something to eat (we didn't know just where to look) we said, "Wouldn't old Helen love to be prouging [prowling] around like this?" And she would have, Mam. So we stayed up all night long, and I got to actually love Maggie Bonham Chancellor. I got a most liberal education on child birth during the night as Mag got to feeling free to express her mind and told about the hard time she had with Bonham, and Carrie Gibson spoke up as freely as if I had been a doctor on a case of hers. Aunt Lill spoke out too. Mag was telling about Uncle Billie passing pus, and about giving Uncle Brown bismuth injections from below and other kinds through the stomach, I call that getting acquainted.

We were so glad we were up when poor Billie Duval, who couldn't sleep, came downstairs. He left home when Helen died and refused to go back and said he never wanted to see the inside of the house again, but did go back for a few minutes early Friday a.m. and, although they told him how sweet Helen looked, he said he knew she couldn't look natural and he had refused to see her except for just one passing glimpse. But when he came downstairs, he said he wanted to see Helen. The poor man is so broken up, and it seemed he tried to feel like she looked herself, but it never satisfied him one bit. He said he could not make himself believe she did look herself, and he supposed it was because he missed the smile she always had for him.

FLORAL TRIBUTES

Well, morning finally came, and we opened the flowers there and those which continued to arrive all morning, and they were such beautiful tributes of love. It is easy to know that every blossom there was sent through the spirit of love; there was nobody to send a piece because of anything except they felt it was doing a last little something for a dear little woman who, as Brother Poague said, "Has given her life trying to obey God's commandments." There were flowers all over the foot of the casket, banked at its sides, around the walls, all over the piano, some tables and chairs. I wish I knew how to describe some of these pieces in detail, but one which Helen would probably have loved most was an immense spray of red carnations tied with a big red tule bow. Mrs. Clark here in town sent it, and Sue Chancellor thought it was inappropriate, but I said it was a perfect tribute, for Helen never failed to have some red on her somewhere. The young men of Richmond sent two immense sprays of roses, Easter lillies and numerous other kinds of flowers. Helen's Bible Study Class, some beautiful red roses and her club a great wreath of pink roses, a perfect gem. Some of Billie's lodges sent pieces and one magnificent piece was of pink sweet-peas and violets. That was a "darling" from Birch Alsup. Then there were all kinds of loose roses, carnations, and spray after spray of blossoms.

DECORATING THE GRAVE

About noon, Carrie Gibson and I slipped out a lot of pink and white carnations and roses and snook out the back and up the hill to the grave which Mr. Peebly had just lined with white cloth. We told him we wanted to decorate the grave and we did so while he went to dinner. O Mam, if you were never down in a grave, you can't know how I felt when I dropped myself down into Helen's, but I was soon busy with pins and feathery asparagus and smilax, and Carrie said she might as well be helping so she would get down too although I couldn't quite figure how we would get out again.

We first made a green background on the white and then pinned those lovely pink and white flowers on so each one was drooping its poor head in grief, and when we tied a bunch of tulle and pinned one at each end of the grave, and to our surprise got out quite easily, after spending about an hour and a half there, Mam, it didn't look like a grave. The sides looked like curtains of blossoms, and Carrie and I were satisfied with the job if no one else even noticed it. But we hope it made Billie feel like the spot was brighter than he had hoped. It would have looked crazy to anyone who might have come, to see us down in the grave like that, but we both felt we were doing a last little kindness for our loved one and we knew she was sayin' "Look at them old sports," if she was able to see us.

Clark's Chapel

Clark's Chapel Cemetary is where Helen (Smith) Duval was buried. The graves of Lilburn and many other Kingsburys and relatives are there.

When we got back, there was a big crowd at the house and the service had as well been held there, as Billie almost begged them to do, though—being lovely enough to say if they wanted it at the church it was all right. Uncle Billie said he wanted it at the church. So the funeral was about 3 p.m. But about 8 in the morning I talked to Mag Chancellor who said she thought the funeral should be at the church, and I told her I thought it would be treating Billie fairer to have it at home, and as A.R. had already dropped some remark about having to change the plan for music on account of "some of them being so set on having it at the Chapel," Mag decided to feel hurt, and she went to Aunt Lill and said enough to make Aunt Lill think someone had made remarks which Mag might have overheard. Aunt Lill asked me what on earth was the matter with Margeret, and I told her all I knew—what A.R. and I had said, and Miss Lill said Mag was "so easy to hurt." So I called Mag out on the porch and talked to her and got A.R. to say she never meant no harm, and A.R. said too, "I think, Margeret, after we have all been under a strain like this, any of us are likely to say things which may sound worse and very different from what we mean," which is so, and Marg. said she guessed she was just having the cry she had been holding back, and that it was all right. So, after running everyone down stairs. I left Marg. and A.R. to arrange the flowers. Mag said, "I'd like to help if I can do it without somebody thinking I'm a Butterin," and I 'lowed, "You go on and we will feel so much better and so will you." When she looked around with tears in her eyes and patted me on the cheek, I knew I had won her back, and Mag will always be more to me on account of that loving little pat as I left her and Rosie to look after the flowers.

FUNERAL SERVICE

Aunt Lill didn't want any of the music which A.R. and I could suggest, and it was a relief when she said to leave that part to Ada Lee, but I knew Ada would have "*Asleep in Jesus*" sung as sure as fate or some other real mournful things if we didn't tell her what to have. Aunt Lill said only two songs would be enough, and we asked that "*Abide With Me*" be first and "*Beautiful Isle of Somewhere*" at the last. And that was all the music desired.

As the casket was being carried down to the front gate, Aunt Lill and Uncle Charles stood at one of the upstairs windows and the former looked dazed, just transfixed, as if she couldn't understand. When

Lilburn at Clark's Chapel Cemetary

they told her it was time to go, she said to wait until the hearse had time to get ahead of the carriages, so that the casket and flowers could be arranged at the church before we got there. This was done. Emerine Green was playing something doleful as we entered the church, and I thought she was going to keep it up for a life-time, but in a little while the choir began to sing "*Abide With Me.*" It seemed like it was five minutes to the verse. Did you ever think what a combination there is in an ordinary little country choir? They look sad on the best of days, but on funeral occasions, well, one woman looked to me like she had lost all but her voice. A.R. had said, "It just seems too bad to have just anybody sing for dear little old Helen," and I felt the same, but there was positively no one else to do it. After the choir finished that song, they commenced "*Beautiful Isle of Somewhere*" right off and I wondered why. and was glad when Bro. Poague said, "Two verses," in an undertone to them. After the prayer, which lasted an hour and made me wonder why Bro. P. hadn't some regard for the family who had asked him for a *short service*, Leota Moser sang "*A Perfect Day*" which was unexpected. I hope Billie and some of the others liked it, but I never can feel that Carrie Jacobs-Bond wrote it for use at funerals. It is for sad occasions besides these. The first part of Bro. P's sermon was *read off*, and I thought "Well, I do think you might not say any more at my funeral than you can remember," but the last half of his talk was beautiful. There are so many things to be said of a dear little girl like Helen. In a little while, the lumps in our throats were worse than ever, and we had started home after leaving the little body, which had been such a cousin to us, up there on the hill. Mam, it was just awful for a minute when we realized it was all done, that there was nothing more any of us could do to show our love for the little kid. She is the first person to leave me whom I loved awfully hard, no one ever made this much difference to me before. And if I have told you incidents in this letter that seem to you I might as well have left untold, I am telling you because it is a part of me to do it, and that I just naturally feel better for doing it. Right this minute I'm looking through my tears and there's an awful lump. I'm beginning to think I have a heart.

My heart hurts most for Billie Duval. He says, "It never occurred to us that this could happen. We were planning only to live." It is pretty bad to have a wife, a baby, and a home taken all at once. Very little can seem worth while to him. His sister, Savannah, is going to put all of Helen's things away and change all the furniture before Billie goes home.

HELEN'S ORDEAL AND DEATH

Helen became ill about 7:00 p.m. Wednesday evening and said she still had one little dress to finish, that everything else was done and she wouldn't let Nary Smith do it, but whipped on some lace herself between pains, in order to get everything she wanted finished before the *event*. They joked about the affair and walked the floor together. She said as they were walking, "Wouldn't you love to have a picture of us now to show little Billie after while?" After the struggle had continued a long time, Billie said he was just scared so bad he lost his nerve, and Helen told him, "You needn't take it so hard. It isn't hurting you." Another time she told him he couldn't stay to the party if he couldn't act better. She was so brave and never had a thought that everything was not going to work around all right, until the second nurse came. Then Helen suspected something. Billie had felt toward the last he could not stay in the room and be of any encouragement to Helen and was out when they finally told her it would be necessary to take the baby. They administered the anesthetic and just before she lost consciousness she said, "Where's Billie? I'm so afraid." In a few minutes she was asleep and her heart ceased to beat. Dr. Buchanan, the doctor who has been such a friend to Helen all through the trouble, just cried to think, "O Anna Rose! We've lost the little girl!" And he stayed at the house and did everything possible to help them. He said it would have been a physical impossibility for Helen to have delivered the baby because her pelvis bones were so close together. Another thing which may have brought about the end was that the baby was carried very high and almost immediately under her heart and the pressure doubtless affected that organ.

Possibly she might have been saved at a city hospital. If so and so had been done, it might have been otherwise, but how can we tell, and Dr. Buchanan says nothing could have been done that was not done, so I guess it was God's will for Helen not to be with us any more.

The most pathetic thing of all yesterday was old Aunt Jane who came up to look at "Baby" as she always called Helen. The poor old darky's grief was so sincere and there was such tenderness as she said betwen sobs, "O you pore little thing, you pore little thing, you *pore* little thing. Yessir, *don't* she look sweet? just beautiful! Well I guess I will go. I can't do no good. If I could, I'd stay longer." And the poor old thing took Carrie Gibson in her arms and just wept so hard. And she expressed such tender thoughts trying to comfort "Mr. Billie." To me old Aunt Jane's devotion was the most touching of all. It got me after I had up to that time been able to behave my self.

I am just making myself believe Helen is still up in Richmond and won't be back for a long, long time. And I get along very well except at times when I get chokey and I know if I was succeeding in making myself believe it, I wouldn't sit on Sue's front fence and talk to her and just feel the water run down my cheeks like I was a baby. I always told myself it didn't do any good to cry, and I've told that to others. There are some circumstances I find, over which we have no control whatever. And by circumstances, I mean my feelings.

Your wet-eyed, hurt-hearted, though trying to be happy child,

Libus

April 5   *LANDSCAPING—A NEW FAD*

I may have told you I was starting a new fad, that of landscape gardening. For weeks I have been writing off and on to a firm to whom I sent a diagram of our place, and they have asked me for more details and so on. Well, last week, if their architect didn't drop in on me all of a sudden !!! I took him out home and he went around with his little blue-print, checking off the things he had designed to plant at the different spots, and when he left I was sure in *the notion*. I am going to plant about a hundred shrubs such as: honeysuckles, wiegellias, barbary, kerrias, flowering almonds, flowering crabs, magnolias, burning bush, and red bud, and I don't know what all. It all looks so pretty, as he told it to me. There are some golden bells, too, which begin their blooming in March. I am so anxious for the shrubs to come so I can go ahead with the planting. Practically all the planting will be right around the dwelling. Later on we can take care of the groups out in the yard. I'd like to have a drive lined with a barberry hedge, but it wouldn't thrive with its roots in my pocketbook. I hope Dad is going to paint the house, and if so, it will be white. I have been rearranging a privet hedge I started last year. The landscape man told me how to change it. I want to tell you I am not used to digging, and I did not forget for a few days I had done some work.

April 14   A REGULAR BEAR

Yesterday, Lillian was out home and told Mother, "It is reported all over town that you said Carl was a regular bear to his children." Last night Mother called me into the kitchen and told me about this and said, "I was so astonished I never said a word." And she has had tears bordering her eyes ever since and has been racking her brain to find out who could have started such talk, or have expressed it that way. This morning she said she had *thought* it, but she never remembered calling him a "bear." The little kids do *toe* the mark and are perfect angels, but I don't like to be around where angels are made, for it seems a severe operation but Mother's goat is got by having "something Mrs. Kingsbury said about Carl reported all over town." Something is always crawling into our scales of equilibrium and unbalancing them.

April 21   IF WE DON'T GO TO WAR

It is such a foolishness that I did not catch the landscape bug long ago, for by now our place could have been a peach if eveything had grown. Right now my back feels like it will crack off if I don't sit up awful straight, but I don't mind. I got that way by digging and setting out shrubs which came yesterday after I thought they would never get here. They came in a box about three feet square and ten or twelve long and the contents proved most interesting. About fifteen different kinds all labelled so I could plant them right into the spots I had spaded up according to the diagram the gardner made for me. I got about half of them out last night and early this morning and I hope to spend all afternoon on the job. The shrubs are all fine large ones, and should make a fine growth this summer, enough to produce "the effect" in a small way. There will be something in bloom from late in March until late in October, and then some will have berries on them that will stay red and look pretty when the snow comes. I'm excited by the promise of great beauty in the years to come, if we don't go to war with anybody and have bombs explode in our yards.

COULD THIS BE LOVE?

Gertrude Ramsey was down for the week-end and likewise Mr. Will and the latter stayed until Thursday morning although "he had to be back home Tuesday evening." Mr. Will gets nicer as he grows on us and Miss Annie must lean toward him when he is here. But Charlie Watkins will be here in the morning to try to lean her over the other way. He can't stay any longer than Sunday afternoon. And then I hope neither of them will come back for a couple of weeks. I think Father thought Mr. Will was staying a terribly long time, for one morning after breakfast, Dad was at the table with Mom and me and we said something about Mr. Will staying over. Dad began, "Well it seems to me ——" and here Mother tapped him on the hand and said, "Now you were young once," and Dad said he reckoned he never stayed that long because he never had far to go and Mom came back with, "Why you just lived at Pa's." I just love my Mom and Dad more every day.

Gertrude is such a sweet, spontaneous sort of girl, not a bit spoiled by anybody or anything, and is clever as I like a woman to be. It is lots of fun to be nice to her, as she is so appreciative. I think I could work up quite a case with her, but there is such a difference between like and love. It is grand at times when you feel like you are in love, but awful when you feel like you aren't but thought you were yesterday!! I'd like to fall in love so hard I would never get over it.

April 24   LOOK FOR THE SILVER LINING

Some folks always see the worst side without looking up to see if there is a rift anywhere in the sky.

Ernest W. Chancellor is running a small feed-mill at the Junction and Edna is running him and it both. She is one breechy woman and comes in the bank with him and does the talking. I always feel sorry for a man in that fix. He will try to say something and the wife will put in and say more than he does, and say, "I'm going to run the bank book after this." I would just as soon be a watch chain charm as to be husband of a woman like that.

Mrs. Tom Heath said Bridelle had always been used to nice things and her husband wasn't able to support her and that is why the divorce is proceeding. On the other side it is claimed that B. is one of these cold, nice women. I reckon Hall [her husband] thought by not buying her any clothes she would have to warm up in self-defense. Speaking of garments, it keeps getting reported that our bookkeeper is going to marry Oland Jones, and to prove it to me, someone said she had 20 night-gowns and 24 corset covers. I don't hear whether she is short on the other things or not.

TOO MANY HIGH NOTES

We had a song service last night because it was Easter and practicing for it, I had told Lillian not to go too strong for too many high notes. She had a solo, some sacred words set to the music of "The Rosary," and when her turn came she stood up to do herself proud, but just as she was at the end of it on the highest note, somebody's baby in the back of the house tried to holler that way too. Everybody giggled and laughed and smiled—even Mother and I. You'd have laughed too. But now for the tragedy. Lillian was so busy with her own tones, *she did not hear the youngster*, and it was with dismay she saw the audience burst out with laughter and "just knew they were laughing at her high note." She says she thought she would die, it made her so sad, but thought at first to keep a high head in the face of all the ridicule, but it was too much. Said various ones in the audience looked at her and smiled and this just seemed *too impudent*, and she sent back the blackest looks she could muster. Finally, the storm broke, she clouded up and threw her song book down in the aisle in front her as evidence she "was done with them" and showered throughout the rest of the program. Cousin Minnie Lee said when Lillian threw her song book down, Mother saw it and her eyes could have been knocked off with a stick. After the benediction, the mother, grandmother, and aunt of the noisy brat came up to apologize and not until they explained why their apology was forthcoming, did Lillian know why the audience had laughed. She was so outdone by the whole experience, she is almost sick in bed. Guess she hates worst of all, the display of temper. Those who knew she *threw* the book are telling those who thought she dropped it, "Naw, she never dropped it. She was *mad*."

"GETTING OLD AND CRANKY"

[*My earliest memories of Fairview include Louis Williams. As a young man, he became the Kingsbury's "permanent hired man." He had a room in the bungalow, built originally to house the sons of the growing family. He was a skilled cooper (barrel-maker), making all the apple barrels. He also supervised temporary helpers such as Eli, a Negro. He had a weakness for alcohol and every so often would go on a weekend spree in Boonville. He ate with the family, and we grandchildren always called him Uncle Louis. He was a great reader of pulp Western magazines and endeared himself to me by saving them for me and permitting me to read them in his room while he was out in the fields. When I was in college and discovered Frost's "The Death of the Hired Man," I thought of Uncle Louis, for several times he did go away, but he always came back, and always was taken in. When Louis became too old to longer look after himself, Lilburn found a nursing home for him and visited him there regularly until he died.*] Our Louis Williams is getting old and cranky or something. He has decided we don't consider him our social equal and he is no better than a negro, and the other day he got mad because Mother wouldn't let him eat in the kitchen at the same time Eli was eating.

[Negro day-workers were fed in the kitchen.] Louis insisted he wanted to do it, but Mother told him "When you have a house of your own, you can entertain and eat with them all you want to, but you can't eat with them at my house." Louis has decided never to eat with us in the dining room again, and if something is not set for him in the kitchen, he eats cold bread and molasses and hurries out. He says he wishes we would run him off, and when told that all he has to do is quit any time he wants to, he says, "I haven't got the nerve to quit." He told me Saturday night after he had asked me to come in and take a drink (he was in his room acting silly), he knew I thought I was better than he was, but he didn't think much of me or my mother or father either, but he reckoned there wasn't anything he wouldn't do for us, he reckoned he would *even jump* in the river for any one of us.

LOOKING AT NATURE

Mr. Will has got A.R. going around smelling the apple blossoms, and seeing how beautiful they are, and she thinks this is the first year they ever bloomed pretty. People have such a good time when they begin to look around at nature, when they have spent a lot of years never seeing anything of it at all.

❧ ❧ ❧ ❧ ❧

June 5   TWINKLE-TOES

I have had such a funny disposition lately. I think it is from trying to keep from "playin' aroun'" as you advised me. I have tried to fade into oblivion, but I must be too fast a color for that. I am sick in mind and body through the effort. It made me feel so *old*. I realize the first time I let go my interest in *petticoats*, I am a goner. I have been doing fairly well on the tricks and turns that have come from meddling about. As many as have been played on me, I am still sweet on the world, and I just know that a few noticements of Gertrude's worthiness won't do her no harm. I'm not going to mess up Gertie's goodness and her innocence. I really don't believe I am that bold and bad yet. Adelaide Broeder and Lorena Dalton are at our house and they are the sweet things. Adelaide is so good looking and Dalt is no shab either and is the cutest little cuddler that ever was. Ad has been teaching me those dance steps that amused us at the Jefferson Hotel last winter in St. Louis: the single and the double twinkle, and I think I told you how the girl has to put her arms clear around her pardner's neck almost and they shuffle the feet so funny and twinkle their shoulders, and are so close to each other. I stepped all over AD's feet at first, but am learning to keep them on my own territory.

❧ ❧ ❧ ❧ ❧

June 12   LONG DRAWN-OUT GOOD TIME

I know I *never did* have such a long drawn out good time before this party. There is not a rested bone or tissue in my body, but it makes me sicker to think the rest I need will come only with the departure of our dear humdingers who have been with us for ten days. The worst feature of the whole thing is that we have just disgusted our Ma and Pa with our late hours, and in spite of the fact we always stayed quiet until we could hear them snoring, they claim to have been kept awake and threatened to call time on us but only had the nerve to do it twice. When I wrote last, Will Darneal and Helen and Ad and Dalt were here. Gertrude was here too until Thursday. Albert, Taylor and Teale Middleton came out and we had a theater party, seeing "Won By Waiting," sitting on reserved seats that were so hard, we were afraid of creating corns on ourselves. The tent show is such a lot of fun and the drama and comedy so ridiculum. The vaudeville between acts is good in spots and other spots are so poor it nearly tickled us to death. Four of the bunch sat on a little bench made for three and Anna Rose slipped off it and tore all the blue tail piece out of her suit skirt and had to trade coats with Ad to get a long one to go home in. The fireplace has been so inviting these cold nights we just like to nearly never have gone to bed until 2 o'clock.

Thursday a.m. Gertie left with Mr. Will and her halo was on just as straight as it was when she came.

I never even blowed my breath agin it. The rest of the girls marked Will's and Gertie's suitcases with placards "Just Married!" and when they got on the train at Estill, showered them with rice and congratulations to make people think they were bride and groom. And no sooner than the train left, they sent a telegram to Will Duval to the effect he was "just married" and signed it Will Darneal. It wasn't long before Austin Riggs called A.R. from Richmond to confirm the message and when Will got to Lexington Junction, Jim Woodson and Will Duval were there in a car to meet them, but Will wouldn't ride with them for fear they would take him around the square a lot, so he went up on the motor train.

The morning before Will left, when Dalt and A.R. heard him go down to the bathroom, they slipped into his room and got into his bed. He was fussed to pieces when he returned and made the discovery and then he wouldn't let them get up for about an hour. Our maid-servant, Ella, heard A.R. tell Margeret about it and later made Mother throw a fit of regret by telling her she heard Miss A.R. tell Margeret "she and Miss Dalton got in bed with Mr. Darneal." The next night Taylor and Teale and George Van Studdiford, who came that afternoon and stayed until Sunday a.m., and I took the girls out for an all round evening and saw "The Girl Out Yonder" at the show and afterwards Edgar Settles played in Foster's and the tables were pushed back so everybody but me and Geo. could dance. I do not believe in restaurant or caberet doings in a little town, but I couldn't raise no voice of protest. It was about 2 a.m. before we got to bed, as we had a down-stairs meeting and then George and I had to comb and roll up the girls' hair and get them ready for bed, and then we all sat around and talked forever. George is one sweet old kid, and he is so big and athletic and yet so gentle, he never once pulled a hair all the time he was combing. I just couldn't have no interest in rolling up Gertrude's hair though. The girls have kept my nails manicured beautifully and have brushed my pompadour for me and it has been just lovely. All but the getting up at 6:00 a.m. regardless of the retiring hour. Of course all the rest slept until dinner time.

"SUCH SWEET KISSING"

Saturday night, after going to the show, *"Don't Lie to Your Wife,"* we got flash lights for the camera and at 11 p.m. started to take pictures. The girls all dressed up as boys and Geo and I made some swell ladies as I shall soon prove to you if the pictures don't go wrong. Then the ladies all dolled up in curls and short dresses and were "children again just for tonight" and looked mighty sweet. It took until 1:30 to take seven pictures and Mr. Taylor Kingsbury had hollered upstairs to know why we hadn't gone to bed. We had a picnic and it was a lot later when the last light went out. Sunday a.m. we saw off Geo. Van who plucked the dew off of each pair of rosy lips in departing, and then they all said he was such sweet kissing.

Lewis Means, Rimer Kirby and Albert Smith came yesterday and after the best dinner Ab and Ad and Helen and me went almost to Lisbon where the road has been rocked and is terribly rough. There Helen and I got out and walked up the bluffs some distance and it looked so wild and wooly up there we listened to hear wild-cats but didn't hear none. It was so picturesque with the rock and the wooded hills behind us and the crops and water on the other side with a great multitude of moonlight over us.

Undated, but written soon after   **SOME FACTS OF LIFE**

The last meeting of the Women's Club must have been a prize number for choice expressions of opinions and fancy discussions. Helen Wagner went with Anna Rose and came home and asked me if there was any reason why a couple on their honey-moon should not occupy the same berth on a pullman?

"TERRIBLY SCANDALOUS"

She said it all started by Anne saying Robert held her hand all the way from K.C. to Estill the day they were married and Lizzie said she did not think it was a lack of affection if Rodes didn't hold her hand when they went on their honeymoon. She didn't ever care for hand-holding anyhow. And then Lizzie related for the benefit of the association some story Rodes had heard about a couple just married having the sleeper berth made down in Fayette before they got on or something terribly scandalous like that and added that she thought it was out-landish for the newly weds to sleep in the same berth the first night and that if her husband wasn't able to buy each a berth, she would pay for her own herself. Helen said she never heard of such goings-on and expressed the opinion that she would leave all that to HIM and she expected to be so crazy about him that she would be perfectly happy with him in the chair car if they couldn't afford a berth. I assured Helen, it was a matter of choice on the part of the parties concerned, that often people thought a berth terribly crowded for two persons, and then they live across the street from each other in the car. Helen said that the old hens just sat up and talked about their husbands' doing or didn't doing this, that, or the other thing and Ann testified about the worst ruckus she and Robert ever had. Said once they had a swarm of company and she had so much to do and it took Robert so long to primp and she went in and found him fileing his nails and said, "If you wouldn't file your nails so much we would get along better," and he gave her a look dipped in devil's blood and said, "These are my finger nails and I'll file them whenever I damn please." Anne of course opened up the irrigation ditch on her face and "cried and cried and cried," and Robert felt awful about it and apologized.

"HE DID SO AND SO "

The general run of the conversation must have been, "Well, Gentry did so and so." "He did? Well Robert Kingsbury never did me that way, but he did so and so." "I'll have you know Rodes wouldn't. I'd never stand for it!" "Mr. Ross is so so and so about so and so" much to the edification of Helen, A.R. and Palmer, the husband-hunters. A.R. said it was one of the most interesting meetings they had ever had.

≈ ≈ ≈ ≈ ≈

May 4   TRAGEDIES IN BIRDDOM

We have been having some tragedies in Birddom out home. As usual, the blue bird which built her nest in the mail-box got broken up some way just as she was beginning to set. She is just a fool to want to live there every year when she never does have any luck. And in one of the trees Dad cut down yesterday, there was a dove home and it was broken up in the crash. Dad was positively grieved as the eggs were nearly ready to hatch. The dove couple acted very sad yesterday evening. But I guess they are the ones that disturbed Charlie Watkin's morning slumber when he was here. We didn't mind their cooing though, early in the morning. This morning along our back fence I discovered two little furry white chickens dead. Knowing there was not a white chicken on the place, I wondered and when I went into breakfast no one could explain their presence at all. Curious, Annie went right out to see and when she said "Why they are little owls" I was some surprised. But sure enough they were and they had fallen down out of the bird house, where Mrs. Screech Owl had evidently had her being. A.R. had seen a picture not long ago on the *Country Gentleman* showing an owl nest full of fluffy little white owlettes, and that was how she knew what they were. We wondered what happened to the screeches. The little ones were not old enough to be so sassy their parents would push them out into the world. Sly old detective that I am, I have it. The very riff-raff of birddom, the Sparrows, just about villa-ed *[Pancho Villa, at the time was making raids along the Mexican border]* into the Columbus haven of the Screeches and killed all the male babies and the female too. Wouldn't you just bet on it? If I see any sparrows in that bird house now, I am sure going to shoot them in the leg so they will be reported dead from gangrene poisoning. We are so sorry for the screeches, but Mother says we should be glad for "Owls are just awful with chickens," but Father said he thought the little ones of the owl family were not so wicked as reported. I bet nothing happens to old Mr. and Mrs. Jay who moved last week next door to me, in the upper story of a tree by my window. She sure was a busy woman for a while and it took all of Mr. Jay's time to fetch the lumber she used. All I can see of her in it now is her blue tail. The mocking birds have moved out to the Plum Orchard Suburb and we hope they will get to raise their family like they want to. Sparrows multiply so rapidly I think not only must the men have lots of wives, but each woman must be lousy with husbands. The rest of the birds ought to get out a paper against them and call it "The Menace" like the Protestants have at Aurora for fighting Catholicism.

SUMMER SOCIALIZING

Friday Anne and Robert Estill killed a pig in honor of the coming of the Sedalia Estills and asked me to supper. Nannie is such a changed woman. She was such a perfect stranger, I hardly ever cared for her company, and she reciprocated the feeling I guess for she yawned incessantly, assuring me it wasn't the company at all, but many late hours, but I never did care for a gaping girl. It is all kinda sad and unnatural for two people who have had such good times together to find a reserve built up in a few months between them which just mildews the association.

Monday night I hauled Teale Middleton out to Ethel's with me, and they, with Virlee and myself, socialized on the front porch and in the automobile and had a spry time. All of us at our house party had a lot of fun at Teale's expense (but it is the only way we can put him to any expense.) Financially he really isn't able to *do much*, but we need the harmless little fellow to run around with us and he thinks his services keep him free of any obligations to any of the rest of us. Whenever we go to Foster's or to the Greeks' in Fayette and he eats and drinks the same as the rest of us, when two or three of us have a good-natured round at the cashier's as to who shall pay the bill, Teale is the gallant who always busies himself with holding the wraps for the ladies until the account is settled and then, occasionally, he will saunter up to the cashier and offer to pay and then drop dead with surprise to find he is too late.

Yesterday morning Helen Wagoner and I had a nice little visit with Miss Alice Kinney at Riverscene, and she is nutty like I am about shrubs and flowers, and such things are such joy when they bloom. She had a poppy bed and a lot of lark-spur and other things in her "Friendship Garden." In it are perennial flowers given her by friends and when these bloom, she always renews her friendship pledges with the donors by sending them blossoms. Now isn't that a lovely idea for old maids and old bachelors with whom "it is might nigh Saturday?"

FLOWERS THAT BLOOM IN THE SPRING

My indigo blue lark-spur blossoms look like the petals were made of georgette crepe and are so large. I sure am going to plant some. I have planted a lot of cosmos among some spirea thunbergil which has feathery foliage and they will grow and bloom in the fall when the shrubs are resting. The pink and white wiegelies have blossomed their little heads nearly off and if our shrubs live and keep their health, our house will be one flowery spot in a few years. The holly-hocks are giants in size and are a magnificent sight. A.R.'s sweet peas are lovely and she made me promise to keep them cut faithfully and to send her a lot while she is away. The nasturtiums are getting free with bloom and the crazy colored zinnias come out in the oddest combinations. One big shrub we mourned as dead all spring, awoke one day and dressed like it was late for breakfast, and has caught almost up with its companions. But it sure did sleep late.

DISTURBING THE PEACE

There is something so funny, but I'll be jiggered if I know how to tell it. Maybe you can figure out the offense for which Locke Amick was arrested. One day on the street Locke told Tom Conole to pull his (Locke's) finger, and when Tom did it, Locke made a noise. Now if you can't figure out what the racket was, I hardly ever care to tell you any more about it. It happened that Sylvia Dodson, the telephone operator, was crossing down the street, and it is supposed she was an *ear* witness to Locke's conduct. Late in the evening, the Marshall arrested Locke, telling him Miss Sylvia had "filed information against him for disturbing the peace," and he would have to appear before the mayor and stand trial. It just scared him to death and when brought before the magistrate who was so full of laugh he had to go back and work with some boxes to hide his face, he said in his little lispy tone, "Mr. Fisher, this is the first time anything like this ever happened to me."

John Fisher said, "Well, is this charge true?" "Yes Sir." "Well, do you want to plead guilty?" "Yes, Syl Dodson filed information against me, and I guess she heard me." "Well, don't you know that is a very grave offense in the presence of women? I shall have to fine you $25. As this is your first appearance in court, I shall give you a stay of execution for the fine and parole you for sixty days, but if you do it again, it will not go easy with you."

Locke thanked the Mayor for his considerate treatment, and not for some minutes did he realize it was all a put up job and they were having fun with him.

Mid-July   THE FLYING CIRCUS

Dad, Mother, and Evie sat on the back seat, and Helen, Rosie and I held down the front when we drove to Swope Park where there was the greatest crowd ever seen in K.C. It was estimated at 125,000 at least. The number of automobiles was estimated to be 25,000 but after the show everyone wanted to get out of the park at once, and at times automobiles were blocked in a solid mass, four rows wide and 14 blocks back - and at times not a wheel turned for as long as ten or fifteen minutes. Engines were not shut down down, so many a gallon of gasoline was used. It took an hour of glacier-like travel to get out of the park, and twice on our way into the city we were caught in blockades and I'm thankful to have driven a car on Los Angeles' Broadway, else I couldn't have gone to the circus, or couldn't have driven out of it. Mother would keep saying, "Let me out! Let me out!" when cars were packed solidly around us. She couldn't have gotten out and Cousin Evie was clenching her hands in silence. It was trying I'm sure to them but it didn't sweat my back like Broadway did.

The aeroplanes flew very gracefully and there was an interesting sham battle and we saw the famous tail spin where a plane would have its nose straight up and spin like a top and nose dive and barrel roll and do many other thrilling stunts. Mother and Dad enjoyed it so much.

Later in the Summer   EVOLUTION?

The other night, Anna Rose, Bob McGavock, and I assembled at Margeret's and got to talking *Religion*. I almost always keep still at such times but, when Margeret said she believed as did her Nogales rector that man sprang from a monkey, I and Sue arose to the point of difference. We didn't say much but I had the most unkind thoughts and when I saw Susanna the next day I asked her what she was thinking when Margeret made that Evolution statement. She replied with a laugh, "I wouldn't have looked at you for a pretty last night for fear you thought the same as I did. Why I could just see Fred *[Margeret Simpich's husband]* on a pole and Mrs. Simpich in a tree looking at him." And I argued it was association that caused Margeret to have such monkey notions. Everybody to their own ideas, I guess, but my idea is that most of us have enough to be ashamed of in our family trees without having monkeys way back in it.

AN ANONYMOUS LETTER

The Snarrs *[the newly assigned minister]* thanks to my good Dad who ding-donged some others until he got a wagon together, moved to town from Fayette yesterday. Mrs. Snarr is a spry-looking woman. I have watched her over at the "Lord's House" (as Mrs. Burrus calls her bungalow), and she "looks somebody home" to me. Mrs. Duke, our chief rib of church support and spreader of dissension has just moved to St. Louis, and last night I heard Mother 'low to Mrs. Groves, "I guess its a good thing Sister Duke moved before she got to tell the new preacher all about the church members." Last week, Carl got an anonymous letter, the object of which was to tell him (so said the author) why the Methodist Sunday School doesn't succeed. It's because Charles Lee is Assistant Superintendent and Ernest Jenner is a teacher. The author related all the scandal I had heard about Charles and some that was news to me, and one case that must have happened not far from Glenida Place. I am sorry I heard of it. Am told it is true and every time I see the woman, who was just a mere girl, I can't see how it has worked out like it has. Well, by comparing writing, Carl and I proved to our own satisfaction that Mrs. Duke was author of the letter. In making out a check to him, she spelled his name "Carol" which corresponded with the name on the envelope. She told him to get better men in the S.S. and "God will bless you," but while seeming to care for the church, behold how she drags this woman, whom I never knew but to respect, down off her pedestal and through dirty mud of present indecency by insinuating that Charlie still slips around. A woman who isn't always keeping her skirts clear of scandal is a "goner." I am sorry I ever heard of this woman's misfortune.

Lilburn and "A Girl Called Josephine"

July 6   A GIRL CALLED JOSEPHINE

Saturday, Ruth Berkheimer said to come to her house to meet her guests. One was a little girl called Josephine. Josie and I found a common footing in the double-twinkle, and every time we could get any one to play she and I would twinkle, and I hardly ever cared to dance with anyone else, and I got to asking her questions about where she was from and what she was doing and was she going to be there tomorrow and could I come to see her and oh me, yes? and I wanted to take her right with me when we quit dancing to go watch the negroes dance in town at Liza Bowman's Annual Ball. O Mam, how you would have enjoyed seeing the COLORED ONES do the hesitation waltz, the one step, jelly roll and the circular two-step.

Sunday we amused ourselves seeing Boonville, going out to the training school grounds and out to the park looking at all the pretty scenery and all the time I was not liking her one bit less. Josephine Pritchett is a daughter of Stonewall Pritchett of Webb City and is going to the University this summer but comes to Fayette every Friday afternoon to spend Saturday and Sunday. Next weekend, we will spend in Boonville with the Billies.

July 11   WITH THE BILLIES

We went to Billie's, and Julia gave Josephine the "once-over." Julia came to my room after starting Josephine on her dress for the evening and said, "Well, that sweet child!!!" but I did not realize the significance of the remark until the next day when Billie and Julia were saying that when they first saw her they thought I was surely a cradle snatcher. However, after Josephine talked up, they found her rather mature for 22 years, and they were charmed by her affable manner.

Saturday night, Billie and Sister took us to Arrow Rock and Josie and I nearly got lost on the big back seat. We arrived with the auto-appetite. When you have it, you can eat horse and have it taste like milk-fed chicken. We had chicken soup with sliced cucumber and tomatoes, then baked spring-chicken with dressing and gravy, peas, asparagus-tips, potatoes, banana fritters, hot with butter, and ice-tea, ice-cream and cake. Then we strolled around looking at the gardens where every old-fashioned thing you can think of is in bloom.

BOONVILLE SCHOOL BOARD

I surely love the Billies and they are the only "Aid Society" I ever hope to belong to. I get so much good out of our meetings and feel we are doing a great good for one another. I know they feel better after running around with grown up children like Josie and I are.

I am so proud of Billie and have hoped to get him to give me some copies of his "po'try" for you to read. His latest is "Ole Spittin' Bill" inspired by W.F. Johnson of Boonville. And perhaps you don't know the doin's of the Boonville School Board but there has been much doing with the building of the Laura Speed Elliott High since the last local option election, followed by city and school elections. In the latter Judge Cosgrove was elected a director by the negro vote. Messres. Mittelbach, Max Schmidt, Speed Stephens, Wm. F. Johnson, and R.W. Whitlow are also directors. Prof. Crane is the Supt. of Schools, and one day Billie and Julia were in church and she remarked about the expression on the face of Crane, and Billie said, "Yes, he just ought to be named Professor Goose." And then inspiration settled on Billie and he went home and wrote a satirical symposium of the "Minutes of the Boonville School Board" where the directors all stated their qualifications, their mottoes and elected some teachers and put some out. In the "Symposium," Cosgrove is named Booker Washington, Mr. Johnson, "Wm. Shakespeare" from his incessant quoting from that Bard. Schmidt is "Murphy" on account of his Irish antecedents, Mittlebach is "Wm Kaiser" who arises to interrupt the meeting with "Hoch der Kaiser" any time reference is made to Germany. Speed Stephens is named Mr. Peter *[presumably for his alleged womanizing]*, while Mr. Whitlow has the illustrious cognomen "Mr. Lowwhite." It is a fact that none of these men have children of school years except "Max Murphy," and he rises and assures the board that they need not consider the interests of *his* son for even one moment in consideration of the best interests of the *board*.

Booker points out what he has accomplished: the ideals he has set for his boys (by the way, his son, Dan, went to the Stephens' wedding and got so drunk he had to be laid out on the plush divan in the drawing room, with his shoes and hat lost. After sleeping in the car that brought him back to town, he was seen early in the morning going home in his evening clothes, minus shoes and hat, and created quite a spectacle.) Johnson is supposed to have been well-paid for services supervising the architecture of the new building. Mittlebach ordered the paints and oils, while Max Schmidt ordered the fixtures and lights so *no other* tax-payer in the district might get a rake-off. He pays a beautiful tribute to a Miss Wilson, who has long taught there, but who was fired because of her support of the dry campaign. The meeting closes with a repeating of the pass-words "I got mine" and singing "*Blest Be the Tie that Binds*" and I want to tell you that Billie beat the words of the hymn all to smash.

A "RUIN'T GIRL"

I am told we have a case of a "ruin't girl" in town (Alda Dodson) and that Charlie Mason, the barber, has flew the coop. He cut my hair last Saturday and was all shaky but it never occurred to me what kind of worry was on his brain. Be it to his credit, he sure gives a good haircut when his mind dwells on such things. You never would have thought it of that nice looking Charlie, who has been dressing in *snow-white clothes* all spring and summer. Alda is a sister of Sylvia Dodson who is the chief telephone operator here. She had typhoid fever last summer and nearly died, and I guess they never did get the fever reduced, and now I imagine she is mad because they didn't let her die.

Some of our other good citizens' names are getting mixed up in the "common property" that put Charlie Mason out of town. One of our good Methodist erstwhile stewards with wife and two kids, and he and still another are Masons, Mam (not Charlies', but Free-Masons). There are lots of nice people in New Franklin, like all other towns, big and little, I guess, but morals are mighty scarce,

BORATED TAR SOAP

Mam, I have to go put the "Borated Tar Soap" Cousin Will bought where it won't smell so loud, or I will think I am running with carbolic acid. Won't you feel sorry for me when I get over all this brilliantine for the hair, sachet for the handkerchief, talcum for the face, and borrowing of the girl's toilet water, and AGE and rest securely and contentedly in the pefume of Borated Tar Soap? Mam, as I look at it now, if all those fragrant things I smell on my form and the forms of the sweet young things with whom I roam, don't keep me from that then I'm doomed. Especially am I thinking now of the fragrance of Josephine's letter.

MOONLIGHT PICNICS

Josephine came down from Fayette and that night we had a big swim. After we got out and dressed we started out for a moonlight picnic. The girls had prepared sandwiches, pickles and olives, and owing to our inability to get "pop" of any kind, we got some "Bravo" and a quart of ice cream all packed away in ice, and tore out. Old Reo pulls the hills so good, we were down at Sulpher Springs in thirty minutes and stopping the car out in the clear moonlight, we spread the lunch on the running board and got busy. It was right pretty down there with the wooded hills all around and the moon floating in a sea of clear sky. We were so full by the time we got to the ice cream, we decided to hold off for a little while, and not until we got to the big bridge across the Bon Femme creek did we feel we had room for more refreshments. We stopped on the bridge from which the trees along the creek and the water under us looked very attractive. We seated ourselves around the freezer, and proceeded to transfer the contents of the can. Of course someone had to come along in a car so we had to get up and drive the car off the bridge.

"PRETTIEST SPOT IN HOWARD COUNTY"

Tuesday night we all went swimming again and at 9 p.m., with our lunch all prepared as the night before, we took ourselves to the bluffs overlooking the river below Lisbon, before satisfying our appetites. My, but we were hungry. That was the prettiest spot I have ever seen in Howard County. After putting away all of the lunch, we clum out on the rocks above the river and drank in the wonders of the night. There wasn't a sound up there except the singing of the crickets in the woods on the bluff above us and the splash of the rocks we pitched into the water that swirled below us. It is beyond me to describe the reflection of the light on the water, but Josephine said it was prettier than the moonlight on the Pacific Ocean.

FOURTH OF AUGUST

Saturday was the Fourth of August and all day our road was lousy with niggers. When Rob and family got back from swimming Saturday night, they saw a little bit of disorder on their porch. A new pair of shoes Rob had just brought from town were unpacked and set outside, and when they got into the kitchen, the egg basket was on the floor, with broken eggs and eggs shells and light-bread crusts thrown about. In a quiet moment they heard someone breathing and upon investigation saw the head of a negro buck asleep on the stairway landing. Rob "had the law sent down," and several men came out and dragged the drunken negro down the steps by the feet, his head cracking against each step, and as they were carrying him out the door, it seems Robert's fury burst out and he took a broom stick and gave the dirty brute a few cracks with it. He had been upstairs and had prowled into a lot of drawers, but had not disturbed anything in the way of jewelry on the dresser. They found some of the children's hair ribbons in his pockets. The incident frightened Jean so badly she nearly had a fit. She didn't sleep any Saturday night and was sick all day Sunday but got quiet about ten o'clock last night. Alice V., the nerves of the family, did not seem affected at all, laughed about it like it was a big joke.

WINDS OF WAR

Lewis Means who has been at Ft. Riley has been recommended for a commission. Evangeline Boggs is crazy about Lewis now and said last night that if *she* could *she* would make him a Captain. John Talbot, Jr. was not recommended. Four of the Fayette boys were recommended, but more of them were not.

[Supplying food to France and England sent the price of farm products soaring, bringing prosperity to most farmers.]

The wheat is being sold at $2.00 to $2.30 a bushel and is bringing lots of money into the country. Claude Ivory paid all of his bills and had about $700 clear. And just any number of other people have money now who never had any before. The Hutsells and Charlie Long each have six or seven thousand dollars worth of wheat, their share of the crop. Will Bushmeyer has about $10,000 worth and so on down the list.

Horace and Father sold their apple crop this week to a St. Louis firm. Got a bigger price than ever before.

August 5   ON GOOD HUGGIN'

That was a nice little lecture you gave me Mam, and I really appreciated it. Only you just don't understand the speed the world has acquired in the years intervening between the time you and Tom were sitting on the sofa with nearly all of the room to sit on separating you, and the time that I "court" in now. What would you have thought if Uncle Tom had "reached" over and bit a piece out of your ear? Well, the girls just grow ears for that purpose now.

Mam, you write, "Until you find a girl who is not good hugging, you'll never find your soul's mate." Well, I am perfectly honest when I say that if my soul's mate isn't going to be good hugging, I hope to die single. I can't understand why you "wish on me" some plain, unhuggable old stick when you know how I adore pretty things. Of course I may adore some girl and take her for a soul's mate and then discover myself blistered—but you can just count on me believing she is good hugging when I send for the preacher. It is no disgrace to be good hugging or a good hugger, I guess. In all seriousness, I can picture nothing more desolate than to be stranded on some wedded Isle with poor hugging. Excuse me!!!

UNCLE SAM BECKONS

The newspaper reports about the change in age limits knocks the notion of a happy winter in Florida out of my head, and I am beginning to think I may as well enlist and go ahead instead of waiting to be drafted. Archie Jones, whom the "natives" had nick-named "Slacker," leaves tomorrow for Jefferson Barracks.

My fountain of news is so near dry I'll have to close.

Late August   **"STILL LOTS OF PRETTY THINGS"**

Aunt Lill had to *weep* and *moan* to get Uncle Charlie to cut the weeds in the cemetery before Billie Duval got here last week. And then he put it off until the day before the visit. People feel so badly at our funerals, I'll declare you'd never think they would let anything interfere with cutting a few weeds off our graves, in ninety days or so.

Grass chiggers have found me a good cemetery since I went to Sulpher Springs Sunday, and there are lots of little mounds to mark the graves on my legs.

"CONTEMPTIBLE HOUND PUP"

Xena is getting as much "hell" this August as she did *Heaven* last summer this time. Herman is a contemptible nocount Pup, isn't kind to Xena, has told her lies too big to haul in a motor truck, cursed Horace and Minnie to their faces and did worlds else that I tear up when I write it. Poor dear kid. But the baby is a darling. I personally hope Xena will divorce Herman but she must love him so. I don't think he has any sense. Horace gave him every chance and Herman just bit the hand that was feeding him. All these goings on are enough to make me pessimistic but I am not. There are still lots of pretty things and good people, and I'm planting flowers for next summer.

~ ~ ~ ~ ~

September 9   **BOONVILLE GOSSIP**

I don't know what became of Alex Stephens' money, but a whole lot of it can get away from a fellow who runs with John Barleycorn *[whiskey]* and neglects his business. There is good money to made in the automobile business if it is managed right, and just as much to lose if the manager don't keep his eyes wide open.

"FAMILY TREE TORN NAKED"

The Alex Stephens' women and the Speed Stephens' women have nothing to do with one another and would naturally blame each other for whatever happens. The Wilbur Johnson's are all mad at the others which madness is reciprocated, and the Stephen's Family Tree is as if it has been struck by lightning, all tore naked. The Wilbur Johnsons are not supposed to have as much as they once did either. I guess when a person gets old it is interesting to look around and see who has the cash, and then think about who had it when you first began to know what a sweet tongue money speaks in, and note the big changes.

BIRTH OF A NATION

When I read about you going to see "*The Birth of a Nation*," and having such a sport of a time, "my heart just swelled up," as Will Darneal writes to Anna Rose, "with gladness." Wasn't it fine there where old Abe got the bullet? Why, if it had been my own assassination, I could not have been more excited. I know how limp you felt after it was all over, and how streams of tears were just flowing down the aisle flooding the orchestra pit, until the fiddles had to move, as soon as it was over. It is truly exciting and plays all kinds of tunes on our emotions, and after three hours of it, I felt like I had been chased over the cliff, served throughout the Civil War, been assassinated and hung myself. You can imagine *my* condition.

September 12   **BOONVILLE BOOZE**

I am sending you a couple of copies of *The Message [the Anti-Saloon newspaper in Boonville]*. I am sorry to have lost the issue between these two as it listed the names of *all six* of the School Board members who have signed petitions and in another column handed each of them a "bunch." Called no names but asked how could these people sign petitions? The man whose son might have been a bright literary light but had drunk his head off (Cosgrove); a man whose brother through drink had wrecked himself and family (Stephens); a man whose daughter suffers abuse from a drunken husband (Mittelbach); and how can a woman raise cain because remonstrances are made against saloons (Mrs. W.F. Johnson, presumably) and it also wants to know how can a High Episcopal member and one who is a leader in his lodge sign it (Max Schmidt)?

"JUST SWIGGING IT DOWN"

The Stephens' pot is more than boiling. Alex is just swigging it down. The stockholders of the Central National Bank met in St. Louis to elect officers and Alex disappeared. They phoned back here to know if he had come home. It is reported Alex is $100,000 in debt. And that he took Crockett Hickman for $12,000. Some say it serves Crockett right for supporting the saloons that gave Alex his drinks. It is said Mr. Speed Stephens will be financially ruined in the "clean up."

They made Nelson Leonard, President of the Central National and the other banks over there are delighted. Speed Stephens, who is not to have any part in active management is V.P. Alex will cost Central National about $40,000. Nelson Leonard has been drunk half the time.

FARM PROSPECTS

The apple packing is going right along, and so is the corn-cutting and the wheat-sewing. The weather is dry as a bone and the dust a mile deep. Rob is "turning loose" 50 head of hogs this week at .17 cents a pound. He thinks they are 10,000 pounds of pork. There are about 200 more hogs on the farm that are growing as fast as tankage and new corn will put on the weight. Most of them are home grown hogs. I hope every one of them will live in health to a ripe age.

❧ ❧ ❧ ❧ ❧

September 27   DARNEAL FAMILY VISIT

We have been up and doing besides getting "done," so we have been folding experience away in layers in our minds. You remember Will Darneal has been wanting to have his family come down and see us to prove to them, I suppose, that his mother misclassed us. They decided to visit the State Fair in Sedalia and make a little visit to us on their way home. They got to Sedalia on Sunday evening and looked around on Monday morning, tearing out for New Franklin right after dinner. Mother was away. Father, Anna Rose and I drove down the lane to get some golden rod and in turning around Dad backed into the ditch and couldn't pull out. In the meantime we heard the Darneals go by screaming their coming, and on they went to the house where there was not a soul to greet them or act like they had come to the right spot. I cut across a field and got there five minutes later and Father and A.R. came later. Louise, the younger daughter, on whom it seems all hope of marrying the girls off, has been centered, said she just felt so dirty from travel and "Shrub" (old lady Darneal) said, "Lou made Will promise not to stop in town, and she hoped you would not be home until after she got acquainted with the bath tub." And they all had Lou go take a bath, while the rest just "freshed up" and looked fine too. Lou didn't look any better after she had the bath than she did before, though she "felt so much better." Sue is the sweeter of the two girls altho it seems the family has put her on the shelf. Father Darneal is a sweet old thing, never remonstrates about anything and at the conferences A.R. and I had in the kitchen, we decided that *his* tail feathers had been plucked back somewhere in the '70's. Our supper went off fine and the guests whose stomachs should have been as craving as vacuum sweepers minced along like they wanted to be sure of each bite. After dinner I asked Lou and Sue to take a drive with me and we didn't get back 'til midnight, and Shrub was up on her ear about them being out so late. The next morning the wind was blowing a gale and the clouds were threatening and all but Will voted to start home, but he wouldn't do it and Shrub reluctantly gave in and they stayed, afraid every minute it would rain. At supper we had an old country ham. You know, Mam, you and I have been used to country ham all our lives and don't think much about it but as Shrub's plate was passed to her she said, "This is the first ham that looks anything like *ours* since we left home." And after a while Mr. D. said, "I believe this ham is better than ours." And Shrub said, "Well, I was just thinking so, but I hated to admit that anyone had better ham than we do. Maybe it is the way this is cooked." No matter what we had or had done, "Lou" had beat it some way.

"BIG COMMOTION UPSTAIRS"

I couldn't stay with them last night and was out doing other society. The Darneals all went to bed early, except Will and about 11:25 Shrub called downstairs, "Will! Will! Will!," until Mother (who got back yesterday) got nervous and called Will and Anna Rose off the front porch. It wasn't long until there was trouble: thunder and lightning and rain, and I was up shutting down windows when I heard a big commotion upstairs. The Darneals had the whole upstairs to themselves and stepping out into the hall I heard all three Darneal women talking and the old lady said, "This just shows how foolish —" and then they shut the door and talked and talked and talked ten or fifteen minutes and pulled all Will Jr.'s tail feathers out I imagine.

When A.R. went up this morning they said the commotion was about them not being able to close a window! The women all came down with with their hats on, ready to go an hour and a half before train time with breakfast to be et first, saying, "I said it was going to rain, I'm a good weather prophet," or "I just hate rain. Even this summer when it was so dry, I hated it," and the old lady flared off! "*Moral*, never again get 150 miles away from home in an auto; hereafter, I'll do my travelling on a train." Old man D. was just sweet and resigned. not daring to open his mouth I guess. Father hauled them to Estill to the 8:15. I'm glad they are gone. I hope the laundress will put so much starch in Shrub's drawers she will have some kind of feelings, even if it isn't politeness !

October 10   OZARK EXPLORATION

Billy and Julia have talked Camden County so much, since they were there in August, I went down with high expectations on everything. I wasn't disappointed! We left Boonville in the Ford Saturday night at 7:00 p.m. Between Tipton and Versailes (where we spent the night), we had a blowout and when we looked for a tire pump we had none. Warren had removed it from the car to pump up his basketball and Billy gave him a beating by absent treatment. Finally a car came along and we borrowed one and rambled on. Versailes is a high point where the rain which falls to the north side of the court-house runs into the Missouri River and on the south side into the Osage. Leaving at 7:00 a.m., the hills of the Ozarks were unfolded to my view, with mists forming in the lowlands, and I realized I hadn't brought along enough adjectives. The covering of the autumn foliage was riotous. After several hours we arrived at Portage Springs where the water surges forth from under a high bluff and ripples over some moss-covered rocks. The water from this spring is a beautiful emerald color. The next point of interest was Hurricane Deck where the storms literally tear tops out of trees, and uproot them, until the "Deck" is almost bare except for the dead trees. We crossed the Osage River by ferry and drove into sleepy looking Linn Creek where Billie got stuck in the gravel, using the wrong ford across the creek.

REX MANN CLUB

About noon we arrived at the Rex Mann Club house and from that time on, I was so full of admiration, I almost busted. Several men of Boonville, Billie among them, built the Rex Mann Club last summer. It is a bungalow with a great living room and dining room, three bedrooms and kitchen and a roomy upstairs. It is on one of the highest mountains and commands a magnificent view of the hills and Niangua River. While Julia prepared dinner, Billie and I explored the path to the river as far as the Club Spring. We spent nearly an afternoon exploring the bluff Julia had in mind as the place to build their summer bungalow and they liked it so well they decided it was made and saved for them. Fernando Capps, the caretaker of the Lodge didn't return in time to take us on the river that night, so until bedtime we sat on the porch and soaked in the moonlit scenery. It was so still except for katydids, crickets, and the rippling of water far below us. I moved my canvas cot right out on the porch and slept there, until my eyes flopped open to see the hills emerge from the darkness. though of course the hills were perfectly still. The sun just got up and sat on them.

UP THE RIVER TO TONKY

We had Fernando ready Monday to take us out on the river early, and while B. & J. stopped at their "Four Acres" estate to clear it up a little and mark with stones where the house should be, Fernando poled me on up the river to "Tonkie" as they call Ha Ha Tonka. Fernando stood on the back of the flat "John-boat" and pushed it along with a pole whenever the water was shallow enough and paddled with one little oar the rest of the time. The bottom of the boat would rake over shoals and a little farther along the water would be twenty or 30 feet deep. Where there was depth, the water was clear green. And the bluffs or cliffs which rise majestically and abruptly from the water were beyond anything [Wallace] Nutting could paint in a picture, with all their timber caps, and wild flowers studded around in spots you never would suspect them of trying and succeeding to grow. After we passed a lot of those wonderful bluffs we had to walk 3/4 of a mile to "Tonkie."

I always thought the Mansion was on the river. When R.M. Snyder "took holt" there was a great chasm below the bluff on which the mansion stands now and just the stream of water from Blue Spring ran through it. Snyder built a damn at the lower end of the chasm and there is a lake covering 20 acres there now. The Blue Spring is at the base of a great cliff and the pool is a beautiful blue color. It is estimated that 160,000 gallons of water runs out every day. In the lake the water is dark blue with water cress, brilliant green, dotting its surface. And great strings of dark green water moss, waving under the water at the head of the lake, made another picture.

From the water tower and upper story of the mansion one can see miles and miles of wooded hills, just solid masses of brilliant autumn colors. High overhead were to be seen flights of geese winging their way southward in V-shaped military formations. Several of the views from the parapet jump straight down to Hell, its so far. It's a rocky abyss with dark blue lake at the bottom surrounded by beautiful autumn crazy quilts, with the water such an animated shade of green. There is a natural bridge near the mansion and not far away on the Niangua River is a cave in which you can travel a great distance by skiff before you can explore on foot.

FOUR ACRES

"Four Acres" is not such an eminent mountain but rises abruptly from the river. The cliff juts out into the river and they expect to build the rock cottage right on the edge, so you can almost fish off the front porch into water 20 feet deep. From this point you have a view up and down the river and have water rippling over shoals in either direction.

On this particular point we recognized hackberry, mulberry, black walnut, white walnut, hickory, white oak, elm, persimmon, cedar trees, willow, loaded with wild grapevines, and many bushes. The cliff itself was decorated with many wild flowers. The witchhazel trees with their brilliant red and green leaves and red berries are so attractive at this time of year.

I'm in love with the "baby mountains" and I want to go back and play around until I get tired of it. They are vast enough to impress a little person like me with the insignificance of myself, and the big springs and caves are so mysterious.

A few days later

Now comes word of a change on the railroad which takes about 31 families away from here. It is just as bad as having a Lusitania sink on us, so far as population is concerned. The trains do not change engines here any more and the fastest train does not stop here at all. It makes a straight run from St. Louis to Sedalia.

November 18 **CHURCH CHIT-CHAT**

I can't remember another time when I have ever been so "listless" or "indifferent" about the unannexed little female women as this November finds me. Always before some one of them has had the focus of my interest, dragging my eye-sight here and there and pulling at my heart straps. I think I'll call the coroner and hold an inquest over my dead interest in such, pretty soon!

The Preacher's wife is all right, goes and comes like anyone else. I hope she is always at home in her head now. Of course the girls and ditto the son, who is also good at dice and cards, fell in with the dancing set and true to Cora Harris's gospel of Methodism, our church members are wagging their old tongues off, saying, "Bro. Snarr can't preach when his children do like that." Sister Mat Burrus has "seen them standing at the corner after midnight talking to boys," and her conscience has told her to tell it with that slandering intonation of voice.

Old Mrs. Jimmy Dodson was in here yesterday when I was alone and dished up something, saying it always made her feel better after getting it out of her system, and she remarked that it was her opinion that, "Hell is just full of good women like that old lady across there," pointing to Mrs. Mat's house.

I think Mrs. Mat can pray all night and read the Bible between prayers and *not dance*, play cards— or *go to the Post Office on Sundays* and then be no better than the dancing, card playing male sinners if she says insinuating things about girls, who, as far as I can tell, are just plain human flesh and blood.

The Snarr girls handicap their Father in a way, but he can't help it. I know Mother and Father can't be blessed for the things Anna Rose and I do. I am not in the circle of the Smarr's because I do not dance *in New Franklin*, and I don't care to attend and not dance, as Myrtle Smarr does.

A FEW NIGHTS BEFORE CHRISTMAS

Mam, the roads have been just splendid since before Thanksgiving, and while the weather has been so cold the ice harvest is on. We have just revelled in it. A.R. and I drove to Fayette right after supper, did some shopping and were back home by 9:30 and with curtains on the car, we did't know it was so cold. I had some Wallace Nutting pictures framed. One subject, "Larkspur," is a pippin. In the background, amid graceful boughs of trees is an old English house and on either side of an old rock-bordered walk are most beautiful old-fashioned flowers: blue flags, red poppies, yellow galliardias, white and yellow daisies, lavender in blossom, a honeysuckle vine and pink roses. It is just alive with harmonious colors. I am giving Sister Julia one and that nice little Josephine Pritchett another. Anna Rose did a lot of shopping for Mother and Father as well as herself and has a regular Chris Hacker habit of writing on the check what she buys with it, and I guess it never occurs to her I was in the bank where I see what is going on and I fear I am going to get a Gillette Safety Razor, some night gowns and an aluminum hot water bottle, and if it turns out this way, won't it be fine? We are giving Mother a set of white china with gold trimmings, ten of each of the different pieces.

SECRETS OF A GOOD DISPOSITION

My disposition has been pretty good lately and I attribute it to following the advice of a young, old man, Dr. Flynn, known as the Health Evangelist, who has been in Kansas City converting the public. Before I get out of bed, I wake up my brain, my eyes, my stomach and my feet by certain exercise, then I hop out and wake up the kidneys by twisting my back nearly off, and take a drink of cold water and then take a friction bath by rubbing myself all over with a regular horse brush. My skin is plum tough now. Next, I beat it to a cold water plunge and after a rub down with a hand towel, I am plum gay in spirits. I can do all this and touch the floor with my fingers too in less time than it takes to write it. And then, Mam, I drink some cream, let breakfast entirely alone, and walk to town. By noon I have the healthiest appetite and I'm just feeling bully. And if one can survive a cold bath, he can survive anything that comes up during the day.

ARRIVAL OF A NAME-SAKE

Carl Jr. and Taylor looked hard for "Baby Sister" on their Christmas tree, but in vain. However, Santa Claus came back Christmas night and on the 26th instant at 6:30 a.m., little Sister "came with a tassel" (as Sis Armstrong would say) and Lillian insists he shall be my name sake. Just Lilburn. I am delighted to have one, but it isn't a name I care for myself, so I'd never wish it on a helpless baby.

"ACROSS THE ICE BRIDGE"

Saturday afternoon, Father took Mother and A.R. and the "Christmas doings" across the ice bridge to Boonville and came back for me. I took him back and returned home with the car for fear the ice might melt before we could get back. It is quite a novel sensation, this driving over the Big Muddy on ice in a machine. Sunday morning it was thawing and there was a lot of water on the ice, and I hardly ever cared to walk over again. Sunday afternoon Billie took us all driving out into the country. The roads were splendid and the air just sharp enough to make us feel good. Sunday night we had lots of fun fixing the tree and went to bed happy except for Warren who had persuaded his parents to give him his biggest presents a week before. While we dressed Christmas a.m., William played Christmas records on the Victrola, and when we assembled at the breakfast table, Billie read the 23rd psalm and Father gave this "Grace:"

Our Gracious God whose mercy lends!
The light of home, the smile of friends,
Our gathered throng thine arms enfold
As in the peaceful days of old.
Wilt thou not hear us while we raise,
In sweet accord of solemn praise,
The voices that have lingered long
In joyous flow of mirth and song.
For all the blessings life has brought,
For lessons its sorrowing hours have taught,
For those we've lost, for those we keep,
For hands to clasp, for those who sleep.
For the noontide sunshine of the past,
For these brief, bright, moments fleeting fast,
For stars that gild the heavenly sphere,
For the ray that lights the passing year.

We thank thee, Father, let thy Grace
Our loving circle still embrace.
Thy mercy shed its Heavenly store,
Thy peace be with us, evermore!

It was such a wonderfully happy way to start our Christmas Day.

"SO MANY NICE THINGS"

All of us had so many nice things. Mother and Father gave me such a pretty Gillette razor all done up in a nickel case, and Rosie contributed the hot water bottle of aluminum. Nannie Estill sent me a box of pecans, the big fat ones that Anne Estill was laughing at her buying at 70 cents a pound. They are delicious but no pecans are worth that. Mildred sent me a Wallace Nutting picture in a mahogany frame. Its an exquisite one of peach blossoms and I am so pleased. Sister Julia gave me a Nutting entitled, *"The Book Seller."* Josephine sent me a very sweet picture of herself and a little verse, framed in circassion walnut:

"When all the stars have lost their glow
And not a shell gems any shore
When fragrant breezes cease to blow
And evening follows day no more
When limpid streams no longer flow
I may forget you, not before."

Julia had a whale of a Christmas dinner for us and Helen Wagoner, who was in Boonville between trains on her way to Montrose, was with us.

A.R. and I coaxed Helen to stay over until the next morning so I could take her to the Fayette dance. She yielded to temptation and we just danced ourselves down and when it was lightning and thundering at 12:30, Helen and I decided to run for home. We got out of town three miles and the lights on our car faded away. We couldn't go on in the dark nor could we walk because the rain was coming down in sheets. Helen was afraid to stay while I went to a distant farm house for help, so we just wrapped up in the robes as comfortably as we could and waited. Nobody came by except a surrey full of people at 3 a.m. who could pick up no more passengers they said. At 5 a.m., we both waded up the road to Charlie Barrows, and he brought us to Fayette in time for the 6:15 train down.

$5 CHRISTMAS GIFT

We are still busy at the Bank. Mr. Boggs got the Bank to give me $5 for Christmas! When I think of how much I've done in the last four weeks, I wonder why he didn't give me $10 as he did last year!!! I've certainly put forth my best efforts, Miss Ida, and if it don't bring forth some token of appreciation like a raise, when the New Year comes I shall soon decide it doesn't pay to work so hard. And Mam, I can't see how it would ever pay anyone to grind, grind, grind the whole day, every day. I want some playing around time.

1917

NEW YEAR BEGINNINGS

January 19   *"JUST BEAT THE STUFFING OUT OF HER"*

Have you heard the latest about Estherline Tinsley's winning ways with her husband? When John has men call at his place for business and gets to talking along such lines, E. comes to the door and calls him to come in. If he does not come at once, she returns to the door and gives him a good cussing and tells him he "used to run in whenever old Sally Lakey called him," and then if John doesn't respond with his presence, she comes out with a revolver and marches him into their sanctum called HOME. She did this one day last week, and John just beat the stuffing out of her when she got him in the house, and she went right to Fayette with a veil over her marred features and gave information on which Dr. Finn and Fred Wilkerson are both indicted for selling whiskey, both being out on bond at this writing. Dr. Finn has employed Sam Major for $100 to defend him. Fred had Paul call Father to Fayette and talked over the case with him, and Fred told Father and Paul that he had no money to pay a fine, that he was way in debt, but that he did have $50 and if Paul and Father would quash the indictment some way, they could have that amount to divide between them. That was bordering on an insult wasn't it?

"GOING ON BESIDES PROTRACTED MEETING"

This week there was an arrest at Mrs. Isaac's Hotel in which a man and a girl, who arrived there attired in man's clothing, were made to get out of bed. Brock McCauley went with the constable after them. The former was slightly intoxicated. When the search of the prisoners, who were suspected as thieves wanted in Fayette, revealed one to be a girl, Brock wanted to search her. When they wouldn't let him, he begged to be allowed to guard her. His request was denied. All of this has been going on here besides our big "Protracted Meeting." I expect, as usual, there is a lot going on around town we don't know about. Old Mrs. Jimmy Bain at Franklin Junction got alarmed at something that went on there one day and said, "They are going to keep on until the Junction is just as bad as New Franklin."

"TIRED OF THE MONOTONY"

Mr. Boggs has taken tonic until he is better and earns his salt at the bank!!! But I can't go away for longer than a few minutes at a time. NOT since the 21st of June have I been away from the bank at all, and while I am getting along fine, I do get tired of the monotony. Some day I am going to quit and take a vacation sure enough. Just because someone else is puny is no reason why I should make myself puny, too, by sticking constantly on the job. I asked for a $15 raise per month and was "awarded the contract."

But what I can't get over is my feeling about that $5 Christmas present he gave me. It has been $10 heretofore, and after digging like thunder all fall while he had a rest cure, I was hardly in condition to have the usual fee cut in half.

~ ~ ~ ~ ~

February 7 **WINTER WINDS**

It has been so long since I wrote that unless some one else from here has told you about how cold it has been, you and Uncle Tom have had nothing to make you shiver and shake with joy that you are not back in Missouri. Last week the weather man caught up with the bottom of the thermometer, unscrewed it, and the mercury nearly all ran out. Fourteen below was the worst our weather gauge got, but we fear the peach buds had a funeral that night. Last Sunday at 5 a.m., when I got up to take the early train to Boonville, it was down to 30 degrees, and the wind was blowing about 50 miles an hour. By the time I was ready to start, a few bits of snow were in the air. I cancelled my trip and went back to bed and by 9 a.m. the temperature had dropped 26 degrees. It was a fearful day. That morning Mr. Arthur Wallace's house burned. Mr. and Mrs. W. got out with an overcoat and a seal-skin coat respectively. All the beautiful furniture and oriental rugs were lost.

BEING GOOD TO YOUR PARENTS

I get quite agitated at times about pulling up stakes and the last spell I had like this was when I heard Frank Mitchell is to be appointed State Bank Commissioner. I remarked that I was going to get Frank to get me a job as Bank Examiner, and Mother just clouded up and wept and moaned, saying, "Isn't it a shame, Taylor, to raise a family as large as ours and then not be able to keep a single one with us?" Just as if I could ever be driven off with a stick!!! It is most pleasant to be with my Ma and Pa, and I realize it, but they might pick up and unwillfully leave me some time. However, there are times when they do need someone around, and they say they get so lonesome when both A.R. and I are away at the same time. I don't guess there is any greater work in the world than being good to your Mother and Father. So I haven't said a word about promulgating myself elsewhere since that wet season of Mother's.

"HE LOVES TO SING"

Bro. Snarr finally asked the congregation one night if they thought the meeting should go on, and asked for those who did to put up their hands and only seven did, so the meeting was closed. I did not put up my hand because I was sick and tired of hearing him sing those old time songs from the book brought over on the Mayflower. He sang without music and loved to do it because they were in the minor keys. He loves to sing better than to preach, but he has no right to punish us. He gets sore because we do not have the love for the old things like he does. He preaches about his worldly-wayward children and says he wishes they could have some sense about doing the good old things he was so keen about in his youth and prime. And one night he sang, *"Where Is My Wandering Boy Tonight?"* because he could sing the first parts of it as a *solo*, and he had the time of his life soloing it, and all the time it was just ripping open sweet Miss Sallie Edwards's and Margeret's hearts until they cried all through the rest of the service. I guess the preacher thought he was singing with wonderful feeling that night and instead of singing two verses as announced in the beginning, he sang four and I think repeated the last chorus softly.

"NO RESPECT FOR..."

One day he said, "Brother Kingsbury (speaking to Pa), Our children think they are pretty smart sometimes, don't they? (And crowed—that was his manner.) Why, we have forgotten more already than they have ever learned, etc."

I guess I ought to be crazy about the preacher, but I hardly ever care for him, no matter *how smart* he is. I know if I were his child, I wouldn't go near him unless he quit bawling me out. His girls sit up in church and never bat an eye when he hits them. His son, Paul, plays cards in Foster's restaurant a good deal and occasionally Bro. Snarr will enter, approach the table, and say, "Paul, let's go home." Paul will continue to play and never have no ears at all, and Bro. Snarr will say it all over again, and finally go out by himself. I haven't got no respect for a boy that will have his Papa do him that way.

February 23 "I'VE GOT THE BLUES"

Something is always happening to take the joy out of life. Had a terrible blow yesterday. I have only one insurance company that writes farm business and they have written me they want to retire, and will I cancel all policies *at once*. This is very drastic as a company in drawing out, usually allows policies in force to remain until expiration. It seems I'll have to take a new application for every farm risk I have, some $90,000 worth at once, and the worst is I have to find a company to handle it. As usual, Mr. Boggs sat down and wondered why the company got so rushed. There was one incident I did not tell him, for he would never get through laying it on me, whether I am to blame or not. The company has mentioned withdrawing several times, and they have insisted on some cancellations recently that were as good as any company would want, and the last time they wrote me about cancelling a policy, I wrote the state agent to illustrate my point as follows: "You must be German, judging from the way you have been "submarineing" my policies. Are you trying to starve out this agency?"

Do you suppose he could have gotten mad and, like real Germany, severed all relations abruptly? Well, I know Willie Boggs would say, "Yes," so I'll never tell him myself, for he is all times speculating on things I say or may have said, getting to somebody and making them mad—like he figured Hulda Humfield was cool toward him because maybe Clara Landrum told Aubrey Landrum that we (Clara and I) said Hulda didn't smell good under the arms (or somewhere) and maybe Aubrey told Hulda. Now *you* know there is no such thing, although it would have been a good turn to tell her. There was a girl at the dance last night affiliated with *smell* and my dance with her was six weeks long. I prayed for someone to tag me and take her, as all dances were tag dances, but in vain. On the other hand, the sweet things I danced with were tagged from me before we could get around the room once.

"HE THREW A FIT"

I'm still trying to generate love for my superior, Mr. B., but this morning he threw a fit about opening the vault door so the "old dead air" could get out, when I didn't do it as soon as he thought I should, You'd think we had a corpse buried in the vault. This is his latest "fad," opening the door to let out the "old dead air." This a.m. he put up a window and opened a door as I swung the vault door open. And, Mam, it is so ridiculous to me when he don't love to leave the transom open an inch during the day, and one coming in about four o'clock smells air that is redolent with the fragrance of rotten perspiration.

Herbert Royston will just about get my job one of these days to come. I shall either get killed by old dead air, when I enter the vault, or else get fired. And as I said to Mr. Father as he cautioned and advised me not to "cross or antagonize Will," one can't get along smoothly all the time unless he gives up all initiative, all personality, all independence. And what is left? Just so much per month. I'm going to start me a pop-corn stand. That so much per month is a great help, but men in banks who have no stock control all get kicked out sooner or later, and maybe I'm tougher to stand the boot now than I will be in later years.

March 26   **WEDDING PREPARATIONS**

The Billie Smiths were out last night and stayed until after 9 p.m. They got interested in the things A.R. was showing them out of her Savings Box. There are lots of things in it now, all of her napkins are hemmed, she has a completed luncheon set, lots of beautiful guest towels, and night gowns and underwear and things you would find in any girl's Hope Box, things which everybody likes to look at because they are "wedding things." To my notion, the prettiest thing she has is a white satin petticoat which she and Helen Wagoner's mother made when A.R. was visiting Helen in Odessa. On the bottom of it are flounces of lace and six little satin flaps with baskets of flowers embroidered on each flap. Each basket is in different colors, and these will show up through any thin areas, and their beauty will not be lost entirely. A.R. has done nothing at all toward getting her dresses and suits and things like that. The prices paralyze her. Heard her say she was going to have Miss Berndt make her a very simple white wedding dress. The date of the wedding is to be the 28th of June, although sometimes she says she believes she will wait until fall, being so comfortable at home.

April ll   **EXHIBITING GROOM-TO-BE**

Will Darneal was down for several days recently. The first night the Club gave an "open session," and all their husbands were present. It was thought at first it would be an announcement party, but resolved into just an exhibition of the to-be-groom. There was nothing to announce but the date. It has been decided to tie the kinks on the 28th of June. They are planning a porch wedding at noon. Rosie was writing to some of Will's relatives who had written her a welcome home, and said, "I am to be married on our porch, dressed simply in a white georgette dress, "and when I read it over, I told her I thought it was too much to decorate a porch with, and she told me to re-write it. I did and when she read mine, she discovered I had been tactless enough to say to this old lady," I doubt not you will be able to give me some points in tatting, crocheting, tattling, etc." On account of the tattling remark, she re-revised the letter.

April 17   **SISTERLY ADVICE**

Sister Hazel is with us and she has been telling A.R. how to storm the "Fortified Fortress of Antagonistic In-laws," and what she had to say was so sensible. The Darneal family act like they will never become reconciled to having the son and brother marry. Old Mr. Darneal is lovely, but I think old Sister Darneal must have been and still be a Von Hindenberg!!!! *[Von Hindenberg was imperial Germany's Field Marshall.]* She has not written, to Anna Rose, nor has either of the two girls since they found out the wedding was to be in June, and Anna Rose was coming to their town to live.

May 25   **VISITING THE DARNEALS**

Toward the end of the week Will wrote Anna Rose about some changes they were to have made in the little house where they are to live and asked her what she thought would be best, and of course she couldn't say, never having seen the place. So I decided A.R. would never have any idea about what kind of furniture she wanted for a house she had never seen, so we sent word to the Darneals that we would come up and spend Sunday with them.

When we got to Lexington Junction, Will and Sister Louise were there in the car to meet us and they rode us to Richmond, where the family greeted us. "Aunt Al" had come over to spend the day and she and A.R. fell on each other's necks affectionately, while Sue and Mrs. Darneal shook hands only. Louise had already kissed A.R. on the platform down at the Junction. It always rains when I go to Richmond, even on the most beautiful days, and by two o'clock, it was doing what comes naturally—raining like all get-out. The Darneals had a mighty good dinner and just broke every bone in their body being nice to us. In the afternoon, we went to see the little house, which has five rooms and a bath, and a little stone porch in front. It is to be done over in white enamel inside and some changes made in the openings between rooms. The house belongs to Will's Father, and they are afraid the newly-weds will not live there long enough to justify them to spend so much fixing it up, or else they would have built a fireplace. Well this little visit made Anna Rose feel so good, and the Darneals all seemed to feel so good about everything and so pleased that A.R. liked the little house and the proposed alterations.

I think it was the best trip we ever took. That is, it will result in more good. Mrs. Darneal will be so much more interested in fixing things. "Aunt Al," it seems, has been chief adviser to Will, and she shows excellent judgment about everything. She is dear and sweet and is about 60 years old. I came away with the kindest feelings about that family, and if they come to my house again, I shall bust a hamstring to make it a more pleasant time than it was when they were here before. Think now much nicer it will be for A.R. to go up there feeling "at rest" with the family and knowing all of them are glad and willing to do anything they can to make her new home a happy one.

CONFLICTING WEDDING PLANS

Originally A.R. just wanted to go to the Justice of Peace, but nobody approved of that and so the simple porch wedding with just a few relatives was planned, the wedding rag to be a suit. Well, Sister Minnie came along and said it was a shame not to be bridey, as a bride, and Mother wanted A.R. to be, so the next day A.R. and Miss Berndt got together and planned the big dress. And then instead of announcements, the families decided to send invitations. And on account of sending invitations, it was decided the best thing would be to have the ceremony at the church in New Franklin. This was planned at the suggestion of certain members of the family, and the next day along came some of the others who say it will be a shame to have it at the church, and Sister Julia doesn't want it at night and Little Julia's dress won't be foxy enough for a church wedding, so we changed it all back to a porch wedding. One day, A.R. wrote Will he would have to shiver and shake down the church aisle, and the next, he wouldn't, and in the face of so many changes he won't know where he is *at*. A.R. says it is not her wedding at all, she is just accommodating the family and that Sisters Minnie and Margeret and I are "making the extra trouble." Miss Berndt is going to doll up my Ma for the wedding in gray georgette.

June 11 *ARRIVING WEDDING GIFTS*

Helen Wagoner came a week ago, and she and A.R. have been in St. Louis with letters of credit from their brother and beau respectively and just swept the wholesale houses hunting bargains and have brought a lot of pretty things home. I know A.R. won't have time to write what she got, and I will try and do it for you, although I am not much on explaining how things are. There is a lovely wardrobe trunk all lined up with a beautiful pattern of rose-colored chrysanthemums, and she has her shoes and hats and her clothes all in it, and they are so easy to display from it. Her speciality was in what they call "teddy-bears." having about nine in what they call crepe and other stuff variously and sundryly embroidered and they are plum beautiful. Mattie Jones made her such a wonderful underskirt with crocheted panels, beading, edging and more edging and gave her such a lovely crocheted centerpiece for a wedding present. A.R. found a white voile dress and a blue crepe dress ready made, and Miss Berndt sent for her today to try on her things and Mother's dress. Mother went to try on her own of course. I can't describe clothes so will keep you posted as to wedding presents. Aunt Al gave that 54 inch between meals table cover, linen with a seven inch crocheted border that everyone falls into a spasm over it is so pretty. Louise and Sue Darneal are giving them a four poster mahogany bed, and the Senior Darneals are giving them the heater in the cellar for their water system and their oil stove with fireless cooker attached. Some of the Richmond friends have sent a cream and sugar in the silver, beautiful plain pattern, and Luther and Sallie sent a cream and sugar in silver, both of these arriving the same day. Helen Wagoner gave A.R. her visiting cards and some embroidered pillow cases, and Mrs. Mills a pair of elegantly worked pillow cases. Josephine Pritchett sent a bridge set, and Sis Alma, a silver flower vase that just pleased A.R. so much that she is already using it on special occasions. We are going to give her silver in the John Adams pattern which is very plain and pretty. That is, the family, except Horace and Sister, are to do this. As for them, they asked to make Anna Rose a present of the wedding dress and Sister Minnie took that under her wing and told Miss Berndt to go the limit or I might say the unlimit on it, and I am anxious to see just what it will be like. Speaking of silver, we are going to give her eight of the knives, forks, butter spreaders, salad forks, tea spoons and boullion spoons. Miss Lill handed me a ten spot the other day to spend for something. A.R. seems inclined to put her money gifts in silver, and I think that is a mighty good way. She got some beautiful shoes at Swopes, and I gave her her dress-up hat, which came on here at Clark's millinery store, and when A.R. rave and tore over it, I had it put away for her until last week, and surprised her with it.

June 20

ACCOUNT OF ANNA ROSE KINGSBURY'S WEDDING TO WILL DARNEAL, AT FAIRVIEW, NEW FRANKLIN, MISSOURI JUNE 20TH, 1917

Everything in connection with the wedding just clicked off like clock-work. For days before we talked about the details and by the day before, we knew where everything was going to be and what it would look like. Nothing in the way of decorations was attempted until 5 p.m. on Tuesday, except bringing two wagon loads of ferns from the woods for storage in the cellar until we needed them. But at 5 p.m. the wheels began to turn. We used black oak leaves extensively because of their bright waxy appearance and their lasting quality. Of them we made a railing 20 inches high all around the porch by fastening the oak leaves solidly in wire netting, and above this and extending down a foot from the top of the porch pillars we made a solid border of the leaves, which we also caused to grow upon the porch pillars. From the outside, this looked very pretty with all the little green "bushes" set against that background. Inside of the oak-leaf railing, we used asparagus for a lining to make the "airy effect," and in the corners, banked oak-leaves and maiden-hair and sword ferns. The door and two windows on the porch were outlined with asparagus and Dorothy Perkins roses. On either side of the door between the door and the windows, we made irregular banks of ferns and oak leaves. At the entrance to the window on either side of the steps were large wicker baskets filled with sweet peas, and vases of sweet peas adorned the piano which was placed in the northeast corner of the porch. A long green grass rug served as a floor covering, and, except for seats arranged for Mother, Father, Mrs. Darneal, Mrs. Heulett, on one end of the stage, and Frank Brickey and me on the other, there were no others there. Entering the hall through the arch of asparagas and roses, the hall was clear of everything except a couple of large vases of field daisies. In the parlor across the east end, the "prizes" were displayed and vases of the field daisies were used here also for decoration. The fireplace, filled with maiden-hair ferns and a vase of daisies on either side, was much dressed up. On the table in a centerpiece of ferns and roses was the wedding cake. Everybody was so nice to help out. The Club girls, most of them, came to our house on Tuesday afternoon after Lillian, Margeret, Mother and Sister Julia had made cakes and cakes and cakes, cutting them into little square pieces, and iced them with goody. I believe they had at least 180 and some whole cakes left for special emergency. Virginia Burkhardt, Mrs. Rob Kingsbury, and Mrs. Horace all served on the suggesting and helping committee to assist me with the porch trimming and when it was all finished, I want to tell you it exceeded my biggest hopes, and I can prove it by lots of people who were present. It was a very pretty setting for the "BIG ACT." Tuesday evening and night, people were coming and going so much, it made a bit of confusion. The Mama Darneal, the Aunt Alice Heulett, and Louise Darneal arrived and the Van Studdifords from Jonesburg with some Fayette people dropped in to see everything in and out of the bride's trunk, and the rehearsal was pulled off by the hardest at a late hour. And after we served the crowd with eats and took the Darneals to Mr. Foster's hotel, Will and A.R., Helen Wagoner, and I had just sat up "indefinite," it was Wednesday morning. When six o'clock came, I riz up and so did everybody else, and as I came down the stairs I saw A.R. coming out of the dining room with the funniest look on her face, and the next time I looked she was hanging on Father's neck, and I heard him say, "Well, you must not think about that part of it" and just guessed at what was the matter, not caring to investigate right then. Later I learned I had not guessed right. As she came down the steps, her old cat had met her at the foot and said "Meow." This was too much for Rosie on this going-away-day.

By the appointed hour, everything was in readiness, seats had been arranged on the lawn and at 12:45, the people began to arrive. From then until the wedding there was not a time that there was not the worst streak of dust hanging over the road, and everybody arrived gasping for breath. That dust cloud was the most disagreeable thing. The day was lovely, ideal June weather, with the sky shaded by clouds at the wedding hour, so that the people could stand out around the porch and not have the sun grins. Just nearly everybody kin to us was here who was in coming distance. Everybody seemed so happy and there was such a visiting about.

About one o'clock, Helen Wagoner in a gown of gold cloth, veiled in tulle with silver trimmings and carrying an armful of Sunburst roses, with silver foot-trimmings (not the roses but Helen's feet) led Frank Brickey, Myrtle Snarr and me to the porch, and as I played the piano and Frank sawed on the violin, she sang very sweetly, *"I Love You Truly"* and *"The Sunshine of Your Smile."* Then "Bab" Snarr took hold of the piano keys and played Mendelssohn's *"Wedding March"* Alice Virginia and Julia, in much beruffled white frocks with pink ribbons and carrying white baskets, with pink tulle bows and filled with pink sweet peas, headed the little procession. After some waiting (A.R. said she was going to be very slow coming out in order to tease the crowd and arouse their curiosity to see the bride.) Sister Jean with a large white lily and dressed like the other youngsters came out with a smile. (She afterwards said, I had to try awfully hard not to laugh.) Bab Snarr played MacDowell's *"To a Wild Rose"* a long time before Anna Rose and Will appeared, and then the Rev. Jacob Snarr impressively spoke an abbreviated ring ceremony and pronounced them husband and wife together. Then came the kissing and congratulations, and the retreat to the dining room to eat a little ice-cream and cake. The refreshments were ice-cream with pink-pineapple ice cream frozen in bricks, and the pink frosted individual cakes, and pink, white and green mints.

While the bridal party were being served in the dining room, the Club girls served the other guests on the lawn. There was the usual excitement in the cutting of the wedding cake. Little Julia got the dime, Albert Smith the ring, and I do not know who drew the other "valuables." We thought we did the right thing by seating the parents at the side of the bridal party, but Mother will never cease to "moarn" because she could not see Anna Rose at all, could see nothing but the groom, and she says she would have given anything to have seen both their faces. Nearly everybody else could, as they faced the crowd, Bro. Snarr's back being to the audience, we thinking he was handsomer that way. We told A.R. and Will they could just use his nose as a canopy to stand under during the ceremony. Snarr, as I said, spoke the ceremony. A.R. gave him to understand that she and Father just thought it awful for a minister to have to read from a book, and after she said it, he laughed his little chuckle and said, "Well, the Bishops do it" and made her feel silly, but her last word to him was that he should have no book at *her* ceremony.

I was busy looking at the people and watching the groom's face twitch when a fly lit on his face once or twice. A.R. looked just as pretty as a picture, and if she could have seen herself, she would have been contented in mind. She never saw her wedding dress until the evening before and had no idea what it would be like and was terribly disappointed, on the quiet, as this dress was a gift from Horace and Minnie. It just looked like the dress was shorter in front than it was behind and was so loose looking and so short. It was of georgette crepe, hand-embroidered in pearls and trimmed with Filet Venice lace—whatever that is—over white satin, and when she was dolled in it and Sister Minnie had arranged her veil and flowers and had her ready to sally forth, she and the dress were lovely. I never saw Mother look so sweet as she did in her grey georgette dress with such pretty embroidered trimmings. Mrs. Billie and Mrs. Horace both wore dresses of white georgette with hand-embroidered pearls, while Mrs. Rob with all the Club girls were somewhat less dolled in dressy shirt-waists and skirts. To save my soul, I can't think what the Richmond people had on, except Louise was in a white frock of some kind with a blue ribbon on it. She is a very pretty girl, bordering on handsome, with light hair and blue eyes, but give me the little old brown-eyed brown-headed kind and I can tell you what she has on and how she looks as far as I can see. When ready to go to the train, A.R. wore a coat dress of black charmeuse with such a nifty tailored black and white hat of white felt and black straw. I don't know but that I considered this black dress, much plaited and embroidered, the prettiest thing she had, unless it was the white khaki-kuhl suit. There was much throwing of confetti and rushing to get into cars to go to the train, and as Nannie Estill and I were together out in the yard signing as witnesses to the wedding at that time, I just grabbed her and put her in the car with me. At the same moment, I felt coming upon me the realization that Lucy Darneal was not getting in the cars and that nobody was left there who would think to bring her to the train. By that time our car was plum full of people who just piled in, and I never was to ask Nannie to get out, so off we went. The crowd was very considerate and the pullman people even more so, as they would allow no one to get on the train to throw confetti or to put up placards. We saw them fade away and the "wedding" had become past tense. When we got home, Lillian committed the *faux pas* of going up to Louise and asking, "Why didn't you go to the train?" Well, we all felt so badly about it happening that way, but I dassen't try to apologize to Louise, so acted like nothing had happened when I hurried down after supper with Helen Wagoner to take Louise and her Ma driving until the train came. And then came another chance for Louise to think I was not very nice. I had attended to getting the Darneal tickets when Nannie Estill drove up and started to the depot to get theirs, so I went along to assist. And while assisting, the train the Darneals were to leave on pulled in and, instead of leaving me to see they did not miss it, they all piled out with their luggage and were half-way up the platform by the time I got back to them, and Louise just more than walked ahead and fast at that, until I begged her not to rush so. But anyhow they got on their train in time, and I fear they will give me a blue-black eye, but to save my soul I could not help it the way Nannie "come up."

I do not know much else to write unless I tell you about the wedding prizes which Aunt Fannie and Aunt Lillie say should encourage Albert and me to put ourselves in line for matrimony. There's just too much to list but someone sent such beautiful little silver salts and peppers, and I said if I could have them and the little doll cream and sugar, the hammered silver pitcher, and the mayonnaise bowl in silver, I would get married right away.

By the time I got home the other guests had left and there was no one left but Father, Mother, Helen and me.

Helen and I progued until eleven and when I got to sleep I bet I snored like Mother and Father did when we came in at eleven. We were all so tired. (For the benefit of those who don't know, "progue" is A.R.'s and my word for "prowl." One of Aunt Lillie's cooks used to say that "John Thomas, the cat, was such a proguer, he just progued up on the table every time he got a chance.") And when Helen Wagoner leaves me, I will surely feel lonesome. Mother embarrassed Helen and me (?) the other night by saying to us she didn't see why Helen and I "don't fancy each other," as if we didn't. We since have had lots of fun talking about fancying each other.

We were not right sure the lady Darneals would shut up all the "cats of their dispositions," but evidently they did, for Rosie and Will have been eating with the family until today, while staying in their own home.

※ ※ ※ ※ ※

May 16   **INCENSE**

I am working on Josephine to get her to come up here soon, and she thinks she will be able to arrive about the last of the month. Did I tell you she has an incense pot down to her house, and it was sitting on a little table in the parlor and when we would come in late of an evening, she would pour a little powder in and let it burn. It reminded me of getting up out of bed and lighting Mother a saucer of Shiffman's asthma powder, only the smell is entirely different. I couldn't see how incense helped any, but I guess I will write Vantine's to send me some for if Josie is an incense fiend, I will want her to feel good and at home in my house, and it will look good burning in my parlor anyhow.

※ ※ ※ ※ ※

June 11   **VISITING WITH NANNY ESTILL**

Mam, I had such a lovely visit over to Nannie's house and since then she has been over here and we just drove out at night to see the moon come up and had such a nice time. Why does any woman prefer one man to another? Why would I rather sit on the river bank and watch the moon come up and build a silvery bridge across the water and make me want to travel in the bright path with Nannie more than with Josephine? I would rather sit there with Nannie one night than to spend a year there with Josie.

Josie doesn't interest me like Nannie does. Now if you can tell me why I feel this way, I can perhaps explain why Nannie loves Dr. Campbell more than she does me. And sometimes she does not love Dr. Campbell so much as all that. I just naturally cannot understand all that comes along, but I am worrying along somehow, mighty low in mind some times and mighty chesty with delight the rest of the time. But between you and me, Mam, I sometimes wonder if there is the person in the world—woman, I mean— who, well, I know you would never understand how I mean it, if I say it in a letter, but it amounts to this: I measure every woman by Nannie, and, "Oh Hell!"

It is so sweet of you to be all time thinking of the roseate paths and so on you want for me. I appreciate all of it and you are a plum sweet one to be so solicitous. I am not doing any one an injustice to renew the old relationship with Nannie. We just couldn't help it. The whole works may blow up again, but I want to tell you I sure am interested as long as it lasts.

※ ※ ※ ※ ※

July 9   **"BEWITCHED, BOTHERED, AND BEWILDERED"**

What was it you said about running off with Nannie? No, Mam, she isn't queer like Etta, and if she had a baby who was a little queer for some reason, she would not try to hide the fact from the public forever. If she liked you, she would just bust a string in her corset being nice to you regular and not every four months. Well, me and Nannie are still acting crazy about paying each other the compliment of a letter every day, which I would miss if I didn't get it, but sometimes the letters drift so along the impersonal, I just think I can't stand the drain on my stamp supply and wonder if she don't feel the same? And then something will come along and crush us all up so close in a letter that it is interesting. The situation is this, Miss Ida. She loves me about 95 cents worth and Doctor Campbell a dollar's worth. Now is that plain to you? And if you were in her place, wouldn't you stand up for your dollar's worth? I would. And as for snatching her off, there would be two at the snatching. But, even taking successful snatching for granted, how would I feel to wake up some morning and find her crying on her little pillow for Dr.

Campbell? I would say a cuss word and "I wish to thunder I hadn't listened to my Aunt Ida." I don't guess she is one of my "vitals" anyhow, though I sometimes think nobody else looks as sweet, smells as good, and has a hand that feels as warm, etc., and other qualifications that would not interest you, and yet, there are times when I forget all about her.

I am a terrible mess, Aunt Ida, and I am in a sad condition when I can't have the same feelings for more than a few days at a time about any one person. I guess maybe it is because all of them have regular changes of feelings about me, but the crops are all so fine and the harvest promises to be so good, I should not have any regrets about anything so nice and worrysome as love. But you would sure be surprised if I would up and marry this fall, wouldn't you, Mam? But if you were to see me all married off happy, you might feel like you didn't have anything else much to live for, and I am not inclined to take chances with you.

Anna Rose's friend, that nice Helen Wagoner, stayed with us until Rosie and Will came back from Chicago, and then I persuaded her to stay on until after Rosie left for Richmond, and I would have been pleased to have had her stay longer. Helen said I was a regular serpent about persuading her to stay. She is Taylor's girl, you know, and being somebody else's girl always makes a girl doubly attractive to me if I like her at all. Aunt Lill is just head over heels in love with Helen and is hoping and praying for the time to come when she will have her for a daughter-in-law. Well, all the time Helen was not down to Taylor's visiting, she and I were just driving around and eating ice-cream and touring the farm and swinging in the swing and getting out ice and turning the ice-cream freezer, and she was taking me to town and coming for me and we were going around to our friends' houses singing and playing, and sometimes in public like at the Patriotic meetings, I don't know how much she and Taylor care for each other, but he is not very thoughtful in lots of ways and I want to tell you the women like to be noticed, and I just busted my hamstring opening the door of the car to help her out and easing her down at the dining room table, and pinning roses on her at all times of the day, and I was that Motherly, I always sat up until she came in from her travels with Taylor, so I could light her lamp for her, and it got to be such a pleasure to wait on somebody like that, I am might nigh *in the notion*, Mam.

My family all sick me on to get a wife and they wish I would cut Taylor out, but even if I could, Miss Lill would never be the same.

July 17   "RING IN HER NOSE

About Nannie? Well, last Tuesday I asked her if Dr. Campbell had a ring in her nose by which he was leading her around, and all I got since was a post-card saying she did not think she deserved the remarks in my last letter.

Yesterday I heard someone holler lady-like and looked up to see Gentry Estill going by with them THREE WOMEN from Sedalia in the car. So I bet they would go on back home last night and was at the train for a quarter of an hour to see them and find out how I had cut up so unpardonable. Nannie said she hadn't written because of what I said about the ring in her nose and that she thought I owed her an apology. And about all we got to do before the train left was for me to laugh at her for acting mad, and for her to astonish me by asking me when I could come over. Now that is such nonsense for us to carry on at all, but it seems like it is just natural to keep on, and not just quit each other stone cold dead at once and forever.

We have oiled the streets here in town and it is such an improvement.

July 27 **SWIMMING, A DANGEROUS SPORT**

Last night at the reservoir was the first time I ventured across water over my head, about ten feet deep. It was dead easy and I feel a lot of confidence since I made the round trip. We are having such a good time. There is always something to be enthusiastic about isn't there?

Sometimes things kinda drag and then is the only time I ever think real hard that I need a wife to make things interesting for me. Every day I see married people have to leave undone things they want to do and would do if they were not married. Their wives don't want them to go swimming where there are other women unless they can be there to watch them, and then they are not right sure about letting them put their arms under another non-swimming woman to teach her anything.

August 20 **PRIDE AND HONOR AND MARRIAGE CHOICES**

Now Miss Ida, if you get to worrying about *me*, I'll think you don't have any other trouble to keep your mind busy, and besides I'll have to censor my "life report."

I will admit one accusation you have made in the letter you caused to arrive today. *I just never have grown up* in some respects. When I wrote what I did about being an "engagement protector" unless I was crazy myself, I knew it sounded childish, but I didn't have time for my idea to take a mature form. And didn't I get a "tonin'down"? But I know we do have different ideas about "engagement protectors." I think you are the kind of woman who, if you were a man, wouldn't pay no mind to a girl if you fell in love with her, providin' some friend, neighbor or your own intuition told you that another man loved her and was engaged to her. Is that right? Well, if I fell for her, and I had any reason at all to believe she cared for me, and if after proguein' and maneuverin' around I found out she would just as soon marry me as the other guy and later, if she felt like she would rather not marry the other one at all, do you suppose I would be ungentlemanly enough to leave her at his mercy? Don't you believe in the survival of the fittest? If I ever marry, it will be to somebody I sure want to marry right, and I never would thank her to go on and marry me if there had been anybody else she would have preferred, but let her false honor keep her tied to me. Mam, it sure is a fact that pride and honor are both accused of being false, but I am trying to keep enough of both to tide me over.

When I get married, I'll sing all the songs in the *same key*, and there won't be near as many to sing to you, although the quality might make up for the loss in quantity.

Early September **RESIGNATION FROM BANK**

Listen, Mam, maybe I have been awful foolish or will be before the thing is all done, but I may get to see you before you get back to Missouri. I am tired of living with a crab apple crossed with a green persimmon in the day time, and only this morning when the sun was shining beautiful and everything was calm and lovely and cool, I announced to the President of this Institution that I would be resigning, the resignation to take effect January 1st. He 'lowed, "All right, I will call a meeting of the Board," as though that was necessary when every last one of the board does as he says to keep him in a good humor. I have had this resigning feeling on me for over a week and have talked it over with my mama and my papa, and while they acted just like they always did about keeping me tied down tooth and toe-nail, I think they see the matter more in my light than they used to. I don't know what I will do now. I just want to do nothing in particular for a while. I always did want to do nothing for a while. I never had any chance along that line. There are such a lot of things I want to do and such a lot of places I want to go. I would like going to California to spend a time, although never having "retired," I would have to find me some work to enable me to stay awhile. I would just love to toddle on up to Montana and look in on that sweet Miriam's home [Tacoma] as I passed, and next summer "jine" Hazel with her people in Colorado and do a bit of camping which is being planned now.

Alice and Taylor Kingsbury

On the other hand, if I can persuade Mother and Father to go some place in Texas or Florida to spend Jan., Feb., and Mar., I should love it to death to go with them, providing they will go some place near the water. I am getting dissatisfied with my bathing suit. It is too high and too long. I think I will get me a trunk as soon as I develop a little more muscular appearance!!!! Now Mam, I know you just think nakedness on the beach is scandalous, but don't you admire an athletic looking man? Don't you think the body is pretty when it is built right? I am not commenting anything on the women's look at all. I said men.

I just bubble up at the idea of leaving this job, but I also wonder if I ever will bubble up and spill over with regret for having made my "resign" today. I may be dependent on my family farm henceforward. But don't say nothing about what I have done yet to nobody that will announce it back here.

Late September   "STAY WELL OFF'"

Old Mrs. Mat Burrus was unkind enough to call me and ask me to come over and see her niece. If I take her out driving and we don't get back early, Fattie will just walk the floor from ten on. There never was a woman who had more nieces than Sallie Burrus. Mat Burrus, a good Christian gentleman, came in here the other afternoon and just ran down my Sunday School teacher, a widow with no income except what she gets from art lessons, for not paying church dues, and for being late sometimes to class, and for her daughter not always coming to toot the piano or getting a substitute. Mat was a sight, talking like he did. He is getting too old to criticize that way.

Monday night I took Mrs. Burrus's niece, Mary Wilhite, to Fayette to the picture show. Mary is right pretty and quite interesting, for the man she used to work for gave her so many things to tell. He was married and was all time being called up by other women, and once he put one out of the office very forcibly, and she sat on the steps and wept. Mary is passionate about marriage and advised me to stay "well off." I liked her for that because I'm tired of being advised the other way!!!

August 21   READYING FOR WAR

Lewis Means and Evangeline Boggs were married in Fayette yesterday. He got a second lieutenant's commission at Fort Riley and is celebrating. Will honeymoon until the 19th, and then poor little Evangeline!! She will, as Margeret Blackwell said the other night, just tag along with us all winter, and we will have to pet and humor her to keep her contented, like we did all this summer since Lewis went to Fort Riley. It would be no lasting comfort to me to have been married ten days.

Early September   SOME GO; SOME GET EXEMPTED

[The United States Declaration of War against Germany sped up development of United States' armed forces through institution of a draft. All men 18 to 30 years of age were required to register. Later the upper age was raised to 33.]

Robert Estill's claims for exemption from the draft on the ground of having a dependent wife were turned down, and last week he was all wrought up and rushing around to get affidavits to the effect that his farm can't run without him. It would be a great loss to him in a way, to have to leave it just as he is getting it on a paying basis. I think he and Anne began scheming to avoid the draft just about the time they realized Robert was within the age limit. For where they had been slackers in one way ever since they were married, because Anne did not care for a "child," they evidently decided a baby would be a great help, but the little thing can't quite keep him home like the children are doing for the young men who now "have a wife and baby to support." There is a difference between the already here and the coming features, and Bob is just scared and worried like the mischief lest he will have to leave home. Nearly every man in town who is of military age seems to be trying to have more and more family to support, and those above 31 who may get called if the age limit is raised are aiming to sure be on the safe side. I will not be surprised if there are not a lot of twins for that reason now.

Well, as the time comes for Johnny Cox to leave for Fort Riley, I begin to value him more highly myself, and am plum sorry for him as I see him farewelling in that smooth-gliding Cadillac. He has to go next Friday. Now Mam, I sure did think Johnny would get out somehow, and until he actually gets there, I will still have some hope of my expectations being realized. In Fayette there is some scandal about Paul Prosser going to Joplin in the interest of William Agnew and Paul Pealer, two young unmarried, single fellows who have been exempted by the District Board.

Early Fall   "SOLDIER BOY FAREWELL PARTY"

Florence is back from the East and says it is *just afire* with war preparations. She said Dr. Alden is going to France to be in one of the base hospitals.

Tuesday night we had the last party we could for our departing soldier boys, and about 100 of us attended the picture show and had a good jazz orchestra to play. We danced in the show building some, until refreshments of red, white, and blue brick ice cream and home made cake were served in Foster's store where we danced in his store, his lobby, and his barber shop.

"WHERE'S THE JUSTICE IN IT?"

Will Jacobs is still cutting up. A couple of years ago when he was intoxicated, he shot his daughter in the leg and as she lays dying day by day from tuberculosis, he got in a fight with his son who was on crutches and struck the boy with a crutch, after which the boy slashed his father across the face with a knife, cutting him terribly. Why is it, Mam, that Bill couldn't have had something fatal happen to him, instead of being allowed to be the cause of so much trouble and suffering both mental and physical to his family? He has a deaf and dumb deformed child and not long ago, he threw her out the window. If, as some people say, there is no Hell except on earth, I can't see why I should believe there is a Heaven hereafter, and I just wonder where poor Mrs. Jacobs will come in for any of her happiness.

FAMILY CHRISTMAS AT FAIRVIEW

Our Christmas was a very delightful one with all the children home, except Xena and her family and Will Darneal. We had despaired of having a Christmasy Christmas, the winter has been so open, but on the night of the 23rd, a twelve inch snow blew in and decorated everything outside, as you have seen nature do so often when the snow is wet and sticks to everything. It was cold enough to put a tingle into the air and make a warm house smell with cedar, a welcome haven after a ride from the train in the big wagon.

I spent a good deal of time making festoons and wreaths of cedar and buckberries which were so fat and red this year, and with these and poinsettias, red ribbons and bells the house was quite festive. The stairway railing was banked with evergreen.

Each daughter-in-law and daughter brought some of their unsurpassed "eats," Minnie, a nut cake and a pound cake, a boiled ham, several pounds of butter, and several dozen eggs; Julia, sixty cheese-pimento sandwiches and an angel food cake; Lillian, a nut cake and a preserve cake; Anna Rose made a preserve cake and an angel food, and Margeret brought two freezers of vanilla ice cream for dinner. For our paper plates and napkin picnic supper we had chicken salad, ham and cheese and pimento sandwiches, ripe olives, cranberry jelly, potato chips, coffee, custard (brought by Minnie) and cakes. Everybody helped serve and clean up and after supper all of us enjoyed fixing the tree, eating stuff, and admiring the tree which was simply loaded down with gifts, and there were stacks and piles of things all around its base. And nothing added more to the happiness of all of us than the roaring fire in the fireplace with its little cedar trees at either side. We went to bed reluctantly and got up soon after.

For "picnic" breakfast we had grape-fruit, scrambled eggs, hot biscuit, butter, cherry and pear preserves and coffee. Needless to tell you how happy were all the children, big and little, and how they enjoyed the fruits of the tree!!! Nor will I have time to enumerate many of the gifts. We gave mother a right handsome Hudson Seal Scarf and muff which which delighted her until she beamed.

At dinner we had two tables, with twelve at one and fourteen at the other, and as a center piece for Fathers' table I made a representation of our house and yard as I remembered it at first. I had made out of cardboard the house and outhouses (one of which I never heard of being used on a table before) and will you believe it, a fly lit right on it during dinner and we had the houses water colored. Every little tree was in place, and the whole works set in cotton covered with artificial snow. By gaslight it sparkled very brilliantly and everybody seemed to enjoy it.

For dinner we had a turkey that weighed about fifty pounds before he was dressed (he had to be cooked in a wash-boiler) cranberry jelly, potatoes, dressing and gravy with peas in patties, olives, celery and bread, fruit salad, ice cream and cakes. Everything was as good as anybody ever ate—and ate is right!!

[Among Lilburn's papers is a letter from my older brother, Bill Kingsbury, at the time of writing, an Editor of the Nashville Tennessean. *It was written shortly before Christmas 1938, the year Grandfather Kingsbury died. The letter contained Bill's remembrances of the Christmas which Lilburn writes about in the preceding letter. Bill expressed the feeling all of us present had:]*

CHRISTMAS REMEMBRANCES OF A KINGSBURY GRANDSON

Christmas of 1917 at Grandfather Kingsbury's stands out in my memory because I was old enough to be perceptive *[he had turned fifteen in January]* and it was the fullest and finest.

Our nation was not yet fully caught up in the World War and I had ceased to be a child without yet concerning myself about the future.

Twenty-eight of us spent Christmas eve under one roof and next day the same number assembled for dinner.

Earlier that year Grandfather had undergone an operation. I believe he had the feeling he might never live to see another Christmas, and he made a particular plea to have all the family together. He was to have more than a score of years left to him.

My uncle Lilburn, who lived with my grandparents, had ravaged the hills and hollows for boughs of cedar. He made garlands for the mantels and swags for the stairway.

His most imaginative creation was the center piece for the Christmas dining table, a reconstruction in miniature, of the house when it was painted red and there were two rows of tall cedar trees between the front door and the gate. The grounds were represented even to a rail fence made of toothpicks.

I remember Grandmother Kingsbury's consternation and reprimand when his realism extended to placing the smokehouse and the icehouse, and between them that indispensable object reached by a plank walk.

Grandmother was voted down by the younger members of the family as unduly squeamish. The outhouse was allowed to stand.

FOR THE DINNER there was turkey, which demanded cranberries.

Not bought, strained cranberry sauce, but a home-made mash of the berries, sugar and water, cooked to almost jelly consistency, and chilled.

Turkey demanded giblet gravy with hard-boiled eggs chopped fine, enriching it, and cream and butter-softened mashed potatoes, and hot biscuits to put it on if the mashed potatoes were not enough.

There were sweet potatoes desecrated by marshmallows (considered no desecration then, but a noble vegetable needs no gilding) and escalloped oysters. And there was a big country ham, thinly sliced, marbled with gray flecks, sufficient warranty that it had been properly cured and mellowed.

There was fruit salad with orange, banana, grapefruit, and pineapple; a Waldorf salad with chopped apple, celery, pecans and raisins.

And of course there were dishes of olives and celery (somehow understood to represent in that day and in that society, the difference between an ordinary and a special meal).

Salsify, a root vegetable seldom seen nowadays, was delicious with a cream sauce.

The jellies, preserves and pickles of various kinds were welcome reminders of the summer garden and bore witness to the productivity of the farm.

The women in the family justly prided themselves on their cakes. A foreign visitor to Cooper and Howard Counties described these counties as the cake belt of the world. Coconut, chocolate, pecan and the seasonable fruit cakes.

The cakes called for the accompaniment of boiled custard. Because our was a dry family [prohibitionist], the custard always lacked the flavor which in the egg-nog belt of the South is said to make it more delicious.

But this year somebody brought a three gallon crock of custard with the explanation it had been scorched to hide the disagreeable taste. One would never have suspected it had been exposed to the fire unduly.

Not all of the food was prepared in Grandmother's kitchen. The daughters and daughters-in-law brought the cakes, custards, mince pies and other things which could be prepaid in advance and easily transported.

Smoking in the house was taboo on account of Grandmother's asthma, so the men retired to the "office" in the yard for their cigars. The weather was mild enough for some to take a brisk walk about the farm through the snow.

AN HOUR LATER, the family gathered around the open apple wood fire near which stood a half bushel basket of apples, cool and fresh from the cellar.

I know of one household in which a dose of castor oil was administered to each member and guest as a bedtime ritual on Christmas night, but that was never necessary with the Kingsburys.

I can see the apples disappearing slowly from the basket. It was before the cult of "roughage" had a hold, but some ate them peel and all.

The smaller of us, who had indulgent fathers or uncles, were treated to apple pulp scraped out with a knife and eaten cautiously (for we were no fools) from the sharp blade itself.

The family talk, if we can believe somebody who observed us closely and commented on our foibles was mainly about food and teeth. But the twain were made to go together. I am sure there were other topics of conversation. And inevitably there were disputes among us youngsters which had to be settled by firm hands.

As dusk neared, somebody played the piano and we sang, not Christmas carols, but hymns and old songs. Then train time came.

We were bundled up. loaded with suitcases and packages into the straw filled wagon bed on the sled. Away we went with sleigh bells jangling on the mules which drew it to catch the 7 o'clock train at Estill.

Over the years which followed, to all who remembered, was a sense of towering, upright love and goodness stemming from the grandparents who had grown old together.

1918

Lilburn at Mount Ranier

[*Lilburn's resignation as Cashier of Bank of New Franklin became effective January 1, 1918. Despite efforts to persuade him to reconsider his decision, he held to his resolve. In letters to Mam written in the Fall of 1917, he had declared his intent to go West. He did, visiting with her, his Uncle Tom, their children, and the Montana Kingsburys. He probably wrote frequently to his parents, but any such letters were not preserved.*

Exactly when he left Missouri, the details of his travel and the time of his return are not clear. Content of subsequent letters to Mam indicate Lilburn was home in early Spring. Uncertainty about being called for military service caused him to settle in at Fairview and help with the farm-orchard work. He writes of this and of offers to participate in purchase and reorganization of the bank. The 1918 letters are undated, but their content has indicated the placement of these excerpts.]

Early Spring

Since my last letter, I have led an upright, uneventful life. The monotony of orchard apple tree trimming has been broken by ten days of sawing wood with Will Humfeld's steam engine, which he let me fire when I wasn't carrying wood to the saw. This I enjoyed, and also I assisted at the murder and dressing of a hog which has afforded our innards great satisfaction. There were no *spare* ribs when we got through!!!

Henry Harris says he "wouldn't stay in the bank with his uncle [Will Boggs] for $500 a month," and is quitting December 1st. Nobody else will be able to stay either unless they are dependent, because a little more of the sugar wears off that old Pill, Boggs, every year.

FARM ACTIVITIES

Father has planted potatoes, onions, lettuce and sweet peas and there are indications Spring is here. As soon as the frost gets out of the ground, we are to have concrete steps in front and walks at the side of the house and a driveway, maybe, and a new wire fence at the south side of the yard to support ramblers, honey-suckle, and the like. A few little showers have freshened up the grass and started the wheat, and the first real rain for months sounds good beating on the roof tonight.

"FUNERAL OF THAT GOOD MAN"

Yesterday we went to Fayette to the funeral of that good man, Bro. Marvin. Centenary Chapel at the college was filled with friends and five different ministers took part in the service. There were flowers in profusion, and the tributes paid to the life of the one who had gone on *[to Heaven]*, were beautiful indeed. I don't know when I have drunk in all of a service as I did yesterday. I have never heard one word to lead me to believe that a single word of praise given to Bro. Marvin was unmerited.

So often we hear things from ministerial lips at a funeral service, which we know are untrue, but yesterday I could accept every word at face value. Aunt Georgia *[Mam's sister]* was very brave through it all. So many have remarked at her strength to bear up under the trials through which she has passed.

"INSIDE DOZENS OF HOMES"

[When Lilburn left the bank, he retained his representation of insurance agencies and actively sought new clients on his return from the West.]

I was out on the road on an insurance trip three days and visited so many places and saw inside dozens of homes. Mrs. Ed Watts told me how she loves their car. Said she had never been in New Franklin *at night* until Ed got the car, and if she ever sees the white way of Heaven, she won't bat her eyes with delight any more than she did at the vision of New Franklin at night!!!

I discovered Mrs. Chas. Watts has a handy arrangement of throwing clinkers *[fused cinders]* from her stove out into the front yard through the living room window.

≈ ≈ ≈ ≈ ≈

Mid-Summer

Today has been the hottest of the summer. Anna Rose and Will left us this morning early, and Mother was all "down and out" from so much Chautauqua going and heat. And the house was so upside down, I got "very feminine" and cleaned it from top to bottom, a process which required about five hours. Don't you know I was a sight!—working upstairs stark naked, and with only a pair of pants on, on the lower floor. But I was the coolest person on the place, I'm sure. I have slept all afternoon, and things were so quiet and clean and peaceful when Dad drove up in the car with Lillian and Carl and three "spring-offs." Mighty glad to see them but sorry to see the apple cores on the piano and Victrola and strewn over the rugs after I had labored so hard. But so it always is at a Grandmother House.

≈ ≈ ≈ ≈ ≈

Late Summertime   THE WEATHER-MAN WILL TELL US

Nobody but one who has lived here knows how dry and dirty it is when we all feel like praying for rain. (As if we were living fit enough lives, to ask such a favor with any hope of getting it on the merits of our good behavior.) A wonderful corn crop is right at the point where it will be much or little according to what the weather man decides very quickly. We have bedded our road in front of our yard with straw, so passing cars do not annoy us with dust-throwing.

OCCUPATION CHANGES

My occupation changes often now since July came in and apple-trimming went out of season. I hardly get on a load of hay before I am called to take the manure-spreader out for a practice run, or maybe I am delegated to prune raspberries and blackberries and get scratched out of myself. Then there are early apples to gather and sell at $2 per bushel, and plums to pick up, and quarterage *[Church quarterly payments on pledges]* to collect. Father sent me out Saturday to raise the church money, and I had such good luck it is a shame for me to have to tell it myself. I went to see any and everybody, and at every place but one, I got what I wanted, and then I let the other stewards know I had $250 in my pocket and told them they wouldn't have to do a thing. I guess I had been away long enough to be just a little strange, so I was able to "put over" collecting like a stranger can sell sewing machines and charms and everything so successfully through the country. One old fellow (Mr. Young) saw me chinning some Rags *[women]* in town and came up and gave me $1.00 saying, "I like to help a good cause," and after a few minutes came up and asked what I was collecting for!

I enjoyed visiting at homes last Saturday. Went to see several elderly people and lots of others I hadn't seen since I got back. Mrs. Josie McKinley showed me a very beautiful bed spread. I admired it as it deserved to be, and thanked her for showing it to me, and she said "Well, I knew you were kind of feminine like George (a nephew) and could appreciate it." I rather resented that, until I thought how much she cares for George, and then I decided she meant to be very complimentary. I haven't shaved since Sunday, and I must say my face doesn't look or feel very "feminine" today.

KNOWN AS A "BAD WOMAN"

I called on one of our members generally known as a "bad woman" and got the $22.50 balance on a $30 pledge–a woman whom good Christian church members told my Mother not to see when the latter called upon her one day. I never saw this woman do anything wrong, and I think more of her than I do of the woman who was more able but handed me only $2. No danger of any man spoiling her $2 character.

CHURCH SERVICE

Sunday, I went to church and as we drew up in front and looked in I saw Nellie *[Blankenbaker]* with her eyes buried in a song book and hitting the wrong notes on the piano, so she had to carry the tune with her voice. Mam, if she didn't sing through her nose, her voice is so sharp it would cut her throat. After it was all over and we were having dinner, I gave excerpts of a hymn a la Nellie at the table and was playing like my eyes was glued to a book and pawing the words, and Carl Jr. hollered and laughed and said, "That's just like Cousin Nell." We hadn't called any names. You know we heard Nell was bad off and never found out what was the matter. It was a case of high blood pressure and doctor told her the least exertion might prove fatal. But after seeing her Sunday and hearing her raise and use her voice to stab the song, I think she is out of danger.

Bro. Snarr preached, but I was a deaf man and bored to death. Only his deep wrinkles, which seem deeper than ever, interested me, and I kept wondering if he could keep these wrinkles clean in the harvest field where I find the dust has absolutely no respect for my anatomy.

"SO MUCH CUSSIN'"

Since I wrote last, we have had threshers, and I want to tell you I never heard so much cussin' in any five years of my life as I heard that one day. I get so tired of hearing "G___ D___." It just rang in my ears for two or three days and I'd think them myself at the least provocation, but it has all "passed by" now. I have called down [reprimanded] Louis and Bill every time I heard them cuss, and now their vocabulary is getting to be quite gentlemanly—and they get just as much work done.

Dad is keen to put out an orchard for me if I "feel like I'll stay here on the home place and care for it."

Mid-September

"HIGHLY COLORED" APPLES

We have had more rain and a week of chilly nights and crisp days with a tiny bit of frost last night, but all vegetation is just beautiful. I never saw such a lovely grass carpet as we have in our yard—without a weed in it, and my "shrubs fairly shine." We finished the Jonathan apples in our orchard today after four days of steady picking and packing. These apples are as highly colored as I have ever seen. Now is the time we had expected to start for St. Louis, but Father and Rob have bought 400 barrels of Grimes Golden and Ben Davis near Glasgow, *[Missouri]* and this deal promises to interfere with Dad and me leaving just now. They bought and turned these apples at a profit of $1 per barrel, which is a real nice little bit of easy cash.

We will have to be in Glasgow to receive and ship these apples, and it seems I may have to go there to inspect them as they are packed. I would rather stay home. Father went up there today to see about the Grimes'. The man in Glasgow uses women to gather and pack the apples, and Rob says it is funny to see girls way up on a ladder, but says he didn't go stand under any and look up. I told him I was not superstitious about walking under a ladder.

"JUST THE KIND OF DINNER"

Last night we were invited to dinner with the Noah Kingsburys and had a delightful visit. Their home is the prettiest country home I know of. Cousin Evie is lovely and had fried chicken, ham, butter-beans, mashed potatoes, asparagus on toast, jelly, bread, ice tea, fruit salad, and carmel ice cream and angel food cake. Just the kind of dinner I enjoyed at Glenida Place at weekend Parties.

TALKING WILLIE BOGGS

Henry Harris was out last night and "set" until after ten o'clock and we talked *Willie Boggs*. Henry has the same tale of woe I wailed, and I was so glad he was wailing it instead of me. It seems Willie wants to sell his stock and get out of the bank by fall. He has priced his stock and Henry wants me to go in with him and buy it, but I can't enthuse. Last night was the first time I ever talked to Henry very much and toward the last I decided he was a "blower" and moreover he was terribly *Boggsy*. Mam, he laughs like Willie Boggs, and looks like the very spirit of him as I imagine him (Mr. B.) to be in the younger edition. He don't nicker *[whinny like a horse]* like Willie, but I guess he would in later life. I'm afraid to unite in business with that strain, and the more I consider the matter, the less inclined I am to go back to the bank. As you know, I am some distance from it now. I would rather haul manure than get tied up again.

SORGHUM

Mam, I had you and sorghum on my mind all fall and was going to send you some. We ordered 5 gallons for Billie, 5 for Horace and 6 for us, and Dad went for it the other day. In due time we completed it *[managed to eat it]*, but we are still disappointed. It isn't like Mrs. Joannie Johnson's usual sorghum at all. It's thin and tastes scorched a little. We called her about it and she said she was sorry but that all sorghum they made tasted that way on account of the effect of the dry weather on the cane. She said she would be glad to take it back but we didn't send it back because we had to have something to substitute for sugar *[war rationing limited the amount of sugar which could be purchased per person]*, but we don't anticipate any feasts of hot biscuits, butter and molasses. Mrs. J. says sorghum all over this end of the county is poor. I am sorry I can't send it to you but feel you wouldn't care for it any more than we do, and it would not be a credit to Missouri.

REGISTERING FOR THE DRAFT

This week has been uneventful except for my registering to go on the road for Uncle Sammy. I presume I'll be gone a month from now as I am at the ripe age. Birch Alsop and Henry Harris will no doubt be given deferred classification since the new ruling was made that banks are necessary to finance the Liberty Loans and their employees will be allowed to remain out as long as possible. Albert will file claims for exemption on agricultural grounds. So you see, of all the young fellows around here, I will be it. But I have no regret at being it instead of staying in a bank with Willie. And as my time comes, I get more enthusiastic about going. I must confess I have had a very "gone" feeling at times when I have contemplated the prospect of going into something I don't know what it's all about, but that doesn't bother me any more. I think maybe I can make a very good "buck private," and in as much as I ought to have gone sooner, I think I'll feel real good about it after I once get in. It's just rank selfishness to want to stay out just because I have a happy home.

OPTIMIST

I found quite an optimist the other day. I saw John Stapleton, an old negro, and said, "How are you, John?" To which he replied, "I'm all right Mr. Lilburn, only I'se got de flu and de piles." Said he thought he worked too hard last Friday when he got hot and "noticed a little chronical diarrhea." This is the old man whom someone asked "Isn't Aunt Mat your wife?" and he answered, "Yessir, but she ain't laid in my arms for nigh onto 18 years."

FARMERS' WEALTH

The apples have been sold at $4.00 and $5.00 a barrel so we know what we can count on. I think I told you Horace was going to "mop up." He had 15,000 bushels of wheat on his farms.

Will Chandler blew in on us yesterday afternoon and still lingers. Many a chicken has died here since his arrival last Sunday and something took all our sugar. *[He strained the Kingsbury hospitality eating most of their sugar ration.]* We were not able to get the usual "ounce per day" for company like Rosie did in Richmond.

A NEAR ESCAPE

Two weeks since I wrote. The time has been given over to apple work and visiting and the latter is more interesting to relate. We left here Wednesday morning, the 25th, for St. Louis. My Dad and Mom, 70-and-68 year old young things, Aunt Lena Bell, and I had a jolly good trip although the last forty miles were mighty slick and wet from rain. We broke a spring on our car and had to run slowly about 30 miles but got to Webster Groves about 9:30 p.m. Near St. Charles, we were stopped by a young fellow in a big car who wanted a half dollar to slip under his carburetor to keep it from leaking. We had no half but asked him if two quarters would do. He said "yes" but that he would have to give us an order on his father for $1.00. Of course I do not accept stranger's checks, so Father told him to cut a piece of wood, and we drove on suspecting he needed money to pay bridge toll. Well, the next day, we read how this same fellow had murdered, by shooting, his chauffeur and had searched the body for money to pay bridge toll, and finding none had pawned his watch with the bridge man. We were pleased he did not shoot us.

MISSOURI IN OCTOBER

The Kardells would have used a "crowbar" to "turn every stone" to make us have a good time had it been necessary, and we had a most delightful visit until Monday noon when we started home, and at 8 p.m., we were here without any trouble on the way. You can imagine what a delightful trip it was through Missouri at this time of year when the foliage on the trees and vines is so highly colored. All the summer flowers, whose growth was so delayed by the drouth, and the fall blossoms were in full bloom, whole fields of golden rod and daisies and lavender wild asters in the Mineola Hills. We just raved and raved, and I did wish I had my California friends to show them what Nature does for us in the fall.

"I WAS SO ASHAMED"

Not long ago, I read some old letters to you, which you have returned, wherein I "raved" about Miss Dorsey and I was so ashamed I declared in my "innards" I would never be so silly again. But I am toasting my thoughts here before the fireplace and trying to live over my last ten days to see what is worthwhile to write. No frosts have come yet and our garden is at its very best. Sunday, Mr. Estill sent us roasting ears and eggplant, so we had fourteen vegetables on hand the latter part of October.

INFLUENZA EPIDEMIC

I understand Dr. Fleet has 250 cases of illness and one day made 127 house calls. Dr. King was dangerously ill, got better, relapsed and, after doing his worst, is walking again. Mrs. King is going to have a fourth baby. She has one to correspond with each Liberty Loan.

DRAFT WORRIES

Dad was mighty good to me on my birthday. Went to the bank and got into my bank box and filled out a Baby Bond card on which 16 more bonds were needed and then came home and told me he had put a little present in my box, which I could see when I went to town. He still talks of a new orchard for me. And I think if I could always be as happy here as I have been this summer and fall I might as well live and die here as anywhere. But cold weather may freeze the fringe off my contentment, if I should be left alone by that local draft board. Have heard no more about my examination. Men from here are being sent to points in Texas and to Little Rock, Ark., so I stand a chance of getting to a warmer climate. I am in no hurry to get to a camp. Don't think me a slacker, for I think it is not too much for a man to die for his country. Only my patriotism makes me want to die and get done with it, if necessary, instead of spending so much time thinking about it and making myself in the meantime of some worth to live.

November 6   DRAFT PHYSICAL EXAMINATION

Monday I spent the morning assisting at the examination of draftees and taking part in the naked parade myself. Except for a defect in my left eye, I had no marks recorded against me so I am still in Class I-A and subject to call at any time. However, the prospect now is that I'll be home until December. I would have been terribly disappointed if I hadn't passed the examination. I suspect a more stricter doctor might have turned me down on account of the eye. About half the men were dismissed. I felt awfully sorry for two or three of them, not because they seemed to care whether they could go or not, but because of their physical infirmities. I'd rather go to war six times than to be in their shoes! Well, Gertrude Hoffman [a "Strip Tease Celebrity"] is seasoned until she doesn't mind stripping off before an audience, and I would get so bold like it, too, but to me, stripping before a lot of others for the first time was novel, but it was a sight to see the naked candidates or victims hopping first on one foot, and then the other foot, about the room. Don't you know I was cute?

Wednesday Night   ARMISTICE DAY NEWS

The bells and whistles everywhere were nearly worn out celebrating the Armistice news today.

Mrs. Nelson Leonard is dead. The "Flu" changed into typhoid-pneumonia, and she was buried yesterday afternoon in Boonville. How much better, it seems to us, it would have been for the little children if they could have lost a father instead of a mother.

Today we have fixed a barrel of apples each for Aunt Rose and Ernest, assorted varieties—with cider, preserves, jelly, sweet and ordinary potatoes, and we hope they will be happy to have them. Mother has a wonderful assortment of such things in the cellar, and Mr. *[Herbert]* Hoover would be amazed. Our weather is splendid again and tomorrow I begin pruning trees. If I could only get through by January 1st, I might feel warm in winter again.

CHRISTMAS NIGHT

We had all planned to go to Billie's but Mother wound up with a cold or asthma, so Rosie and I went last night, and Dad came for dinner today. Lillian and boys went out to stay with Mother. The Billie's had a beautiful tree and a lavish dinner, and we had such a good time. ... I just "natcherly" don't know how things are going along without help here. Mother has thought or has persuaded herself she would have a good as new arm *[broken in a fall]* as soon as the splints are removed, but we know better. Her arm hurt her a good deal today, and it will be a long time before she gets any real use of it. She says she would rather cough all winter than go away, and I have over-persuaded her all I can in vain. I can't say any more. If they had gone to Florida, it would have been better for both. Father, when the doctors in Excelsior Springs gave him a clean bill of health, decided he was a humdinger so overdid himself lifting barrels. Now he finds the rupture reappearing and will go to the hospital for another operation right after the New Year. He is keen about the Sisters at the hospital, and takes them something every time he goes over. They seem to love him dearly too.

"IF JOHN WESLEY HAD SAID IT"

Lillian is reading *"Science and Health"* and just read a passage from the Bible and then the explanation from *"S & H"* and remarked "That is all so clear. I never thought of it before." Mean things we are, we asked her to explain it to us and she couldn't. I am *plum* away from Science. Lillian just said, "Dad, aren't you ashamed? If John Wesley had said it, you'd like it."

WHO'S THE MEANEST WOMAN IN COOPER COUNTY?

Margeret had a turkey dinner Sunday. It was lovely. Robert and Anne Estill, Betty Anne, Mrs. Ellis, and Mrs. Mills besides us. Mrs. Mills and Mrs. Ellis have each proclaimed the other as being "the meanest woman in Cooper County." We heard it from Margeret *[Mrs. Mill's daughter]*, and we heard the other side from Anne, but both women were so sweet last Sunday.

"CAUGHT WITH BRITCHES DOWN"

Christmas caught me with my britches clean down. I didn't even get cards and letters written, but those who love me will understand, and those who don't will think of somebody else, maybe. I shopped madly after I got to Boonville last night (for myself). I got some good-looking tan shoes and a velvet hat. I had to order a new suit the other day as I am getting so fat my old clothes don't feel good. I have gained over 20 pounds.

I got the usual things for Christmas, with a few more than usual, leather bill books *[bank notes were much larger then, requiring a different type of bill fold]*, memorandum books and note cases. etc. Gave money chiefly, as I didn't have time to do buying. I had less Christmas in my bones than *ever before.*

NEW YORK LIFE AGENT

Am now agent for New York Life Insurance Company, and am picking up a little commission now and then. Wrote $7000 insurance last week.

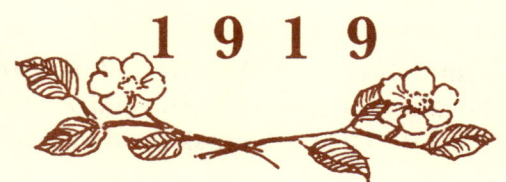

1919

[Lilburn, despite misgivings voiced in the Fall about returning to the Bank, yielded to importunings and to the promise of greater responsibility. He helped buy Will Boggs out and was again Cashier. The Officers and Directors of the reorganized Bank contracted for a new building. Some of this year's excerpts reflect Lilburn's greater interest in the bank because of his more active role.]

LET IT RAIN

The rains we have not had in May for several years are upon us, and we're trying to be patient, hoping the water is all for our best interests. We have found we cannot do without it. It is rather a wet trip into town on these down-pouring mornings, but I am not disposed to move from the country into town.

MONTANA VISITORS

Bess Kingsbury Agnew, a first Cousin from Montana, and daughter, Elizabeth, have been with us nearly two weeks. Cousin Bess is a regular old faithful about reading her *Science* lesson every day. When she first came, she said I was to read the lesson with her every day, but it seemed we couldn't get together more than once a week, and I must admit I was not very keen to do it because it made me seem so dense to be unable to grasp Sister Eddy's line of thought as quickly as Cousin Bess does. You see she has read it for ten years plus and nearly knows it by heart and sees it so clearly. She asks me if it is not plain as everything, and it hardly ever is, but just to keep from saying "No" all the time, I sometimes say "Yes." Sometimes she lets me read *Science and Health* and sometimes it is the *Bible.* Either way, I can't get the connection between the references as we hop, skip, and jump over the Bible and back and forth among S. and H. *[The strong family bond between this daughter of one of Taylor Kingsbury's brothers caused Lilburn to feel an obligation to accept her effort to convert him to Christian Science.]*

Elizabeth and I spent the day and first half of the night at Ethel's. Teale Middleton and Taylor and May Belle Long were there also. We had a real festive time. May Belle is a young grass widow. She is real interesting and as I had always wanted to rush a grass widow [divorcee], which is something I never tried, I may avail myself of the chance!!! Elizabeth stayed all night. May Belle told her some stories that don't have parlor atmosphere and I think Elizabeth was so thrilled she wanted to stay and hear more. Elizabeth is innocence personified about many things, and it is a shame to have her eyes opened. She sprung one of her stories on me without the slightest idea of the real meaning. In fact, the story was about asking what is a *real* man? When I asked "what?" she said, "It is a man who can make a deaf and dumb woman cry out, "Oh! Daddy!!" Elizabeth thought it was the cutest thing. I heard May Belle saying yesterday she nearly died at Elizabeth being unable to understand some of the things she told her. I guess the sooner Lizzie gets her eyes opened the better it will be for her, but it is a shame one can't get through the world with a trace of innocence about one. If one person doesn't snatch the veil off, another does.

BEAUTIFUL MISSOURI

Missouri has been perfectly beautiful this spring. We have had such wet, cold weather that there has been no sunshine to burn up the vegetation and it has just gone wild. Aside from the flowers of California, and the well-kept premises, Missouri has the Golden State skinned when it comes to real nature's display.

WORK STARTS ON BANK BUILDING

The material is being assembled and work on the new Bank building will commence as soon as the weather clears. We won't be able to get in before the early part of September. I am already sick and tired of the bother of it all, but know we will be mighty proud when once we do get in. It is going to cost a lot more than we thought. If we get off at $15,000, we will be mighty lucky, or I should say good managers. I think Will Boggs believes he could get off with less, but of course he could if anyone could because he would do without a lot of the little nice things that are so big in usefulness.

July 11   "GOING ALONG THE SAME OLD WAY"

It has been so long since I had any news of you. We are going along in the same old way, only I have been busy just lately along a little different line. I spent my 4th of July and several afternoons and evenings riding over the country explaining the advantages of fire insurance on grain and wrote policies totalling over $125,000, short term risks. It paid for the gasoline all right, and afforded me opportunities to meet the men at their own farms or in their own homes. I always feel differently towards people whom I see *at home*. Since I got tin Lizzie [*early slang for Model T Fords*], I have explored parts of Franklin and Boonslick townships I never knew before. I hop in Lizzie any evening and go out to see somebody, and now and then have a chance to talk a little for some future business. One afternoon, I made a round of all the threshing outfits. Mam, I sure do enjoy meeting people outside the bank. I have been in Boonsboro more in the last month than in the last two years. Can always find someone to ride with me on these trips and nearly always run into someone on a trip who says he used to do business with this bank until he tried to borrow $75.00 on two mules from Cousin Will and couldn't.

"LAZARUS STINKETH BY NOW"

Last Sunday we were spending the day at Horace and Minnie's and Bro. Snarr was there. I asked him why he used that text about Lazarus "stinketh by now" when he preached Mrs. McCully's funeral and told him it beat anything I ever heard. He said that was not the text but he read it for Scriptural reading. It was all the same to me though. Mother asked him if he preached at the big Centennial in Columbus, Ohio, when he was telling about how Bishop So-and-so and So-and-so preached? Father asked him if the Bishops were supposed to preach any better than the other preachers? Mother asked him to tell the story about the lady putting sugar in his nose. We had a lot of fun.

CHRISTIAN SCIENCE TEACHINGS

I have my *Science and Health Quarterly* and am doing my reading these days. Luther Lee brought me a very enlightening book, called *Paul Anthony, Christian*, which is a novel based on Scientific facts and it was most interesting to me. I haven't gotten anywhere much yet, but it seems to me if one can live up to the teachings of Christian Science, his life will be a lot more satisfactory than mine has ever been. In fact, I think there is something very beautiful about it all. Of course there are some things I can't understand. I can find no satisfactory explanation of them but to learn to be patient, to love everyone and to feel like everything that.... Oh shucks, the funny thing about it is I can't express just what it seems to me at this stage of the game. But, really Mam, I like it, and I really enjoy the lesson Sermon and the *Bible* together. I never got to reading the *Bible* any other way, but it is positively interesting this way.

When you quit talking about sickness though and always tell people you are all right, which you are, except for a mortal illness, it bores you to listen to other people telling about their pains and ills and it seems like they do it more than ever before. I don't find a lot of things in C.S. which I had been led to believe were there before I took time to read some of it myself. Some of the articles in the *Sentinel* are the best things I have ever read, and I don't see how anyone could read many of them without getting inspiration from that source. But I feel like I don't know the A.B.C. yet. I must say Mrs. Eddy was pretty smart or something to get all this system up, and I kinda resent it now when different ones say she was a bad woman. Of course she might have cut up some, but even if she did, everyone but Christ has done that so far as I can find out. But she wasn't bad when she fixed up C.S.

C.S. is going to make me uninteresting as a scandal-monger. I will eventually have to give it up and be more charitable and never repeat things which may be errors to do somebody harm in the sight of other people.

The work on our bank building has been tied up three weeks while we wait for door and window frames. Nothing to do but wait.

July 18 COMPLAINING HOST

I do not want to be known as a complaining host, and I do not mind you and Alma knowing I am no gentleman when it comes to keeping mum about my company, but I don't want the rest to know I uttered a complaint against anyone. So do not pass it on. As Science teaches us, we are not to judge the motives which impell people to do things we think peculiar, or keep them from doing things we think they should do. We can best show the Christian spirit by being charitable in our thoughts of them, and by feeling that they are doing what they think is the right thing.

I don't want to be misunderstood. Elizabeth is as sweet a thing as was ever raised up and she isn't in the way but we are a little tired of her hovering over us indefinitely. Elizabeth is the most easily entertained person you ever saw. Any attention delights her beyond words, and if we can't do the things she would prefer at a particular time, she just loves what we do do. If we stay at home and go to bed early that suits her fine, and if we stay out all night it doesn't ruffle her. As I say, she is not in the way and is not a burden to Mother or any one else, and if she is happy here, I think we are doing just a little good in letting her be that way. Elizabeth asked Mother one day, "Really, what did you think of me when I first came?" and when pressed, Mother said, "Well, I thought you were a spoiled child, and secondly, I thought you were the laziest thing I ever saw," and continued, "But I find I am mistaken. You are just as industrious as anybody when you know how to do. Do you remember the day I asked you why on earth you didn't help your Aunt Bess clean up the upstairs?" Elizabeth took it all good-naturedly and seemed to appreciate it. She just loves Mother to death. As I told you, it is sometime since she was the kissingest and lovingest thing you ever saw at first, but she has got away from it entirely, and never so much as refers to getting herself kissed, which just suits me fine, as I don't like kisses that are ripe. I like to snatch them off pre-ripe. Not that I was a comfort to her at first. She just never had been around a cousin she could kiss. Albert and Taylor were even better material than I was, so far as that goes. It was her idea of cousinship. A man who through relationship was conventionally kissable. You get me.

Elizabeth is no swan. And at times when she would gambol on the green like a swan it was appalling. There is not a *cute* atom in her makeup and if she was honest-to-goodness mine, I vow I would not know what to do with her. I would marry her off as soon as I could.

That is a sort of summing up. She is a darling and yet with it all, lacks the indefinable something which just naturally leeches one to others, so the separation hurts more or less when it happens. All the kinfolks are lovely to her when she is with them, but nobody acts crazy to "subscribe" for more.

Everything is fine here, only the windows and doors for our bank won't just come. If they are not here by Monday, we expect to make them here rather than wait an indefinite time for the shipment to arrive. They have just about finished putting up the vault walls this week. So far, the building is solid as a rock. With a concrete floor in the basement and a concrete floor over the whole thing at first floor line, with concrete and brick vault extending up, it looks tight.

LONESOME FOR YOU

Your letter was nicer than the sermon I heard Sunday and touched me and "done" me infinitely *more good.* So much, my thoughts and my heart, have gone across the space which separates there from here. Last night I saw such a pretty picture, "Sirens of the Sea" which must have been taken at the beach caves at La Jolla, near San Diego. The scenery of the ocean, of the surf breaking on the rocks was so realistic that I could almost smell and taste the salt and how I did tingle to be back. I have been quite "in the dumps" today behind my mask of a smile I wear at the bank. And tonight, looking at the pictures I brought back from my trip, I got so lonesome for you all.

OFF UNDER HER HAIR

I wonder if I ever told you about Maudie Watts Spry pestering me? She is off under her hair and is all time trying to get a constable to arrest me "for a crime Jim Watts and I committed eight years ago." She has even called over long distance from Marshall to our J. of P. She is always accusing me of taking her children away from her, or "putting spiritualistic work over her, or of doing things without consulting her about the Apostolic Creed." She came to the bank last Saturday, and seeing her first I fled to the vault. She waited a half hour for me to come in and I waited for her to go out. Guess I'll have to be the complaining witness to send her to the asylum. The women just go crazy over me!!!

Things at the Bank are going along fine and I'm pretty tolerable happy. I hope the new won't wear off this job.

SOME INTENSE TIMES

I have been having a week of intense times and almost had something happen to me. Vera Bridges and I have kinda drifted out to where we had to stop and get our bearings. We haven't got them yet. It is surprising how fast you can drift when you let yourself go. Martha Payne said Vera and I were the best match she ever saw and explained that it was because Vera had had as many beaus as I have had girls. Well, Vera came down to our house Saturday afternoon and after the bank closed we went up to Jennie Pearl Lewis' to eat watermelon. Mrs. Lewis brought Vera a towel to spread over her lap and said, "I want to keep you looking pretty for him" (indicating me). I assured her she looked good to me either made or marred, and Mrs. Lewis felt that gave her license to say, as she started to take some melon into the house to her sick daughter, "Well, I'll take Annie some melon and let you all spoon a while." Neither one of us knew what she meant as Mr. Lewis and the two girls were still present. Wasn't that crude? The girls took up the topic and stayed with it for some time.

Saturday night we went to the dance at Wingfield's and after we got back Mother made us go to bed at two o'clock—just called us to, mind you! Sunday we went over to Moberly for supper and Sunday I took the lady home. Well during the rush of Society I almost let go of Science. Vera said to please never mention it to her or in her presence. She just thinks it awful, but of course that is because she doesn't know anything about it. If she did, she couldn't be so rabid that she couldn't see some good in it. Well, I am going back to it again and I am getting along better in my daily work. Either Science or more sleep is doing good for me. Billie said when I told him since taking up Science, I had enjoyed reading Genesis, it didn't take Science to make that book interesting to the average human. I can't get out of Exodus. The first two books of the Bible are to me just representative of the fact that getting into things is a lot more interesting than getting out of them.

BANK BUILDING DELAYS

Today is the day our contract says our building is to be delivered to us all finished, but it is a long way yet to completion. No plate glass, no wood trim for the interior, and no vault doors yet and no assurance when we will have all of them. We hope to have the plate glass soon and when that is installed, the marble floor and fixtures can be placed. Our fixtures have been here a couple of weeks and they are mighty pretty.

I sold my Ford the other day for $600.00, and I miss the little thing terribly, but can worry along until spring and then get a starter model. It was such a good price I couldn't resist. Walking will keep a pot-gut off this winter anyhow.

"NOT RUSHING NOBODY"

Besides banking, I have been having a dancing good time at Wingfield's, but am not rushing nobody right now. Vera passed on and Josephine came for a wonderful four or five days and I followed her most home, but the little heifer has gone to New Mexico and while she swears she hasn't, she acts like she has forgotten me. In the meantime a bride has come into my life and gone. She married a young fellow from Armstrong whom we all knew quite well and Mary Hunker gave a picnic supper at Wingfield's and asked me. It was on the night of one of the regular dances and it was a wonderful supper and a wonderful night. The upshot of the matter was that I sure was mad at this fellow for marrying this girl. She is from Oak Park, Ill., was five days wed and danced divinely and was so bewitching to look at. Friend husband had to go to K.C. and left Friend wife and made her promise not to dance. Silly man. She came to the dance at Fayette and fell for the music. I had such a nice time. She didn't know many people and I never introduced her to many for I knew if I did they would take all of the dances. I never had but three straight.

BUSY! BUSY! BUSY!

The pen has gone out of style for me, but I must write you somehow tonight and no pencil is in sight. Dad's white cat hopped on the table and walked over the words above and made the blots. He has settled himself for a nap at my elbow. I might get lonesome without the big white kitten with one yellow and one blue eye. You will say I ought to have a baby, but then I couldn't write you so often.

Mother and Father write me every day or two about what a good time they are having on their trip to Florida with Horace and Minnie. I am so glad they are having a good time it never occurs to me to miss them. I am not of a missing disposition much anyhow. I don't see why I should miss them as long as they are happy and I am well and happy too. Only I know it is nicer for me to say I miss them. But I never get home until six or seven and then Louis and I have supper and I try to read law until I go to sleep—and as soon as I wake, I tear off for the bank and am busy all day—so you see why I'd almost rather "batch." Last Sunday when you were feeling sorry for me, I was sleeping until barely time to get to church, then I had dinner with Margeret and Rob and afterwards loaded the Nash with little Kingsburys and took a long drive. Then after supper I came home, worked myself up into a frenzy, and wrote a love letter which I see is over here on the table under the cat. I thought I missed Josie, but on Monday I didn't, so I thought it just as well to refrain from mailing it. Do you reckon I really would like to have her around *all* the time?

I have been capering some in the new car with sweet little Ruth Harris who says she never has loved a man and wants one to *make* her love him. In other words, she wants one to "treat her rough." A fellow comes to see her who is crazy about her since she was a kid (he told me so, staking out his claim I guess) and she says *he is a grand* man but don't make her love him. Says he's too nice to her.

FUNERAL MUSIC

I went to Sallie Blankenbaker's funeral and Nell B., Ada Lee, Maude Short, Ada Tanner and Chas Lee played like they were the choir and we had a hurried consultation about what to sing, while they were getting out the corpse. Finally, Nell whispered "Play something as they come in." Mercy! I racked my brain for a funeral march and none would come and I said, "'*Abide With Me*'?" and Nell, who was searching the hymnal madly, said "Yes, and we'll sing it." So we set the stage and the curtain riz!! I don't want any soft singing at my funeral. I want them to sing loud or not at all. Not at all is my preference. After the preacher's eulogy, the word went through the choir to sing So-and-So (I forget) but Ada Lee said, "It's the only thing she ever asked for (being so stingy, I guess), then they marched out to *"Nearer My God to Thee"* which Nell S.O.S.'d me to quit after the second verse. Then we went out to the graveyard. As they hadn't any more than turned the newly installed water system on when she caught her last spell, she may have got too warm using the toilet and overhet, being used to going down in the garden during cold weather. *[Indoor plumbing was just being installed generally; people had typically used out-houses.]*

I didn't know what a fine year we had at the bank until the various income sources were balanced out this week. Will have another good one if the glad hand, hard work, and my few brains permit, and the good Lord helps me. I like to think of Him as being in on the deal too. I must make up my bed and lie on it.

❧ ❧ ❧ ❧ ❧

November 19   A DIVORCED WOMAN

May Belle is mighty interesting company, and quite sufficient unto the day. I like her. Last night we went to the revival in town and then to my house to sit by the fire and eat apples and dance to *"My Cairo Love"* on the Victrola. That is a keen thing to step by. I surely did enjoy myself. I'm almost in love with May Belle but am afraid to fall in, her being a widow with a living breathing husband alive. You know what the good book says about marrying widows. If I was going to break a commandment, I don't see any use in being married do you? Well, it is just too bad that such a talented sweet girl should have divorce papers.

BANK BUILDING PROGRESS

The marble setters are at work on the bank fixtures and they are going to look mighty fine when completed. The grain in the marble is beautiful, and there is just enough of the mahogany in the marble to match the wood of the fixtures. I tell you, you would be proud to see us all fixed up. The large plate glass has never been set owing to our inability to get some copper settings, so it is cased up and sets right in front of the building. I think it will be a month before we can occupy the new building as there are so many little things to be fixed up. It we get moved and settled by the first of the year, we'll be fortunate. The wood trim is of birch in the banking room and oak in the directors' room. The grain of the wood is beautiful. We won't be able to get a concrete walk down before spring or to do any of our landscaping.

Say, there was some stink in social circles in Boonville because Mrs. Mahon petitioned the county court to defray the expense of keeping little Mittie, who has tuberculosis, at Mt. Vernon Hospital, when Mrs. Mahon dolled up so to marry and took such an expensive wedding trip and is remodeling a house to live in. Of course her husband is defraying such wedding expenses, but wouldn't you think Captain Irvine would be willing to help take care of Mittie until she dies?

1920

AS THE YEAR BEGINS

January 4

NEW YEAR'S DAY

I managed to feel young enough to take Harriet (White) to Boonville to the party, and Mrs. Billie was mighty nice to us and chaperoned us to the New Year's dance at the Golf Club. Harriet was beautifully dressed with lots of neck and shoulders, etc., showing, and I got her some dark red roses to wear with her black dress. She was right stunning looking, but I was not stunned. I just wonder what it is she lacks that keeps her from being awfully interesting to me. I think it must be just a little shortness on pep, for the way she *flows* when she walks is too dignified to suit me. But she is a sweet-mannered girl. Maybe I have lost some of my pep that used to make any girl interesting to me.

TAKEN TO ST. LOUIS

They have finally taken John Kingsbury to St. Louis although Cousin Bee said she was afraid they wouldn't wait on him good at the hospital, *[and]* that she gave him a glass of milk about six times a day. We all said we bet good white sheets would cure him if they were not too much of a shock to his skin. All the time he was at home, they had him on a double cot, and instead of fresh sheets they had an old comfort under him. Cousin Bee and Palmer finally said something had to be done, they were just about worn out.

"A NICE NEW BUICK"

Earl and Laura Blankenbaker have a nice new Buick car, and they already look different. It sure will bring out people. Remember how it brought me out? Earl rides on the front seat and Laura on the back, and they just ease along. They haven't got the speed craze yet. I am so glad for them.

"TWO DAYS TO GET BACK"

Julia has asked me to the Golf Club dance in Boonville Thursday night. I don't care much to go. One dance is enough for me for a while. I danced every one at the New Year's Eve party, four hours straight, and it took me two days to get set back.

"SAT DOWN ON THE SCISSORS"

Helen Wagoner came after Christmas for a few days and sat down on the scissors. She was hurt in the sitting room and the blood just spurted. She was lame for a couple of days, and I hoped she wouldn't have lock-rump!

January 27 BANK'S GRAND OPENING

Mam, you should have been to our bank opening. We all had the best time, and you would have, too. We had lots of beautiful potted ferns and used the 300 carnations as favors to women, in large vases to add color. Then a friend, Lionel Davis, sent a dozen American Beauties; a Mr. Laughlin, a Kansas City banker, a large bouquet of roses and narcissus, and the Boonville National Bank a beautiful basket of flowers. The latter I sent over to the Chancellor girls' home today to cheer up their sick room, and Ada Lee phoned they were delighted to see and keep it. We had lots of congratulatory letters and a few telegrams. Mrs. Leavenworth and Ethel Smith pinned the carnations on the women, and some of the teachers passed the cigars and lit them for the men; other girls gave tin horns to the children. To each horn was tied a card: "Toot This Horn for Bank of New Franklin," and the kids sure "blew up the town." We gave out 200 horns, ten dozen pencils and 300 cigars, so we had some company!! The day was cloudy and warm enough that people could wear a flower without the flower freezing, and they came for miles though the roads were slick. We had an Edison machine going in the back room, and the music did sound so pretty in the front, but by 1 p.m. there was such a jam and racket you couldn't hear yourself talk. The lobby and directors' room were packed tight. After all the delays it really feels good to be moved in and ready to go.

March 24 JOHN TINSLEY'S DEATH

John Tinsley is dead. He had the flu a month or six weeks ago and got up about two weeks ago and went out and got soaked in a rain. He didn't take off his wet clothes when he got home and later went out doors in his sock feet to talk to someone, and pneumonia developed. He wasn't sick very long, the second spell. I was up to see him the day before he died, and while he seemed pretty sick, the doctor didn't think he would last only so short. Well, I was back Friday night and Estherline was sure sighin' and moanin' and threatenin' to sit by the corpse all night even if she caught cold and died, which is what she said she craved. Then I was back to be a pall-bearer Sunday afternoon, and Estherline was moanin' that she wouldn't have nobody now to love and pet her and say pretty things to her. The funeral was held at Centenary Church, and he was laid away in the cemetery near the depot.

Saturday night Tom Jordan sat up with the corpse in company with a Mr. Fish. Tom was in yesterday and was telling us that he wore a fur cap, and John Tinsley had one like it. It seems the caps got mixed up and Estherline took one which Tom claimed was his. Tom said to Mrs. Burton, "Aunt Llawer (get Tom's accent), I believe Estherline's got my cap." With that, Hell came off E's tongue and she stripped him hide-bare with cuss-words plain and fancy. Finally she moaned, "Oh, I would just kill myself if I had some medicine and it wasn't for the baby." Tom said, "I'll take the baby home with me and raise it. *I'll take* the baby and I'll furnish you the Rough On Rats if you'll take it." Then Estherline turned on the old negro woman until the latter threatened to "lay a skillet on yo haid, if you warn't drunk. You done found the whiskey the doctor done brought fo Mr. John, which the nurse hid." I said, "Tom, it's a wonder John didn't wake up." Tom said, "If he hadn't been restin' so easy I'd sure called him."

As we carried John out, she moaned and groaned, "That's all I got and there it goes." I thought she would do worse and was disappointed that there was no exciting scene at the grave. She just bent over and cried hard without moanin' any. Old Mrs. Burton said, "Daughter, don't you want some flowers to press?" and she answered "Yes, I do, I do, I do!" Then I heard her 'low she couldn't leave the grave.

The way I am telling this reminds me of the way niggers talk about funerals, but one never enjoyed telling about one any more than I have enjoyed describing this one to you. There were lots of beautiful flowers. Since the atmosphere has cleared up, Robert and Gentry Estill and John Kingsbury were called up to the place to assist at the inventory of the estate. At a low estimate, it amounted to about $7500, but he owes some money, about $2300 that I know of. After the inventory was completed, Ben Burton casually remarked, "Well, you all will be the very ones to sign Estherline's bond as administrator." All these men put their hands behind their back, although Ben had the pen and ink right there for their use, they assured him they did not think it at all necessary for *them* to sign the bond. I don't think she is fit to administer the estate but would feel sorry for anyone who had to do it, for they would come in for many a cussing. From all I can learn, Estherline is not anything but "balmy" in the head. The trained nurse in fact told me she was crazy.

"SHE WAS JUST DEAD TIRED"

I just don't know how Mother is going to get along at home this summer. Last night she was just dead tired, and this morning she did not seem to be much rested. Said her nose bled twice during the night. I am going on a hunt for a cook. They say it pays to advertise.

"HAS SOLD HIS HOME PLACE"

Horace has sold his home place of 800 acres. Minnie has a new two-carat diamond solitaire which she wears with the other one of two carats with a platinum band ring in between. I told her I thought she was fed up with diamonds, but she said someone had pawned this one to John Waltz, and she was able to get it at a bargain and did so. It is just beautiful. Minnie looks mighty pretty. Not a grey hair in her head thanks to a hair artist.

"RUMORS I WAS TO BE MARRIED"

My fixing up the house while Mother and Father were in Florida created rumors I was to be married, and of course I enjoyed the talk very much and did nothing to discourage it, but everybody has about forgot it already. Judge Bagby just phoned me that he had suggested to Mrs. Tinsley that our bank should go on her bond as Administrator and "Would I do it?" No wonder I'm ending this letter. I have no other thought but to get out of this proposition.

❧ ❧ ❧ ❧ ❧

Easter 1920   BAD EASTER EGG DAY

I'm glad there were no autos when Uncle Tom was a young man, for girls will sit in them all night. He'd have been ruined. Well, I have just as much respect for her in an automobile as I used to have in a buggy.

I was so glad to have a letter from you again. We have had some wild Sundays. A week ago, a windstorm kept us in all day, and Easter has been a bad egg of a day. It has snowed and blizzarded all day long and turned the temperature down to 10 above zero, and we fear the fruit is all cooked as the warm weather had brought the buds almost out. Snow has drifted in the roads until cars stuck in the drifts.

Betty Chancellor passed out this morning about 5 a.m. Sure will be a muddy funeral tomorrow. Clark's Chapel is all torn up by the storm of the 25th, so I don't know where the funeral will be. We had the worst windstorm I ever saw and lots of damage was done. It unroofed Clark's Chapel and blew in the South gable end of the building. Bill Bushmeyer's house was unroofed; a barn for Uncle Billie, and so on. I have done nothing but write tornado and hail insurance since, but I'm not complaining. Have written probably $100,000, and the commissions are right fat and nice.

Spring   FREEZE AFTER-EFFECTS

More wet weather brings a lull in business, and all the tornado policies are written up. That storm blew me many a dollar. If some living example dies around here now, someone without any insurance who ought to have had it, it would give my life insurance business a boost, and maybe we would all be able to go to California and spend next winter together again.

The freeze Sunday night seems to have just blighted the fruit crop perfectly, and Mother has announced a ban on preserves and canned stuff. Mother also said she is glad I had the house fixed up for she would feel now she couldn't afford to have it done. Poor Ma! But I want to tell you that the freeze knocked some props out from under some plans I was making. I thought a grand piano would set mighty good out there at home this fall, but the stuff is off now. It is not at all necessary to our happiness, and we might as well wait and use harps anyhow

BED BUGS

Mother said a Chinaman washed her clothes while she was in Boonville staying with the Woods family, and when he brought them back, Mrs. W. said they must be gone over to see if there were any bed-bugs on them. One immigrant was found and the following conversation which Mother related amused me. Mrs. Woods: "Now if you had gone away and found this later, you would always have thought that you got it at my house." Mother: "Yes, and if you had found it after I left, you would have always thought that I brought it here." Both were right.

A CHANGED PERSON

Rosie says that since Christmas I have changed more than any person she ever saw. Because I didn't show any interest in classical music records or going to hear some of the great artists in K.C., and said that as for me, give me Jazz and a good picture show, or give me nothing. She says I am getting so I don't care about anything but making a dollar. But I hope she is making a mistake. Rosie has parties and clothes on her mind more than anything, not having no baby, or prospects.

BETTIE CHANCELLOR'S FUNERAL

I didn't intend to go to Bettie Chancellor's funeral, but decided to and got there as they were stretching out the first song, about ten verses it seemed to me. Dr. Moser, the tenor, was standing in the hall door, and Nell B. and Ada Tanner and others were scattered over the house so those in each room could be getting some of the music. I was standing close to Dr. Moser and his breath was bad, but the fragrance of cut flowers was uppermost. The Clark's Chapel Church being ruined, the funeral was held at the house and lots of people were there and it got so hot and close, and right in the middle of the discourse as the preacher was feeling his way along, there was a commotion like somebody was kicking over a chair, the door to one room was suddenly closed after there had been a lot of rushing around. Miss Jaeger, the fat school teacher, had fainted plum dead away. I would have given anything to have been where I could see, but as it was I had to look the other way and strain my eye-balls trying to look out of the back of my head, I don't remember much about the sermon. But as you must know I always take away something, and I will repeat what struck me most forcibly. Rev. Taylor: "Miss Bettie is gone. It's all over. There will be no more paroxysms of coughing. There will be no more contortions of face as she struggled with the ills of the flesh." And then he told where she had gone, and announced that those who wished a last look would pass by the casket and out of the house so that the family could assemble alone around the casket in a last farewell.

Isn't it funny how people stretch their faces to twice the length in the hall at the house and then get normal as soon as they get out on the street again? There were probably thirty persons in the little hall, and everybody had the funeral look until I was afraid to expand my chest right good. When the funeral procession left the house, Ida and Josie and Lillie Cason were swathed in black from the ground up. But I guess the veils were warm on that cool ride out to the cemetery. Miss Bettie was 63 years old. Seems like an awful time to live single, but I can't talk, as I have done half as well already myself.

I have remembered another thing that the preacher said at the funeral. He said one of the business men of the town had summed up Miss Bettie's life perfectly when he said she was a "perfect lady."

EASTER LUNCHEON

Did I tell you about the Easter luncheon out to Annie Scott's? The greatest impression I had was about young Clark's Chapel. The house was just lousy with kids. I remember about 15 years ago it was feared the Clark's Chapel race would become extinct. But somebody has saved the situation. The worst kid was Maud Short's little girl who would stand at the top of the steps and hit everybody who went up or down and accompanied the blow on Earl Blankenbaker's head with the remark, "Old bald-headed man." She nearly pushed Hazel down the stairs, and Hazel said, "Look here, you little imp of Satan," and little Shorty looked shocked. Downstairs, Frances Blankenbaker was giving readings, and she shows promise, and Xena gave a couple of good ones. D.D. wouldn't say hers, but ran to Minnie with "Nannie, you say it," and when she wouldn't, she said, "Mama Xena, you say it," which afforded as much fun as anything she could have said. Lavinia pulled one in negro dialect, but she didn't get the dialect. Louise Chancellor was playing some, and Frances, Minnie Sue, Lavinia and some other little ladies were singing some popular songs. Bessie Smith, the picture of big strong, fat health was propping up Nelson Chancellor, being the backbone for him as he went from the living room to the dining room and feeding the poor thing who makes your heart bleed to see, until you wish you were somewhere else. Mattie's youngsters who look lots better than they used to were running wild, and while they seem wonderfully improved, they look so "balmy," to see them puts a crinkle in your spirits. Emma Chancellor is as fat as Sallie always was, and Will Chancellor stood at attention against a wall with his whiskers cut like walrus teeth as I told Hazel how Alma wrecked his life in your parlor the night she told him they couldn't marry because they were kin. [*Conventional belief of the time was that when first cousins married there was a strong probability of mental deficiency in their children.*] The house was profusely decorated with white and yellow jonquils, from Annie Scott's gardens. Minnie Lee was saying she had brought a list of conundrums but the house was so big and the crowd so scattered, she couldn't get the whole house at attention at once. I never saw the advantage of Scott's big house until I heard her say that. Alice Lee was another of the young girls present. She is a right pretty girl but when she laughs she throws her head back and puts her handkerchief over her mouth, it always makes me think of someone who has her teeth out, during which time they contracted a habit hard to overcome. Maud Short's own teeth are out, and she has new ones that make her look as if she was biting on a nail. New teeth made an awful change in Lillian's face, but since she is fat, you don't notice so much. I don't aim to ever part with my natural teeth until they go of their own accord. Cousin Em Chancellor is bigger than a barrel. She must be nearly as large as Mrs. Arbuckle was. Minnie was there with diamonds on every place she could hang them: ears, neck, brooch, fingers and wrist.

"OLD BIG MAMA"

In all my banking life, probably the greatest *character* to visit the bank often was coarse old "Big Mamma" (Mrs. Jennie Dodson) but a golden-hearted soul. She had double pneumonia and died and was buried today. The old lady looked nicer than she ever did in life and I hope somewhere she will enjoy her pretty shroud. I'll miss the old rough thing. I believe I loved the old lady, "Queen of the Sorghum." She did look so nice and peaceful today. There was an "opening the casket" church funeral, and the relatives were all going up for a viewing when I left.

"I AIN'T SAYIN'"

I heard Estherline T. said, "They are already talking about me marrying again, but I ain't goin' to marry. The man I love is in the ground. Of course, I ain't sayin' what I may do after while."

Mam, there just *isn't* any chance for you to get your wish that 1920 will marry me off. The time ain't ripe yet.

May 14   **UPCOMING WEDDING**

There is a lull in the business, so I'll send off a few words to you.

Sister Fannie Smith up and announced yesterday that Ethel and Frank would unite on the 2nd of June at a home wedding. Frank has been so busy all spring fixing up his house and all such until he looks like he had already been married. Sister Fannie had the club with her for the announcement, so the news spread fast. I sincerely hope and pray I will not be asked to play the wedding march, for I feel like refusing. I have missed several weddings, the seeing of them, on account of beating time on the ivories, and getting old as I am now, I do not wish to miss another thing. But having played off Florence and Nadine and Rose, maybe they will ask me for the sake of uniformity.

"QUITE A CRAVING FOR IT"

Father has been going to Shrine and Council and Chapter meetings of the Lodge lately and drinking Excelsior Springs water until he says he has cultivated quite a craving for it, and so has Mother. He had the car loaded down with it when he came home from Richmond. It seems to do him lots of good about the stomach; his digestion gets along fine using it.

LOTS OF RAIN

We have had another cold week and lots of rain. Until now the foliage has been backward, but things do look wonderful right now, and it is a joy to me every morning to see the country as I walk to town. People who live in the town all the time miss a lot of the pretty things of nature.

"SPENDING LOTS OF MONEY"

Business is still pretty good so far as demand for money goes ,and people are spending lots of money, until it makes my bank statement look mighty thin, but we have 904 accounts now, and whenever the money begins to run back, I am looking for deposits to go higher than ever before. This is always a skinny season, and it is a hardship on your young Hopeful who wants to GROW all THE TIME.

June 8   **WEDDING**

I used always when I was a man of leisure to write wedding accounts before the kisses got wiped off the mouths of the bride and the groom, but this time my flow of account was sluggish. It was a mighty pretty wedding. It occurred on the front porch just as the sun went down at the same time the other girls had faded from singleness. They couldn't have had a prettier evening. Frank's sister sang *"At Dawning,"* and it sounded beautifully *[sic]*. Maybelle Long played, and Dell White and Virlee Pierce preceded the bride and groom. As soon as the ceremony was said, the kissing started and I enjoyed standing off and watching it. I never got but two, Maybelle's mother and the bride. But am just as fat as anybody. The eating was served as soon as the kissing abated. Pink and white ice cream and angel food cake. Then the young ones of us came out to town and got Edgar Settle to play a dance for us, and we had a right nice party for the visiting boys and girls. The bride and groom seemed to be staying all night at home so nobody made any move to give them the devil in any way. The next day they snook off to Boonville and took a train for either St. Louis or Kansas City. Some say one; some the other; but anyway, they are back now. They might as well have taken the train here as nobody was layin' for them. Guess they played like they thought they were going to do them tricks. I write as though nobody wanted to. It isn't that but nobody seemed to be in the humor to pester them any.

I asked Frank before the wedding if they had changed the plans any and he said, "They thought they would at first, but it isn't as if one of the immediate family or an older person had died. It was just a child, and while they all felt awfully bad about it at the time, I think they have all forgotten it by now." Frank can look sadder than he can look happy. He took on at his other wife's funeral a lot more than he took on at this wife's wedding. When *he* mourns, he *mourns*. They had lots of pretty presents but I don't remember very much what they were, a lot of silver eating helps and sandwich plates and china and cut glass and vases and the usual donations. I asked Xena to go to the dance with me, and she went to her mother and said "Mother, Libbie wants me to go to the dance out at town with him, do you think it will be all right?" Sister Minnie 'lowed that she believed it would be perfectly proper beings as I was her uncle. Xena said, "I just wanted to know for you know how people talk out there at New Franklin." Xena looked just fine and seems very happy. The Braggs and Horace Kingsburys have joined forces and have bought them a new farm, and they are going to have a new home right near Huntsville where they live now.

RIO GRANDE VALLEY TRIP

We got back to Kansas City from our land inspection trip to the Lower Rio Grande Valley on Saturday morning. We showed and shopped and got home Sunday afternoon and took Jeffie D. to her house. Jeffie got so tiresome to me before we shed her. She would tell me the same old thing over and over again about "The Valley," and "wonderful opportunities" was and is an expression that makes me almost invert my swallowing apparatus. In a few days after I got home, Mr. Elliott, one of the land men, came down here, and we just busted a ham-string being nice to him, feeling so under obligations and Jeffie was down town talking land trade with Bob Clark. Eventually, Mr. Clark decided to trade his Lisbon farm for 40 acres adjoining the last tract Jeffie bought. A dozen times during the trip, Jeffie reiterated to me she was no land agent, had never been and had never in her life received a cent of commission for selling or helping to sell a piece of land. And it was the last thing she told me after the Clark deal was closed, and she added that she wanted no commission, her only interest was in getting her friends something good in the Valley. About ten minutes after Jeffie left the Bank, in came Bob Clark, saying, "What do you think, the old lady has struck me up for a commission?" I was surprised and told him why I was. Later Jeffie came back and said she wanted to explain something to me. Said maybe I thought it strange that she would jump Clark for a commission after saying what she did, but as she was going up the street, the thought came to her that she had gotten Clark a good bargain, and he just might as well give her a commission for it. And she struck him for it, as she had been to considerable expense on that trip, but "I declare to you, I never thought of it until after I was talking to you. You know we are good enough friends for you to understand I wouldn't have said what I did to mislead you." O, but Mam, I sure was misled! I had been trying so hard to think Jeffie was more than she had been painted to me, and all the time I tried to forget she was reputed to be a Skinner from Tightville, but she wouldn't let me get by with the better thought. She said, "I thought that as people were thinking I am selling land, I might as well have the game as well as the name." Mam, can't you, who know her so well, just see her talking to me? Well I wouldn't buy a flower pot full of dirt from her now, and the package of dirt she insisted on my bringing home in my traveling bag don't mean nothing to me any more. I guess Mother didn't quite convert her on the trip, although Jeffie told me Mother got right close inside of her sensitive skin. While we were away, Tom Black took unto himself that little hair-lipped Holliday girl that got horse-whipped by the women several months ago.

"SOME FORTY ODD THOUSAND AHEAD"

One of the parties who won one of the prizes at our bank opening, guessing how long it would take the candle to burn, has come in with a deposit of nearly $1,000, which has been "layin' here" ever since. This party had always patronized the other bank before this. Our statement has been published, and Citizen's came out the next week. We were some forty odd thousand ahead on the totals. There are so many things I want to do, but just can't seem to get it all done—all things that might bring new business or make what we have on our books into better business. But every day I get the lesson driven home that we can't do it all right Johnny on the Spot, and results are not always immediate. I am learning to look further down the line than the present for results.

"ANOTHER GOOD WOMAN GONE"

Well another good woman gone. Jo Pritchett has announced her bans. She is going to marry the President of a bank in Tucumcari, New Mexico, and writes of "their nest" being all fixed up. She was such a sweet little thing, and now she has passed beyond any reach of mine whatever, I appreciate her more than ever. Girls never are so sweet to me as when they pass *just beyond.*

June 14   "LIKE A MILLION YEARS OLD"

I needn't have bothered about how Delia would have a good time. She has taken the boys of Fayette by storm, and other boys, too. All the boys who were out to Wingfield's dance Saturday night wanted to dance with her, and as all the encore dances were tag dances, nobody got to much. I would see her half way across the pavilion coming towards me, and before I could tag in, three others beat me to it and before I could dance ten feet, somebody ruined my chance to tell her "goodbye, I'm going home." Some boy said she would get her dress torn clear off from having so many grab holt of her. She looks KEEN. She wears her hair in the prevailing cootie garage style, and I prefer it much more than the peeled onion brush-back. She looks like a real kid-girl now, and so much younger and girlish than she seemed when I saw her last. She dances beautifully, and with two dances a week at Wingfield's, she should manage to wear her pep down some. These dances are so different this year as nearly all the old girls married off last fall. I found myself dancing with widows and wives, and I felt just like a million years old and like I must get married myself to hold the respect of the community. I just can't take the responsibility of the next cradle roll. I have brought up four or five litters now, and it seems like I am getting too old to undertake another.

June 30   SOME GOIN'S ON

I used to think you would hear of me getting married, but I don't think so any more, at least for the present. I think I must just wash my slate clean and start all over again. I think Helen Wagoner is one of the sweetest girls the Lord ever let live, but I can't lay awake nights thinking about her like I would love to, worrying lest somebody else might nab her off the carpet. And so far as I know, she has no sentiments about me at all. Anyhow, Sister Minnie don't want me to have Helen, and I have got to accommodate my family.

PERPLEXED

I might say I have never found out just what constitutes another fellow's girl up to the time he gets her tied to him by the preacher. I don't believe I am ever going to get married, Miss Ida. You women sure do lay out Taylor Smith, but I don't reckon he ever did anything worse than many another boy, and goodness knows he paid an awful price at the time. I don't know why T. and Helen busticated, only she didn't find it convenient to have two beaus at the same time. One day she had two devotees and the next day she didn't have none.

JOSEPHINE PRITCHETT'S TROUBLES

I wrote and poured out my soothing syrup on Miss Maggie Pritchett, that sweet little Mother of Josephine's and the day after I had a long letter from Jo, saying she did not care what a lot of people thought of her, but she did care what I thought and explained how all the trouble came about: what she did and did not do, how she had suffered through having caused her parents such distress and that she was going to teach next winter, if she could get her name back which she thought would happen soon.

Then I wrote to her and put my arms around her and comforted her as best I could, and then she wrote back that I would never know what sunshine the letter brought her.

A few days later, I had such a sweet letter from Ma Pritchett explaining everything, and I was glad to get things first hand. From the time the wedding was announced for the 15th, the home people gave nine parties in six days, but the parties turned out to be indignation meetings against Bill, the Groom-designate, and campaigns for Claude who is very popular in Webb City and whom all the crowd wanted Jo to marry. They talked Claude to her incessantly, and she said she could not get them to quit by kindness or through rudeness. In the meantime, Claude was sure pushing his own case, at those parties or calling at the home. Mrs. P. cautioned Jo about it but the latter said she was strong enough to resist the influence. Saturday evening before she was to leave on Sunday, Claude came to the house and wept and moaned and cried on Mrs. P's shoulder about his wrecked life, and some of the crowd came in and begged Jo to make him happy and in an emotional moment she thought she could. The girls rushed upstairs and packed her grip and away they went to Carthage and were married. Then she must immediately call Bill who was in K.C. arranging wedding bells to tell him she had married Claude. When she heard his voice she realized it was "Her Master's Voice" and fainted on the spot. Came to and said she must go to K.C. to explain to Bill and as Jo said, "the crowd could not hold me, and I went right straight home and told Mother what a terrible mistake I had made." The next morning she went to K.C. and upon talking to Mr. Foyvill who was generous enough not to blame her, she collapsed. She realized she loved Bill enormously and never could return to Claude. Bill insisted she should go back and do her duty by her husband, and when she vowed she couldn't see no duty, I am told (through Helen Waters) that Bill said she could come to him as soon as the stink cleared up. Claude called to know if she was coming back and she told him NEVER. But her Mother and Bill persuaded her to go back and look on Claude once more to see if he was the same one she married. But she stayed in Webb City only a few hours and went to relatives in Mississippi. It all sounds like a movie of tears don't it? I don't think Jo was temporarily insane although she did herself proud as one who might be. Claude always had a spell he put over her but other people could break it pretty easy. Claude is one of those beautiful brown-eyed devils. He is suing for divorce on the grounds of desertion, so he will not stand in the way of Josephine's happiness. Anna Rose and I have a bet on whether Mr. Foygil will take her on the rebound. I said he would and she took the negative, saying that no matter if he did say it would be all right, when he got back home to Tucumcari and had to move his things out of the bungalow he had furnished, his pride would swell and he would rebel. Incidentally, a girl he jilted for Josephine, lives in the home town. Jo sure did act crazy, but I know she did not want it that way, and to me she will always be a wonderful sweet little girl.

WHO FLUNG IT?

I don't know who flung it to Aunt Helen or whether anyone did, though we always give an old maid credit for it, except some old maids we have around here. We know they never had even a fling. And I wish they had had. I think everyone ought to have their fling, man or woman. Well, Helen was devilish popular as a young girl and even yet I understand has a prospect. She is about to leave for a swing around the western states, sort of a last casting of the net, and if the fish aren't there, maybe she will settle on the old man down at Webb City.

"NONE OF HIS AFFAIR"

Clara Woodson owns the movie-theater in Richmond, and one night she demanded a woman in front of her remove her hat. Lady refused and Clara said, "Indeed you will. I own this house and I will see that you do." But the lady didn't. Next day the same incident was repeated and the lady got up and left and waited in the lobby until Clara came out. Then she, the LADY, grabbed Clara and shook her all to pieces and gave her a tongue-lashing. Clara's husband is Justice of the Peace, so Clara went to him to have him arrest the lady, but he said it was none of his affair and he wasn't going to do it, so she got mad and went to Jefferson Barracks to visit Tom and recuperate, and soon after that husband Fleet got drunk and had a crap game in his garage and shot his pistol off at the concrete floor until he scared all his pals into nervous wrecks. Clara told all the girls up there that she did hope while she was gone Fleet would get out and go with other women, that she wanted him to do it. Mrs. Liza Crispin, Mother's friend, spent last week with us, and she has lived next door to Clara forever. She told Mother things about how Clara used to get drunk and poor little Emily would have to go over to the neighbors until C. sobered up. Hell! Why do women turn out so bad? It was right cute to hear Mother and Liza talk. It sounded like two children trying to out-tell each other. Mrs. C. would say, "Now this is my new dress and it cost $20." Mother replied, "Well, I expect my new one Miss Berndt is making for me will cost $100." Mrs. C.: "I always give a dollar a Sunday to the church, no matter whether I go or not." Mother: "Well, I give more than that. I give $5 every Sunday. I give $60 a year!!!" Well, we just had more fun out of Mother's arithmetic. A.R. said, "It sounds like you all are trying to out-do each other," and both joined in "Why there isn't a bit of rivalry between us."

"SUCH A FINE NEW SON-IN-LAW"

Gentry Estill's wife went up to Aunt Fannie the night of the wedding and said, "We want to congratulate you on having such a fine new son-in-law. We think he is such a fine man." Mary was dumbed somewhat when Aunt Fannie said like only she could say it, "Well, we *hope* so."

July 17   SHOCKING BOONSBORO TRAGEDY

Boonsboro has had another shocking tragedy, although it happened in Fayette. Emmett Ballew deliberately shot down Ben Sartain Wednesday evening in Fayette.

It is said by some Ben wrecked the Ballew home, but we don't believe Ben was guilty. We hear all kinds of tales, but everybody who really knew Ben believes him innocent. Emmitt shot him in the forehead which killed him instantly, and after he fell, shot him twice more. Then he cooly threw the shells out of the gun, reloaded it and walked away. Lots of people were within a few feet of the shooting. Jeffie D. Marshall saw it all. She was in the court house and looked right out of the window at it. She says Mrs. Ballew is a lovely refined little woman who had not been able to tolerate the overbearing husband and finally left him, but had returned to Fayette to take steps about getting the children from her husband. That she was industrious and one year raised 400 turkeys.

And the next person said that Mr. B. was crooked as they made them and he ought to have been shot. Lots of the Boonsboro men do not believe Ben was responsible for busting up the home. Someone said Ben was there papering the house last winter when Emmett abused his wife terribly and Ben took up for her. She had been in Fayette several days. It is just awful. Mrs. Emmitt Ballew told Bessie Sertain, the widow, Ben didn't have anything to do with her trouble with her husband. She was at the funeral yesterday and looked on the corpse and "took on" more than any of the family. She said in Fayette she hoped she would get to go to her husband's hanging.

I went to the funeral, and it was a real Boonsboro funeral, the funeralest place in the world. The little pasture in front of Bob Ballew's home was just packed with automobiles, and the casket was moved out into the yard, which was packed with men, women and children, where the sermon was said. I couldn't hear the funeral discourse as I was so far away from the preacher and people on the ragged edge were talking amongst themselves. But I got one remark, "It's a serious thing to be born. It is the beginning of a life you can't get away from. It is a very serious thing to be born." Preacher Cunningham may have told what we ought to do about it, but some giggling girl and her beau made too much chatter for me to to hear. Finally he got through his sermon and they opened the casket for the last look. For at least a dozen verses of *"God Be With You Till We Meet Again,"* about seven sung loud and five soft, the crowd passed by to view the remains. It sounded as if the choir was just sung down as it kept getting softer and softer, I bet they did it on purpose so they could hear every word the widow moaned over the casket. Finally, the crowd got to moving around to the cemetery, and I hopped in my Lizzie and drove over there to see what was doing,

The widow arrived at the head of the grave just as they placed the casket there ready to lower it, and she commenced to moan, "Please let me see him just once more and I won't take on! Please let me see him once more, and I won't take on," so they let her and she kept her promise. The preacher dismissed the crowd and so did the undertaker, but Dad, who was sitting out in the road, said nearly all the crowd stayed to see the last shovel of dirt put in and the flowers put on. Somebody from Boonsboro told me they were expecting another funeral in B—— right away as they had just heard that Kimmage Widener had been knocked in the head and killed *dead*.

August 11   *INSUFFICIENT FUNDS*

I am racking my brain to think of something social or scandalous to tell. Perhaps I can relate something in high finance. Holman Lee bought the biggest part of the wheat in the country, early—at a high figure. Owing to his inability to get railroad cars, the wheat was stored in an old elevator and in sacks on the right of way at Kingsbury Station. There were 2200 sacks of wheat out in the open. Well, Holman kept on giving checks for the wheat as it was delivered and now there are about $18,000 or more of his checks which the Boonville National can't pay on account of no funds. He is still giving checks. He has all the wheat on hand and claims that as fast as he can move it out, he will be able to take up these checks. It puts things in a devil of a shape for those who hold the checks. Bill Bushmeyer's check is for over $11,000; Halstenberger's for over $5,000. Then the Slees have a check for something like $1500 and numerous others. All these people are not on calm street by any means, and they all feel like doing something, but what can be done? If one attaches wheat, the others will, and all will be thrown back on the producers who would have to sell at a low figure. Holman claims to have the wheat sold at a price that will clear him. And everybody is just hoping and praying he has. It would just blow things up for him and everybody if anybody pushes him to the wall, so the inclination seems to be to let him work it out. But this will undoubtedly cripple him or his credit as everybody will want to be paid in advance hereafter.

September 4   *BANK COMPETITION*

A Mr. Edmonston from near Sedalia has bought an interest in the Citizens Bank and taken charge as cashier. All we know is hearsay and that is that he had to pay above $200 a share and bought $20,000 worth. One report is that he bought Birch's stock and Mr. Alsop retained his. Birch holds the insurance business and is to have an office in the bank. To show our good will for the new banker, we sent a large bouquet of gladiolas to him this morning. It was a very scrumptious bouquet. And he came right over and thanked us for it and said as soon as he has time he wants to come over and talk over "regulations." I am keen to know what he has in mind. I hope he wants to open not earlier than 9 and close not later than 4.

Well, our statement skinned them a little worse this time than last, and we of course are much elated.

Mam, I am not having a good time except in banking. Everything else seems kinda cut off, no time for anything but monkeying with bank business. I must get some more outside interests, or I will be going to rot. My head spins at night thinking how to do this and what to do about that and sometimes I nearly fly off the handle. And I just wonder if it is worth the energy. Maybe this new banker will solve the situation so we won't compete so hard, but then not to do that would sure be stagnation. I believe I would rather stew than stagnate, wouldn't you?

❧ ❧ ❧ ❧

September 25   A NON-RELIGIOUS STAND

Our physical being makes such a difference in our viewpoint of daily proceedings. I have been getting all the sleep I need for the last two weeks. Have been beating a tamboreen [sic] of a piano at the revival meetings every night for two weeks. It beats going to the picture show so much, as it saves a lot of eye strain. Picture shows get to be such a habit anyhow. They can be so satisfying to me tho, but I doubt such satisfaction is good for anybody because one might be doing something which would give one a finer sense of accomplishment. I have no aims on marrying. Maybe I will before I get to be forty, but right now I am going through the "process" where it sure doesn't make any difference to me whether anybody says "yes" or "no." The longer I stay single, the longer I can keep you here. For haven't you extravagantly said you think you would be ready to pass on if I were happily settled? Why, Mam, under the circumstances I can't afford to marry.

You asked about Jeff and Blanche Clayton. Blanche has always been here in town. Was born here I guess. She is a real pretty, slender brunette with big, brown eyes. All I have against her is she is the most tactless remarker I ever saw. It sounds as if she says things through excitement, as if she tried hard to make clever repartee, and it sounds like a saw, and often feels like it too. One can't think she does it intentionally. That is the cutting things she says, seem to be said in a nice sociable way, but oh! ye Gods! It makes you feel like you tripped and fell down on a porcupine. Evidently she has not crowned Jess with thorns or else his skin of appreciation is tough. I think he did fine to get Blanche. I think she will make him a fine wife.

At the meeting the other night, the preacher asked for testimonials as to the condition of souls, and after Father and a few others of the old members had the nerve to get up and say that all is well with their souls, a little boy sitting in the juvenile choir on the platform got up and said, "My soul feels pretty good."

Rev. Corbin is from Glasgow, and I don't mind hearing him preach a couple of hours if he wants to. Then there is a singer and our regular preacher, who just scolds and abuses us.

The first night, I queered myself. He asked the Board of Stewards to dedicate themselves to holy living and to come up and give him their hands and stand with him facing the audience. He knocked me off the piano and put Alice Lee to doing the tune so I could come too, and said now which one will get here first. All the other nine rushed forward, and I was the only one who for some reason refused to go. He bawled me out and said, "Bro. K. won't you join us?" and I wouldn't. I didn't want to do it. Well, Mom thought I was just awful when she got home from Richmond and heard about it, and I supposed Father would too, but he said he thought those propositions were misleading sometimes and he hardly believed in them himself.

The kids have been going to church with "Ranmother" as Babe calls her, and Carl Jr. has been keen to join the church. He and Alice V. talked it over and decided they "might as well go on and get it over with." And they planned to do it the same night but Carl didn't get there and Alice wouldn't wait. So Carl Jr. went the next night but went to sleep during the sermon and when the singing commenced, he tried to arouse and got to crying. Mother told me on the way home that Carl Jr. just cried, and she guessed his little heart must have been touched. But the next day I asked Carl what he was crying about and he said, "Well, I couldn't wake up and my foot hurt so bad I couldn't join the church." But last night he made it all right, and Sister Jean said she was so proud of him. The kids are all so sweet and cute and I just love them all. Bobby is a dandy.

MISSIONARY SOCIETY MEETING

A picture of life at the Missionary Society meeting. Mrs. Charlie McElroy is in arrears a long time, and the other day at Cousin Bee's meeting, Rosie was in the kitchen helping serve when Mattie Jones came rushing in hunting change for a ten dollar bill. No one could bust it. Someone said, "The idea of Mrs. M. coming out here with a ten dollar bill. She just did it because she knew we wouldn't be able to change it." When Father was told of the incident, he said he wished they had brought the bill outdoors to him (he was chauffeur that day), for he could have changed it and kept out for that crate of strawberries he sold her year before last, so she could have squared up everything at once.

BANKING PROMOTIONS

I have hardly seen Mr. Edmonston since he has been here. Presume he has been mighty busy and I know I have, but whenever we do meet we say we must get together soon and make some new regulations and quit this coming in before breakfast. As long as I am used to coming in at 7:30 and enjoy it, I don't care how long we keep those hours, but I told Mr. E. I would open and close at any hours that suited him. And *every holiday* no matter what it is, so it won't be long before we may have hours from 9 until 4. Much decenter. One day last week we had eight new accounts opened.

We have just got in our new safety deposit boxes and my chief job now is to get them all rented. Am writing personal letters and showing them to customers who come in and before long I hope to have that job off of hand. Next month we are going to have a corn show. Everybody to whom we have mentioned it seems pleased with the idea and we are sure it will draw lots of people into the bank and give us some splendid advertising. The thing for us to do is to keep doing something that will get the minds of the people on us. And the business will just naturally follow. Lillian and Carl often laugh at me for "talking shop" at the dinner table, and Anna Rose says I talk nothing but BANK.

༄ ༄ ༄ ༄ ༄

October 20   RUSHING HARRIET

Thursday I rushed Harriet White to the picture show, and it just poured rain so I had to stay in town all night. The next night I assisted her to Wallace Leavenworth's 21st birthday party at Mr. Pearson's. There was a big platform in the yard and a string band of nigger music, and I stepped around right lively, as Harriet just loves to dance, and nobody seemed to ask anyone but the girl he brought to dance, and I was it all the time. The sore throat I had and the good time almost got me down but thanks to *materia medica*, I am shining like a light by now. I like Harriet very much, only it is such trouble to go see anybody when every thing don't just suit, and I hardly ever have the time. I would rather write an insurance policy anytime than to call on a girl.

CUTTING SCRAPE

Last Saturday evening just about dark Will Rouse walked up to Bob Wayland at the garage where he was measuring oil for somebody and struck at him. Bob put Bill down immediately, and they were up before anybody knew they were fighting, but that quickly Bill had cut Bob terribly in the back of the thigh and twice across the back with a knife. Bob did not know he had been cut until people noticed him bleeding. It took 125 stitches more or less to close up the cuts, and Bob is laid up in bed for at least ten days. Bill Rouse is at large. He had been drunk all day and had threatened, I am told, Dr. Fleet and Mr. Foster. Fleet because he refused to write Bill a whisky prescription. A very shocking affair and there seems to have been absolutely no cause for the assault, other than that the parties disagreed over a horse about five years ago.

APPLES ARE SELLING

Apples are selling for from $1.00 to $2.50 dumped right into the wagons and automobiles in the orchard, and they come from places within a radius of 60 miles. I think there has been $1,000 worth of apples a day dumped into wagons in the Horace K. The Taylor K. and the Robert K. and the Todd orchards. Father and Rob have not contracted their No. 1 apples and what they do not sell here are going into cold storage. They do turn into money right fast. And that $1,000 a day has been going on for some time.

ɞ ɞ ɞ ɞ ɞ

November 1   NEW BANKING HOURS

Today we begin to open at nine instead of 8:30 and I am taking the hour between eight and nine for a letter to you. Tomorrow we close all day long, something unheard of on Election Day in New Franklin, but Mr. Edmonston, and I have decided to close on every holiday.

SHOPPING WITH MOTHER

On Saturday, Rosie, Mother and I went to Kansas City for the day. We met Helen Wagoner up there and after lunch started on a shopping tour for Mother, getting her ready under protest for a trip to Florida. We had lots of fun with her. At one store she bought a Kimona and the sales lady thanked for for the purchase and asked her to come back. Rosie said, "You can wear that on your second honeymoon," and Mother, thinking of trips as honeymoons, said, "I have already had three." The sales lady looked so funny and we all giggled as we went on to the elevator. At the milliners' she picked out a cheap little hat and just clung close to it, feeling she did not wish to pay "big, large money," and it did look good on her, only it was not very good material. So we went on up to the higher floor and finally the sales lady put on a hat, and Mother fell for it at once until she took it off and looked inside at the price mark. She decided at once it was too much and laid it off while the sales-lady tried others on her. But we could see Mother looking around to see if the hat in black velvet and silver cloth was still close by. She couldn't seem to get away from it, so we just naturally said we would take it, and I told her that if she didn't tell the price of it at home, Taylor, who is rebellious against present prices, need never know of her folly. $32.50 just seemed the height of folly for a woman like her to pay. As we went along I said, "Mother, if I were you, I'd get me some silk bloomers while here." And she replied with a disgusted "No," but immediately tempered it with, "Do you reckon?" But we never had time to look for them. We left K.C. at 6 p.m. and just had time for a nice dinner on the diner before arriving at Lexington Junction. Mother tickled all of us again by looking at the menu and saying very loudly, "Chicken salad, *sixty cents.*" My, but we were hungry and everything was so good, and Mother has the best appetite just like the rest of us and had the best time.

ESTILL TEA

Anne Estill had a tea yesterday and invited me along with about thirty Columbia people. They came on the 2 p.m. train and Robert, Gentry and I met them and conveyed them to Greenwood farm, where everything was merry until time to leave.

At 5 p.m., Anne invited everyone to the dining room and we got our plates, napkins and utensils and, cafeteria style went around the table where different ones served old ham, turkey, cranberries, peach pickle, candied sweet potatoes, dressing and gravy, fruit salad, stink cheese, coffee and hot biscuits, then candy. We took our plates anywhere in the house we wanted to eat, and eat we did. Everything was done to perfection and et well. It was a nicer party than the one the Governor was at.

Among the guests were the Mitchell girls whom I had longed to meet. They impressed me as being as different as night and day. Helen is the sweet, unassuming one, while Frances reminded me of a cackling pullet, and it seemed to be on her mind that she must be cackling or humming a tune or picking up her skirts and stepping around coquettishly every moment of the time. But her leg and ankle and feet were above criticism. She was handsomely dressed and was rather pretty, only at my age I feel she is not at all necessary to making my existence happy. Helen, on the other hand, was so quiet and had quite a charm about her. They impressed all of us home folks at the party the same way and we had such a good time talking over the party after we got back from taking the Columbia people to the train.

"I MUST GET TO WORK"

I am running around too much socially now and losing money by it. All the time I might be talking insurance and closing prospects, I am shillyshallying around having a good time. Must get to work. This morning when nine o'clock came, and we opened our door there were about a dozen people who flocked in and there was no flocking to the door across the street at all.

November 18   **ANNA ROSE'S PREGNANCY**

A letter from Rosie tells of her trip to K.C. to see the doctor who had her stripped for examination and as she expressed it, measured her chassis and her wheel base and everything and finally told her that if she got to the place where she couldn't have the baby, he would have it for her. He is a baby specialist and Rosie is to go to him every month, and eventually to the Christian hospital for the party. Mother said she had eight and the doctor never saw her until the time came!!! All this high priced doings "gets her goat."

"HOUSE CAUGHT FIRE"

Rob's house caught fire from a flue last week, but it was discovered in time to prevent a disaster. Margeret was upstairs and heard the burning embers dropping down on the plaster overhead. Almost before they turned around after the alarm was given a lot of people were there from Estill, and the kids stood on the road to hail passers-by.

December 8   **NO TIME TO WRITE**

My correspondence has just run wild for some time, and I am heartily ashamed of myself. When business gets so pressing that it leaves no time to do other things, life is not what it ought to be. I have arrived at the point where I never attempt a letter after leaving the bank, and in the last few weeks it would have been impossible, even if I had thought of such a thing.

TURKEY DINNER

On Wednesday before Thanksgiving I went to Boonville and in the evening out to the Walnut Shade Church near Clark's Fork to a turkey dinner. It was equal to one of Clark's Chapel feeds: turkey done to a turn, cranberries, dressing, and gravy loaded with thousands of livers and gizzards cut up in it, celery, pickle, salmon salad and fruit salad by the barrels, I am sure, as they heaped it on the table so bountifully. Then they gave us a plate with four kinds of cake. All of it was the best, and none was better than the other kinds.

"AN OFF NIGHT"

Last night was an off night, but I worked right through at the bank so I could get this letter written first thing this morning. We have 200 more accounts than we had when we moved in.

"CHRISTIAN SCIENCE HAS SAT BACK"

Lillian has had a right sick child, and Christian Science has sat back while the medical doctor has taken charge. But Babe is lots better and able to be up and around the house. I just naturally think maybe Bessie done more harm than good by coming in here and spreading all the Christian Science propaganda. How can anybody with as many kin-folks as Lillian and with a husband who can't see anything in Science, when it comes to actually taking the place of medicine in curing sickness, ever get anywhere in it. Just about the time Lillian gets to sailing along good comes old man croup and a lot of other ailments like ear-ache, and we all hoot at the idea of calling up the C.S. reader in Boonville.

ROSIE'S ANNOUNCEMENT PARTY

Rosie was going to have an announcement dinner party Tuesday night, For favors she was giving a basket with a doll and had cut out a baby-dress with a needle in it, in the basket and she wanted some verses to put in the basket, so I will send you what I was able to compile.* She has to go to K.C. every month to pee for the doctor. Mother and I have laughed at her about making such a fuss about every little thing and going to such a lot of expense, and she just naturally set down on us and said she did not want Richmond saying she was "another Helen Smith who died of neglect." And so we will shut our mouths and let Will pay a million dollars for this baby if he wants to. We had no business meddling anyhow.

> * LAST SUMMER ON LAKE MICHIGAN
> *My love and I did wish-we-can*
> *That is to say,*
> *Sometime next May*
> *The stork will bring our BILIKEN.*
>
> *You all know the nosey Mrs. Kewpie*
> *And her cross fence neighbor Mrs. Snoopie!!!*
> *Well, I simply burst*
> *To tell you first,*
> *We're going to get us a KEWPIE.*
>
> *Pretty soon you'll hear this old town say,*
> *"Did you know Rosie Darneal was that way?"*
> *Love me and my beau*
> *Grab needle and sew,*
> *Help clothe our child next May.*
>
> *To hang up town is mighty fine,*
> *And the hangling life has sure been mine,*
> *But come next May*
> *I lay hanging away*
> *Except hanging small squares on a line.*

❧ ❧ ❧ ❧ ❧

December 20   OLD TAILS SANITARIUM

I tell you this business life deprives me of a lot of fun I used to have and I am not right sure it pays, but I am in the midst of it right now and am surely its goat. I really should have a wife *right now* to do some shopping for me. If I don't get one by next year my folks will begin to compare me with the Willie Boggs who never bought presents because they said he was too tight. But maybe its because we can't find time to get around and see the "pretties" and find out just what people would like. It is to be hoped you would like a letter from me. It is the first off a real new ribbon, and if it doesn't look Christmasy, it is.

Mr. Estill came to Dr. Mat Burrus' "Old Tails Sanitarium" for an operation about two weeks ago. Last week Mat had an article in the paper about the diseases they had operated for. Well, it seems everybody's trouble is located in the tail, and they are even circumcising women. Well, Mr. Wallace will just kick the cover back and about the time he gets better he errorfies and gets a cold. He is very impatient and tired but Mat says he will do well to get out by Christmas. They worked over Mrs. Mat, and she came out a lot reduced and looks lots better. I suppose there have been a dozen or fifteen operations over there in the last few weeks. A surgeon from Detroit comes down here to take the money.

"END WAS QUITE SUDDEN"

Mr. John Herndon surprised us all by removing his mortal coil last Saturday morning. Had hardening of the arteries and the end was quite sudden. Yesterday was the funeral and the crowd was all one could hope for. And the usual two-thirds were so curious that I, standing in the back of the church, had to crane awful hard to see over the craners in front of me. Mr. Johnny was a powerfully good Christian man, I guess, and if he didn't store up any valuables here on earth, he will probably draw a nice crown in Heaven.

"TO HEAT THE PLATES"

Cousin John Kingsbury has nerves or something and at times has awful shooting pains and moans and groans, and Cousin Bee said she had to hustle around considerable to "heat the plates." Father asked to be explained to, and it seems that they have a hot water bottle but it leaks and they just put plates in the stove and heat them when they want some heat for his body. Some think the new house is so nice John just can't rise to it, or else Bee can't mess it up to be in keeping with John. But it does look like they ought to compromise somehow. John always has to unshoe himself before stepping on the hardwood floors, and they all live down in the basement except when they come up for air or company. Cousin John is right porely and something should be done for him besides what is.

BANKING PROBLEMS

These are close times right now. So many people expect the bank to carry them for all their expenses while they hold their wool, wheat, corn and stock for higher markets. We are just getting along fine but it keeps me watching mighty close, and right on the job. We have not had to refuse anybody any money they really wanted and we are hoping we will not find it necessary to call in any loans. Thanks to a lot of good friends, we have sure sailed along good. Have not had to borrow any money until today, and all the Fayette banks showed $20,000 or more borrowed. And the Citizens showed $55,000. If the Lord will help me along as well as he has already, he is sure welcome to the ten percent I lay aside in a titheing account. If the Lord will help those who help themselves, he sure will help me, for I don't lay around *much*. But it is wonderful to be able to work, and I hope I shall always be.

Right now we are struggling with the tax problems of our customers. So many receipts are made out wrong and so many people will bother us to attend to their receipts now and they lay them away until they can bring themselves to part with the money later on. As if they would make something by not paying them now. It just requires a lot of extra time to look them up two or three times. But that is part of the business.

"SUCH A SWEET LETTER"

Nita writes such a sweet letter. Of course you did not approve of her. There is always somebody who does not approve of the girls I pick on. It flatters me beyond words to have people let on like it makes so much difference to them whether I marry to suit them. I think I will marry the one that meets the most opposition, I begin to feel I must *protect her* from the assaults of those who really don't know her. Now for instance, Minnie said she never could consent to Harriet. She just doesn't know Harriet at all. Neither do I much.

But skirts don't bother me much, Mam.

ta ta ta ta ta

December 28   *POST CHRISTMAS MUSINGS*

It is all over with, Christmas, and we have settled down to earth again amid a new resolution to begin to get ready earlier hereafter. We went to Billie's on Christmas Eve and had a very happy time, and the beautiful tree the next morning, and a bountiful dinner, and instead of coming home that night, we just "continued" until Sunday. All of us got nice things for Christmas.

"SPELLS OF VERTIGO"

Cousin Nell Blankenbaker is having spells of vertigo, and when the attacks come she just falls very unceremoniously flat on the floor. She had one Christmas night and another Monday morning, but was getting along nicely when I heard from her last. Our preacher spoke of her as "She won't be with us long," but whether he knows or not I am not taking time to discuss.

A FRAUDULENT BORROWING

I sure had one put over on me yesterday. A country school teacher who has been patronizing the bank for some years sent her brother in to see if she could borrow $50.00. He said she had gone to Kansas City to have her eyes treated and would need the money. I told him to send her a note, which I gave him, and upon receipt of note duly signed, we would forward her a draft for the money. Said she wouldn't be back before next Monday. In mid-afternoon, another of her brothers came in and said his sister had sent me that note. In it she said she had returned the night before from Kansas City, as she did not know whether she could get the money to have her eyes treated, and that she was returning the following night from Glasgow, and as she did not feel like coming down, would I please let her brother have the money to bring to her. I did so, and this morning I heard that the girl was over across the street at Dr. Burrus' Old Tails Sanitarium. I went right over to verify the rumors I had heard, and this girl had come to town one day last week and had gone to Dr. Fleet to see what was the matter with her. There was nothing the matter except she was going to have a baby, so Dr. Fleet phoned Dr. Burrus to prepare for a maternity case and to get a woman to stay with the case. Which was done. The girl who wanted the money gave birth to a baby on Christmas day across the street and sent it last night by her brother to St. Louis to place it in an orphan's home. The idea was nobody was to know about it, but I guess the old woman who waited on her put out the news, as it came to me this morning through a down-town leak.

I have no confidence in that brother, and I bet he threw the baby out the window and kept the money which was to pay its way into the home. The other brother I had considered worthy of confidence, and the girl had always "done right" so far as I knew. I feel worse over having the confidence broken than I do about letting the money go, for I could have spared that much to help a pore girl, myself. And I suspect that is what I will do. I don't see how she can go back to finish her school next week.

Please accept of my best love and write me soon about your Christmas.

1921

January 12   CHURCH FUND-RAISING

We are busy raising money for a new Methodist Church. Don't know how far we will get. Some people think the very fact of Horace Kingsbury being back of it will build it, but I doubt it unless some of the others "cut loose," Mother and Father are just "honing" [eager] to get this new church, and out of $9700 subscribed one day, $7100 was to come out of the Taylor and John Kingsbury families. At this rate it would be Kingsbury Chapel—and other people won't be interested like they would if they "all done their bit."

New United Methodist Church of New Franklin, Missouri, completed in 1921.

OLD LOVES

I noted your remarks about Albert Smith and me. I'm afraid you made them too late to have much effect on me, for I seem to have lost all interest in owning a woman. Albert, however, is going with a mighty fine and mighty pretty girl, but I don't excite because he has often done that before. He may still have something on his mind, but honestly, I haven't. I don't find it as much pleasure as it is troublesome to see girls, and in this frame of mind I create less interest in their minds than I ever did, which never was much. Last year, things happened to my girl friends. I always loved Josephine Pritchett, she was so pretty and sweet. The Lord saw fit to remove her from this life recently, leaving a tiny little baby. My old pal, Clara Woodson, is paralyzed from the waist down and can never walk again. Myrtle Flagg, at whose shrine I worshipped so long, got married in December. I was glad to hear it for she had been going to waste for so long. Another old love owes me $4 for a petticoat, but I'm afraid it will make talk if I just take it off her.

Josephine Pritchett

The girls I have gone with have all been sweet and nice and pretty, but I don't want to get where it will make much difference to *me*, what *they* say and do, or to any one of *them*, what *I* do or say. I can't understand the way they act, and don't have time any more to *try* and solve the puzzles. I'm so happy here at home with my Father and Mother, and as long as they allow me, I'll probably be here.

"FUNNY BLESSING"

We had a nice Masonic banquet last week, prepared and served by the Eastern Stars. And as we sat down at the table, Burke Leavenworth was called upon to return thanks. He said, "Our Father who art in Heaven, bless these brothers and sisters in their intercourse, socially, financially, and otherwise in which they may have dealings, bless this food to our use and save us in Heaven. Amen!" I thought it was a funny blessing, and so did Mother. When we got home, she said she wondered what the man meant.

RAILROAD MOVE-BACK

The railroad division is to be moved back on Feb. 1st and will mean 150 to 200 men thrown into New Franklin, and Heaven only knows where they will be housed. The change was announced on the 5th to take place on the 9th, but the suddenness of it caught so many men unprepared they postponed the change until the first of next month. I have been busy sending letters to prospects who may come here to live. Have written lots of personal letters. Some day I am going to get me a "steno."

NEGROISMS

I didn't tell you about the old negro woman whose mistress sent her to town with a note to get some chiffon. She gave the note to the manager, and after he read it he told her to go to a certain counter, and they would wait on her. As she passed out of the store, he said, "Auntie have you got your chiffon?" She looked at him contemptuously and replied, "Cose I's got my shiff on. Sposen I's comin' down town before all dese gem'mun widot my shiff on?"

Old Aunt Kittie told Lillian she believed Harriet Brown was suffering from "old time exposure." Lillian said, "I never heard of such a thing. Do you mean consumption?" "No." "Do you mean dropsy?" "No'm, I mean she is paying up for some chillern she didn't have when she was young."

Annie Bly said Rodes Estill didn't want to pay her $3.00 for a day's work killing hogs, and they had quite an argument about it. Annie said Mr. Rodes said finally, "Annie does you still contain for $3.00?" And Annie said, "Does I contain for $3.00? Deed I does contain for $3.00 when I see so many automobilses and tractors sittin' aroun' as I does here." She said "Miss Lizzie got mad and sure laid down the god-dams." "Laid down what, Annie?" "The god-dams, Miss Lillian, the god-dams."

ès ès ès ès ès

Early February — UPDATE ON JEFFIE

I must tell you the latest about Jeffie Marshall. She called me to see her on Monday of this week. Lynn had returned to Arkansas and Jeffie looked fine, was lying in bed, but had on a festive kimona and seemed to have as much sense as I did. She laughed about the things she did when I was up there before. It would take me all day to write the things she told me going over some correspondence with her, and I guess Jeffie has had some shocks as she calls them which have just naturally set her nutty for the time being at least. Earl's bank at El Campo was closed on the 3rd day of January. Jeffie insisted on me being her best friend to the extent of requesting me to copy a diary she had made of her illness from the time she left Edris until Lynn left. I have done so. Wild!!! It sure beats all. I think she must have had a big row in Oklahoma with Edris' husband. Anyhow she ends by saying they have all gone out of her life, never to return, so help her God. She explained so much stuff to me that it almost sounds sensible when I read it. She is delighted to have Lynn back in her life again and says his wife is coming up here to stay until she (Jeffie) is strong enough to travel to San Benito.

BIG SAFE DOOR

The other bank has bought a big safe door that weighs 11,500 pounds and just the weight of it crushes us. And they are going to have marble fixtures, even marble where we have mahogany. But believe me, Cousin Ida, before they get all their fixin' up done, this old boy is going to bear down on getting the business, and we are trying to get all we can before the new bank cuts its swath. We are almost over the 1,000 accounts mark.

ès ès ès ès ès

February 5 — "SHE WAS NUTS"

I must have written my last letter to you just the morning before all the Jeffie excitement. But did I tell you they were taking her away? You can call it meanness or whatever you will, but Jeffie was more than on a tantrum. She was *nuts*.

Lynn's wife, Mattie, hadn't been here more than 24 hours before Jeffie had her backed off, and Edris, coming a little later, had a terrible time. In the meantime, Jeffie had run off the George Lowes who were staying in her house, without any clothes (construe that right). She threatened to shoot various ones and assured them she could shoot straight. Edris later found the revolver in the bed. Sunday night Edris got scared and went through the mud at mid-night to the Lowe cabin to get old Emily. She didn't dare to let Jeffie know she was out of the house, and when Mrs. Lowe came she told Jeffie she waked up thinking she heard Jeffie call, but she guessed it was a chicken crowing!!!!

They arranged to start to Little Rock on Monday afternoon and came to Foster's hotel about eleven o'clock. Edris' son, Billie, was afraid of his grandmother after hearing her talk as she did and wouldn't go near her, so Jeffie thought Edris had poisoned his mind against her and that made it bad for Edris. She came to the bank Monday and talked sensibly about the situation. Said she was just worn out as her mother did not allow her to sleep and she had been 74 hours with about 2 hours rest.

Jeffie sent for me to come to the hotel and, after mushing me with "the best friend and only confidant stuff," signed some papers for me to pay her taxes for her, but of course I wouldn't dare advance anything with her mind like it was. She could talk business to a perfect clearness. I went over a lot of things with her two times and she knew absolutely what was what, but not for long could she keep her mind off her family affairs. After talking with her some time in a private room upstairs where she was eating her dinner, Jeffie rammed two letters in my breast pocket and told me to read the letters before I left the hotel. I did so and one was from her son, Karl, telling all about his troubles and assuring her he did not expect any help from her as she had done so much, yet all through it was the underlying hope, it seemed to me, she would come to his help once more. He assured her he had nothing left, hardly any money except what he got from selling a trinket, and so on, and on. The other letter was an answer to it, and Jeffie sure had spread it on, and after commending Karl for the success he had been that paragraph trailed off in "I want to kick you." Then she went on to say how he and others had kicked Lynn when he was the down dog. How old Jack Rose had said to Mrs. Casey over the phone that scoundrel Lynn was in the pen and his old mammy ought to be there with him. She sure paid tribute to Jack Rose for saying a thing like that to a woman who knew her as "a pure little girl." She finally said Mr. Marshall, she herself, Edris and Lynn had each lost and found the big diamond, so why shouldn't Karl have his turn? It was crazy!!! They took her to Little Rock and I have not heard a word from her since.

Messages have come from Texas, however, to the effect if she did not meet obligations by the 4th of this month, her creditor would foreclose. Mr. Rob Clark, just back from Texas, says her water rents are delinquent and one of her tenants is losing all he has on account of no water. Her affairs up here are in good shape judging from the records. In spite of her mental condition or nervous condition, whatever it was, she was negotiating to get an eastern loan on her land here to take up one held by a man at Glasgow. But everyone was afraid to take anything she would sign, as a dozen people would testify she is incompetent. She wanted me to take 1100 barrels of corn and a lot of growing wheat as security for the taxes here in Howard County and talked clearly of having the corn insured, and turned right around and asked the silly question, "Are you keeping all my letters?" Jeffie pretty nearly got me out of my mind before she left.

MOTHER'S PRAYERS

Haven't been doing anything lately but working. I am able to shout the glad tidings that we have over 1025 accounts, which will soon be 1050, or a gain of 50% if I live, keep my health, and the respect of the population, which I am trying to do with the help of my Ma's prayers. Mam, you know she has seven children and she prays especially for Horace on Monday, so that makes my day, Friday. Nearly every Friday, she tells me it is my day. Isn't that sweet of her? I guess I will always remember Friday as my day.

~ ~ ~ ~ ~

February 14 COUSIN JOHN'S DEATH AND FUNERAL

Cousin John Kingsbury died on the 10th inst. and was buried at Mt. Pleasant after a church funeral in N.F. on the 12th. Big funeral crowd and lots of Masonic doings and scads of flowers.

During last December he became ill and suffered intensely from some bladder affection. (I declare I never used that word "affection" just in that sense, but I suppose it is all right. I sure do love mine.) All the doctors around here had a chance at him to diagnose the trouble which they called cancer of the prostrate gland. They said nothing could be done for him so they took him to St. Louis, so the finest doctor in the city could treat him and he had the prostrate gland removed and the operation was successful, but what killed him was cancer of the rectum and bladder. Somebody asked me in the barber shop what was the matter with him, and I told him of the operation and he said he believed that would kill *him* too. People are not as serious as they should be.

Palmer, the daughter, was like a piece of stone. I think she had suffered during those five weeks and more of attendance at the hospitals until she was just numb. She looked like she was suffering agony of grief but didn't shed a tear.

Noah Kingsbury and ourselves were to meet the family and corpse from St. Louis, and Noah started to the Flyer before we did and got stuck in that mud hole near Herndon's. He went up to their house to phone us and began to knock on the door in great haste. Susanna came down to the door and asked who it was, but Noah is so deaf he couldn't hear a thing so he just continued to beat on the front door. Then he ran around to the back door and the same thing was repeated. By that time Sue and her mother and father were frantic, and Sue phoned into town to send help at once, as there was someone trying to break in the house. Mrs. Herndon, peeping out a window, got a side-view of Noah's face and realized who it was, so Sue called off the police.

We got Noah unstuck, and he went on to meet the train and loaded in the John Kingsbury family and went ahead, while we waited to pilot the hearse over the mud. When we got to the Herndon's, bless my soul if Noah wasn't stuck in the mud again on the other side of the road, and the mourners were all out in the mud. We picked them up in our car and took them on home.

Friday night, I tried sitting up with Luther Sartain, keeping the corpse company, but he was short on entertainment for me after 1:30, and I just had to pile over on the davenport and sleep four or five hours. But whenever I would awaken, Luther was always sitting there reading, and I said to Louis Williams I did not understand how he could do it. Louis said sitting up with a corpse for Luther was like going to a party was for me. Luther enjoyed it! He meant Luther enjoyed sitting up under those conditions just like I enjoy going to a party. When the Coxes came for the funeral, Luther was still in full force and Margeret said Luther kissed Katy. We do not see how that helped anybody. But he certainly is in his element helping grief-struck people, and I shouldn't say anything for I know when I die, if nobody else will sit up and make my corpse keep quiet, *he* will.

WHEN THEM WHAT OWES ME PAY

We went to Boonville yesterday and had such a nice day. Billie was telling us of a letter someone had written to get more time on a loan. It went "Dear Gents: I receive the leter telling of the intrust I.O.U. Ples be pashent. When them what owes me pay, then I will pay U. If you are as unprepared to go to judgement and meet God as I am to pay this debt, you would sure go to hell. I will pay soon. So no more. Yours truly."

ORCHARD BURNING

Yesterday it was so warm we drove out to the Boonville Golf Links and spent the afternoon without any overcoats and today we have had the windows up and the front door open. Unseasonable weather for vegetation. Things are just growing up and the buds are swelling, and yesterday a locomotive spit fire into our orchard along the track and burned that orchard north of the house off and a straw stack with it. Mother said that was what we got for leaving church and going visiting on Sunday.

March 4   MARY ESTILL'S TUMOR

Our weather is just lovely and spring-like yet and the leaves are out on some things and vegetation has begun to grow. People have planted potatoes and made lettuce beds. Yesterday I enjoyed the evening with the Estills in Sedalia. Mary is up and doing and looks fine, but her incision has not entirely healed.

I learned some more about her tumor. The doctors decided that she had always had it. The day before she felt it, she slipped and fell and the doctors said that the force of the fall turned the cyst over and twisted the neck of it so that circulation was stopped. Immediately this body commenced to swell and it would have busted in a few hours had it not been removed. A Dr. Hill from Kansas City came to Sedalia and operated. They later cut open the cyst, and in it was a small ball of hair and what looked like two grains of swollen corn. One theory is Mary came very near being twins but she was the stronger of the two and just absorbed the weaker. You have no doubt heard of such things, but I never had. Guess the two bodies must have been teeth.

AUCTIONEER'S STORY

Horace's sale was a crowded one. Someone counted 280 cars and when they sold things the people just shoved and stampeded until you couldn't see what was being sold. They all wanted to hear the auctioneer's good stories and cuss words. He said, "You have all heard about Mary, the hired girl, who got sick and they sent for the doctor. The doctor came, examined her and said, 'Mary, there isn't a thing wrong with you,' and she said, 'Well, doctor, don't let these people know it. They owe me $20 and I am going to stay in bed until they pay me.' The doctor said, 'Well move over and I'll get in. They owe me $50.00.'"

Mr. Wallace Estill bought 60 cans of fruit on the strength of Minnie's reputation as a canner. He was boasting about getting it to Horace, who said he felt he had to tell him it had been put up since Adam, and Mr. Estill told me the first night after he bought it, he just wondered how much ptomaine poison was in the fruit.

ea ea ea ea ea

March 17   XENA'S BABY

Sister Minnie stayed up at Xena's for ten days and every night they would arrange their clothes for an emergency call, but none came. They sent D.D. into town to stay with the other grandparents but finally brought her home, and Minnie called a family meeting and they all got to figuring and Herman decided the party would not be until April 3rd, so Minnie came on down here to be with Horace and to wait the later date. But didn't Xena up and have the baby girl last Monday. They named it Betty Florence—Florence for Mrs. Bragg; Betty because they like the name.

BIGGEST LIAR IN COUNTY

Mr. Bill Gray died this week, and Bro. Lindsey preached his funeral. Mr. Edwards said he always heard old man Bill was the biggest liar in the county, but he bet Lindsey would beat him at the funeral.

THREE YEAR OLD'S IMPUDENCE

Last Sunday Bobbie Kingsbury was with me when his Mother and Father drove up to get him. We were in the cemetery, and they called for him to come home with them. He said he didn't want to go. He just loves to go around the cemetery and ask, "Who's buried there?" Bob came to get him and Bobbie said, "Dad, you wait here," and he went down to the car and said to Margeret, "Moogie, I don't want to have any foolishness. I'm going to stay here." That was pretty impudent for a three year old, wasn't it?

ea ea ea ea ea

March 18   CHRISTIAN SCIENCE BEAUTY TREATMENT

A Christian Science note: Aunt Lill was up at Lillian's one day when Grannie was there. Grannie had told Lillian to put Vasoline in her hair for six nights and Aunt Lill told Lillian she ought not to do it, that it wasn't necessary, and for her not to use cold cream either. Lillian said, "Do you mean to tell me that if your hands were chapped you wouldn't use cold cream?" And Grannie said Miss Lill said, "No she wouldn't, that they would get all right without it if she read and studied and took care of her self." You know Mrs. Williams has always spent much time making herself pretty, and she could not be convinced that Vasoline and cold-cream were not very efficacious. Miss Lill treated herself to a new suit and hat and looks so much better. I hope my Ma will jar loose and get herself some.

HIS LAST GASP

Mr. John Alsop's estate is estimated to be worth between $250,000 and $300,000. Has $180,000 worth of property and real estate around here, a thousand acres in Kansas, and some land in Wisconsin. Left John and Burch each $15,000 and the rest to his wife. Mrs. A. has announced it is her intention to make her home here. Mr. Johnnie was taken to Okmulgee and as Bob Harris said, "Miss Eller said she had Mr. Alsop so she could move him any time." He was taken ill at 2 a.m. and was very ill all day, and about 5:30 p.m., while the nurse was massaging his hands, he just gave one gasp and was gone. Mrs. A. said he had no idea he was going to die.

୨ ୨ ୨ ୨ ୨

April 4 THE COMPETITION'S LIES

I have had the unpleasantness of a first "Clash" with the new man at the Citizen's Bank. One of our customer's came to me and asked me why I had said I was "sweating blood" worrying about whether he would pay back the money he had borrowed from us. I denied the charge, and he said Mr. Edmonston had told him this not an hour before. I said, "Lead me to him." So we went down and confronted the gentleman and he said, "Well, I was thinking after I talked to you it was Birch or Charlie Harris who had said something of the kind, but I had it in my mind that Mr. K. had told me." I assured him I had never discussed any man's business with him, and he knew it, and if I had, I would have considered it a breech of confidence, and sincerely requested him to sort out the things he heard in his mind, so he would not be quoting the things Charlie or Birch said as things coming from me, that the things they say are entirely different from the things I say, etc., and he said he was awfully sorry it happened. After I had gone home, he told my party I had talked about his affairs to one of the business men in town, and said business man had said if I talked about my customers like that he didn't want to do business with me and drew all his money out and put it in the Citizen's Bank. My party went to said business man and asked him what I had told him. Said business man said I had never as much as mentioned his name and said business man went to Edmonston and asked him what he meant by saying it, etc.

I tell you, Mam, I am plum outdone by such doings and so far as cooperation is concerned between Mr. E. and me, there can't be any such thing after such an underhanded lie has been told on me. He told my party he wouldn't have told him what I said if he had had any idea he would run and tell it. I told Mr. E. that if he was putting out lies like that he certainly wasn't the man we hoped he was when he came to New Franklin. I have had a fly in my ointment lately because of this deal. But lies have a way of reacting. I am pretty well known around here, and people will put the proper construction on things. I feel like I could just mash his face in or get mine mashed in an attempt. Mr. E. doesn't look up from the walk much as he passes here now.

"TORN UP WITH POLITICS"

This little town is all torn up with politics. Two factions in a mayor's fight. I don't see what either one would have it for, but of all the raking up of old stories and criticisms about each other you never heard. One side calls itself "The People's Ticket" and Dr. Moser is the candidate. Wayland Carpenter is on the other side, and such scampering and whispering as is going on you never saw. I hope I may never feel it my duty to run for office, unless there is a nice "plum" to be had.

ON THE OTHER SIDE IT'S NOT SO GREEN

After their sale, Horace and Minnie took a room here in town and have been here ever since. Horace is busy going to his other farms every day and getting things fixed up, so he can get away for the summer. They are planning to go to St. Louis for a time while having their car overhauled and put in shape for their tour through the east this summer. But now they are able to do anything under the sun they want to do, I doubt if they are nearly so keen to do it. Isn't it the way? Half the the stuff we have thought we would just about die to get, don't look like we thought it would when we get it. And lots of time the dreaming of doing things just beats the realization of them all to pieces.

NOBODY SAYS ANY NICE THINGS ABOUT HIM

Yes, John Alsop died right sudden. As our preacher announced from the pulpit: "As you all know, one of our members, Mr. J.A., passed away in San Antonio last week. He was taken sick at 2 a.m. and was ill all day, passing away at 5:50 p.m., utterly unconscious of his danger." That was the extent of the remarks. Mr. John left a sizeable estate, but nobody says any nice things about him, so what good did it do to get it all together, or rather what good did it do him?

"THANK GOD MA CAN'T HEAR"

Old Mrs. Wayland is still around and just pesters me to death coming in the bank to ask me how much "loose money" she has, and if I think she can stand to pay as much board as she is forced to pay. She comes in five or six times a day and this morning when she first came in she said, "Mr. Kingsbury, have I seen you this morning?" I told her I didn't think she had unless she had slipped up on me when I was not looking and couldn't see her, and she said, "Well, I haven't slipped up on you," Poor old thing. She said, "Whenever I am bent with trouble, I come to talk with you." But I sometimes wish she would have a new kind once in a while. She is so feeble and childish, But I may be the same way some day, or my Mother might be, so I'm afraid the Lord might bear down awful hard on me if I were not good, even though I'm a little impatient with her. I sometimes feel like I know how Mrs. Berkheimer felt when she was telling about what a trial the care of her old mother was, and how she sometimes got impatient. She said she sometimes said cross things, but she just thanked God Ma couldn't hear her. The party said, "I would think she could tell from the expression on your face," and Mrs. B. replied, "Well, I just thank God Ma can't see." Unfortunately for me, Old Miss Wayland does both see and hear, so I have to keep on the soft pedal.

"TOO HUMAN YET"

The banking life is a great life, and I just love it since Willie passed out. I wish I had had a little freer rein early in the game. Willie has been in Miami, Florida, all winter and sent back a picture of himself standing in front of some citrus fruit, and underneath was written "Grapefruit and Oranges." I told Herbert, my cashier, that I would have written "Grapefruit and Lemon." Now there I go flying off at a tangent from my purpose to forgive and forget. I am too human yet.

Nothing doing socially for me. I must revise my methods, or I will be like an old stick.

※ ※ ※ ※ ※

[An Undated Letter] "WE ARE JUST DOIN' FINE"

Anna Meyerotto, our bookkeeper, is still out. She has got over her neck trouble but wanted to lay out another week, and I was so gracious in saying it would be all right, but if she could have seen my feelings inside, she never would enjoy this week any more than I am. We have been so busy, and I have had a lot of her work tie me down tight so we just work on the books and don't pay no 'tention to what goes on outside, looking around to find out who goes and comes and when to write the persuadin' notes and letters. We are just doin' fine. I wish to goodness the Bank Commissioner would call on us for a public statement, as we can make one some better right now than we have ever done before.

"YOUR CHECK REPORTED 'O.K.' TODAY!"

The Holman Lee matter is getting settled gradually, The checks he has given have been cared for to some extent with the prospect of all of them being paid off after today. A lot of people holding checks have been on the restless bench, and it does me so much good to call them up and tell them, "Your check is reported O.K., today!"

"SPIRITUALLY UPLIFTED"

Well, I went to Chautauqua every time I had a chance and was sorry I did not get to go in the afternoon. The program was just excellent, and the play, *"Peg O' My Heart,"* was just as good as it was when I saw it in St. Louis, and better to me because I paid more attention to it than I did to the lines in St. Louis. But you probably do not remember who was aberrating my mind at that play, do you? I remember Nannie told me at Vandervoort's at lunch when something was said about nuts in the salad, she thought probably the nuts had gone to my head. If that was the case, *"Peg O' My Heart"* was nothing to me. The lectures were most enjoyable and despite what I said about myself being unable to get the uplift, I was spiritually uplifted and pushed up until I was just as inspired as anybody, and it is a good feeling after you haven't had it for a long time. I am always inspired along banking lines, but there are *other* lines of inspiration which really do one's soul more good.

April 9   "PEACH BUDS ARE PLUM DEAD"

Well the fruit buds came out until we could find as many live ones as dead ones, and the prospect is fine for an apple crop, but mercy me if the temperature hasn't been hanging around freezing all day, and it isn't warming up much, if any, and we don't know what will happen tonight. Most of the peach buds are plum dead, but there are some cherries left.

TALK OF BRIDGES AND OLD PUFFERS

A week ago Friday night, I took Harriet White and went with Rodes and Elizabeth to Columbia to a Commercial Club banquet given to create enthusiasm among people along the Old Trail toward building a bridge at Boonville or Glasgow so a big hunk of that 60 million dollar bond issue voted to get Missouri out of the mud will be applied toward improving use of the Highway. The Tavern dining room was filled and the after dinner speeches were very entertaining. I enjoyed Miss Pearl Mitchell's more than any. It was about the shortest and to my notion the best. She has lots of poise when speaking, is quite striking looking with her snow white hair done very prettily and with green ear-knobs to accentuate the whiteness. She said she was glad she had lived to see two bridges built—one at Glasgow and one at Boonville, as the representatives from these places each built one in their talks—but she hoped the bridges were not burning down as she was tempted to think from seeing so much tobacco smoke in the room. Mam, it was vile, the women's eyes just streaming tears and yet the durned old puffers just sat and blew the stink fumes thicker and thicker. I don't think it is gentlemanly to stir up such a smoke.

MAY 11   "ALL DOLLED UP"

The other bank is about all dolled up and looks very pretty. I hope they are going to let the chance to advertise by having an opening go by. Don't hear anything of it. Our deposits are going down like they are at all the other banks, and in a way it makes me feel like we aren't making headway, but as long as we still have the same clientele I just guess we are going along fine, and deposits will get big when the crops come on. We have about forgotten that we were going to have an apple crop. After you lose out on a thing like that, it don't make much difference anyhow, if you stop to think about what you have left.

May 31   "HORSEY BABY"

Since I wrote you last, Lillian and I drove with Horace and Minnie to see Rosie's baby. The baby was so sweet and pretty. It has such a lovely little head, blue eyes and lots of pretty brown hair. Rosie had quite an experience. When the baby was two or three days old, the doctor advised her to have a baby specialist called in as the infant was not doing well at all. He feared an internal hemorrhage or something like that and injected a dose of horse serum into the baby, and Katie got alright right away. I hope it won't make her horsey when she grows up. Well, Rosie thought the baby was going to die and had a miserable day. I think she will be leaving the hospital soon.

June 3   Dear Uncle Tom Smith [Mam's husband],

In the first place you should know me well enough to realize I don't meddle with other people's business. In the second place, you should know that even if I meddled in how Grannie's estate should be settled, there isn't the slightest reason why you or anyone else should pay any attention to it. I having absolutely no interest in it, would have no legal "butt in," and if I tried to butt in, I would hope to have you kick my butt out.

So, I really should have very little trouble reinstating myself in the good graces of your family. I ought to get insulted that you would question my attitude towards this matter.

The Sunday Dr. Mitchell called me down to his farm, I was sitting in the dining room with Aunt Ella and Aunt Georgia. While I do not remember the details of the conversation but one of the girls either asked me the question, as to whether "Ma's estate would have to be probated," or I may have remarked I thought it would have to be. But remember, I had never until that moment paid any attention in my head to whether such would be necessary or not. One or the other proceeded to tell me Mr. John Mitchell had assured them probating would not be necessary, which I could understand, there being no real estate involved. I told them if Mr. Mitchell had said that, I knew he was right as he had a lot more experience than I had, and after giving it thought I could see no reason for probating the securities. Now if you can get anything out of that which would make Aunt Ella write you I was presuming to say what should or should not be done about affairs, you are a good one. I assure you it was always a pleasure to do anything I could for Grannie Casey, but I assure you just as hard it would give me no pleasure to butt in at this time. Why under name of Heaven should I butt in? I assure you there is not a one of you I wouldn't do anything I can for while you are living, and I'll guarantee not to meddle when you are gone. I actually believe your letter made me sore. But I have no time to be sore. Just wipe it off the slate.

Dearest Aunt Ida   "DONE ME A WORLD OF GOOD"

Your little scrawly letter just "done me a world of good." You will soon be coming back to your old writing ways, and I never will listen to Aunt Georgia again. She just naturally painted things so black about you I was too depressed to write you a "standard" letter. I could not feel you were interested in the things I so flippantly relate.

Aunt Georgia wrote me a nice note after the funeral and asked me to thank the pall-bearers for her and I wrote her it was not necessary to thank them unless *she wanted* to, and if she felt that way, I knew they would appreciate the expression a sight more from *her* than from me. I could have done it for her, only Heaven knows when I would get to see all of them, and I would rather have no thanks than a hand-me-down kind, if I were they.

If Georgia hadn't painted things so black, I would have written you a detailed account of the funeral, but I also thought they would go into detail about everything. How sad we all left it to others. As you know, Granny passed away on Saturday evening, and they phoned to me early the next morning to come. I lit out and was there by ten o'clock. A bunch of the neighbors were there in the sitting room but Aunt Ella, Aunt Georgia and I were in the dining room. Daisy just would hurry dinner so I could eat before starting back home. Daisy had a couple of other niggers helping her, and they had cooked everything. One of the neighbors, a Mrs. Judy, who had been in the community two years but whom neither Ella or Dr. Mitchell knew, came early in the morning and stayed all day. You have heard of people doing that but you don't see it so often now. I got everything arranged and went out to the cemetery with Tom Peebly and put him to work. The monument on the lot is placed so that there was not room (length) enough to put another grave close to your father's, so we had to dig Grannie's grave a little over to the right of the monument. You see the monument is set so it fits right between where two graves should be, but if Tom dug the grave so close, it would have weakened the foundation of the monument and caused it to lean over later on.

GRANNIE'S FUNERAL SERVICE

I told the Mitchells not to start from home too soon. I told them noon would be early enough, but don't you know I was in the barber chair when I looked out and saw the procession going through town. They didn't want to get to the church before the crowd assembled, but they got there at least a half hour before time for the service. When I got there, Aunt Georgia said they had been waiting for me to begin the music, although I was still 15 minutes ahead of the time they were to arrive. They had told me congregational singing would be all right which was pleasing to me. So I asked Nell Blankenbaker to select the songs, three of them, and two verses of each song was to be sung. While I was waiting for the service to begin, I looked around and Nell and two or three others were all lipping me, "Are you going to play something as they come in?" Well, I racked my brain and at the last second hit on the idea of playing *Beautiful Isle of Somewhere* softly, and I believe they sang *What a Friend We Have in Jesus* as soon as the family were seated. I must be crazy, but I can't think of the other two songs, I liked the singing at Grannie's funeral because they did not try to sing in whispers. I want them to sing loud at my funeral. It was soft and sweet at Grannie's service. Just right. Bro. Alexander made such a pretty talk, using the text of the fallen leaf. There were lots of pretty flowers.

$1000 BABY

Rosie's baby is a girl. Will said he didn't care if it was a boy or a girl now that they were both (Rosie and baby Alice Katherine) getting along fine. She will leave the hospital on Sunday or Monday. Mam, it just seems outrageous to spend $1000 having a baby, when Lillian got three such nice ones for $50.00 each. But Rosie was so thankful all the time she was there, as they told her one time the baby was doing badly, and called in a baby specialist who injected a dose of horse serum into its little body.

Rosie was a regular Jersey [cow] for all the babies for a few days, but now ain't so fresh and has to have help to feed *her* baby.

WRITING INSURANCE

I wrote enough insurance the last two weeks of May to give me 11th ranking out 106 agents in the St. Louis area. Had enough applications to make me seventh, but didn't get all of them examined in time. Ain't that fine?

I sure did appreciate your letter Mam. Give Uncle Tom a good kicking for writing that nonsense to me about meddling into Grannie's affairs.

June 15 MONTANA INVITATION

Mother and Dad are really planning to turn westward before the summer is gone. Mother has reached the point where she says so and so won't be necessary around home if they are going to be away. Father wants to go and see Ack, and recently he sent Ack a picture and right back came a letter from Aunt Margeret, which Ack had picked up and wrote a lot on when she laid it down to do some housework. Then she finished it up and just done most cordial with it, as if she had not been the hell-cat she was in the last letter before this one. They insisted Mother and Father just stay on the ranch indefinite.

CHAUTAUQUA HULA HULA

We all went to the Chautauqua and everybody did, and we enjoyed seeing everybody. It was a good natured occasion. The Hula Hulas were here on Sunday and could not shake much shimmy and none at all until the last piece, when *Yaka Hula Hickey Dula* was played and one little fellow just bust with the wiggle, we all craned our necks to see. Father felt it beneath him to go and see the Hula, but Mother went and just loved it.

"THIS RESTLESS FEELING"

It is awfully hot weather to have company, but Mother has a guest, little Edith Crump, and she told me last night that she wanted me to be awfully nice to her and show her a good time. Mother forgets the difference in age. She is so in the habit of turning the young lady guests over to me to learn 'em. Well, Edith is much too kindergardenish for me to take Mother's orders in the true sense. So she can just show her the good time herself. I have not been home in the evening for about ten days now. This restless feeling does get hold of me so. After supper my first thought is to go SOMEWHERE. The idea of sitting around home walking or reading is so out of date. And if I do settle down to spend an evening, somebody, if it isn't Mother or Dad, says "Let's go for a ride!"

CHIGGERS

Tuesday night Harriet and I were invited to the Golf Club in Boonville and I ate heartily. and a half dozen chiggers sucked it all out of me and then died in my skin. We don't have chiggers around home and I don't care much about going where they have their haunts. Never dreamed they would inhabit Boonville's Country Club grounds. Guess I will have to join, as I am over there so much I would be taken for a sponger if I don't memberize. Sunday Harriet and I are invited to a tea at Anne's which she is giving for some St. Louis cigarette smokers and poker players. Anne thinks having all these people for friends now will make it lovely for Betty Anne when she grows up, but believe me I would hesitate to rush a child into the crap-shooting, poker-playing, cigarette-smoking gang if she were mine. I would feel I would like to start her in something different even if she should naturally drift into such things herself.

PAIRED OFF

Whenever a man and a woman go together some, people begin to pair them off, Now I would like it better to pick my own dates with Harriet and go when I feel like it without having it suggested that I do so and so, so much. Let somebody else bring her some, so I can see how it looks.

FAMILY ROWS

Some of my good friends, married ones, have had such a terrible family rumpus between themselves, I have decided not to marry for a great many more years. However, they have made up and it is lovely, but they needed killing while it was going on. It seems I hear about everybody who has a family row for judging by the number I hear about, I think *every* family must have *some* rows.

FAMILY DOIN'S

Last night, I marched in the Eastern Star, which is pretty much a Clark's Chapel organization, which insures that it is lots of fun, like a big family. Five of the seven officers are cousins of mine. I felt free to shimmy a little in the march when the music was right good. Mother had a full day as the Missionary Society met with her, and it was her birthday, too. Today she was so tired when she got up, she felt like going back to bed, which is exactly what I would have done. But she said she had too much to do. She never will get over the habit of having too much to do.

Mother has phoned to bring out the ice-cream in a paper box. Isn't that the tackiest way for country people to do? I haven't sweat over the freezer this year, and it hasn't been done by anyone at our house but once. Do hope you are feeling better.

July 14   BANKING SCAMS

Too much gadding about for writing. Both pleasure gadding and business gadding. As times get tighter for the general trade, I find it advisable to check up and inventory the stock given as security under chattel mortgages, and believe me the things we sometimes find out make us lower our estimation of a part of humanity. We find some stock mortgaged to two or three banks, some "imaginary" stock mortgaged, and occasionally a man will lie to me right off the bat and I will not realize what a good liar he is until I go to Fayette and check the records. Banking is now getting to the place where it takes all the brains and all the eyes I have, and the other bankers say they are having the same hilarious (?) time keeping up with some of the customers.

TOO MANY PEOPLE

Tuesday night I took Harriet and Sallie and George Edwards down to Alice Kinney's to call on one Elizabeth Ravenel from Savanah, Georgia. They had recommended this girl to me so much I had high expectations. But she has adenoids or tonsils, one, and I had to listen hard to understand what she said in her Georgia brogue. Miss Alice called me to one side and told me what a charming girl she was; then Margeret Ravenel privately bragged on her; then I was passed on to Cora Hurt who lisped a recommendation. I bet the girl don't show the same side to me she does to them old girls. Certainly the things that appeal to them wouldn't appeal to me at all. Last summer when this girl's sister went riding with me about midnight and we stayed out until 1 a.m. the Kinney-Ravenel ideals were just ravaged and long since they told me that *this* girl was not the harum-scarum kind like Mary Wallace was last summer. But in spite of adenoids, I gathered Elizabeth would not mind going riding at midnight, and I am going to ask *her* to to do something outlandish just to give Alice, Cora, and Maggie a thrill. Elizabeth is a chemist, got her degree at Columbia and works in a laboratory and will no doubt blow me up if I get rash. George and I did not like her nearly as much as we like Harriet. Harriet is a real human, I suspect. She doesn't like to go in early at all, and the other night after we took George and Sallie home, we drove out to the lake and sat on the bridge and listened to the bull-frogs, as she had never heard any until this summer. Just as we were listening to one that was real close to us, we saw a car come over the hill towards us and we had to beat it for fear somebody would try to ruin our reputations. There are too many people in the world sometimes. This is about all which has been happening to me, which is not amounting to much.

Your loving Lib

EPILOGUE

The July 14, 1921 letter is the last of Lilburn's letters written to Mam and given to me.

Mam (Ida Casey Smith) died August 12, 1921. She was buried in Tacoma, Washington, where her son, Lynn, was then living.

In addition to having no use of her legs as a result of an accidental gun shot wound many years before, she had become afflicted by severe and painful arthritis and a heart condition. Congestive heart failure caused her death. She and her husband, Tom Smith, whose health was also deteriorating had moved to Tacoma to be near their son. From time to time in earlier letters, Lilburn had expressed solicitude and concern for his Aunt's health (apparently responding to her mention in letters to him of problems she was experiencing). It was in character for him to write her regularly at length of the people and places she knew and loved, in an effort to divert her from her suffering and illness.

Mam's husband, Tom Smith, in the summer of 1922 returned to Missouri to visit brothers and other relatives. Lilburn was on a trip through the West with his brother, Horace and wife. A letter written him while away by his father, R.T. Kingsbury, on August 14, 1922, tells of Tom Smith's death.

Dear Lilburn,

I wired you last night concerning death of Uncle Tom, care of New Baldwin Hotel. I hope you will get the message in time to attend the burial at Tacoma.

I think in one of my letters I mentioned that on the occasion of my visit to him at Dr. Mitchell's, I found him so much improved he was out riding with Dr. and Aunt Ella *[Mam's sister]*. I think they took him out three nights in succession, and he seemed so much better, we all hoped he was getting well. One evening he had a bad attack, and it was necessary to tap him again from which he did not rally as usual. He continued to grow weaker each day until Saturday evening at 7:30, when he died very suddenly. He had just told the nurse who had come in with her hair dressed nicely, how nice she looked and then turned over and life went out instantly just the day, hour, and minute, one year from the death of Ida.

Mother and I, Charles and Lillie's family, Billy's family, Albert Smith and Ted Erickson and wife, went down to the services which was just two songs, reading a scripture lesson and prayer, after which the body was taken to the train and left Columbia for Tacoma at 1:30 p.m. Neither Ella nor Dr. was with Tom when he died; only the nurse in the room. I had been down to see him Thursday and Friday before his death. . . .

[Whether or not word reached Lilburn in time for him to attend the service in Tacoma is unknown, but on August 22 he wrote from Seattle to his Aunt Lillie (wife of Tom's brother Charles) as follows:]

"I am sending you a couple of little pictures which will show you where Uncle Tom and Aunt Ida were laid to rest. In the closer view picture, the basket of gladiolas is at the foot of Uncle Tom's grave—and the little flowering plants at the extreme right are growing on Aunt Ida's grave. The gladiolas were lovely. They were the flowers I ordered per Father's telegram for you all.

We are starting home tonight but will stop over one day at three places, so we won't get home until the 1st. Will be mighty glad to see you all.

It seems mere coincidence that Mam's death comes at the conclusion of a phase of Lilburn's life more notable for his many love affairs than for serious pursuit of a career with clearly established goals. Mam's death undoubtedly left a void. Her interest in him, first as a child, and then as a young adult, evoked in turn a deep affection in him for her. Her enjoyment of his letters influenced him to take note of those happenings in the community he thought she would relish and to write of them as amusingly as he could. I think Mam's belief that he had ability as a writer and her obvious enjoyment of his letters were important factors in his becoming a prolific letter-writer.

Mam's feeling comes out in a letter to Lilburn, written August 15, 1917:

Lilburn, my boy,

I've often thought, what a delight for old age and an antidote for "blues" would be a diary from our "teens" on through life, of the pleasant, pretty and sweet things that have come to us.

Wouldn't it chase the wrinkles away and help the sunshine dissolve the darkest clouds? And you, Lilburn can come nearer having one than anybody I know. If you would cull from your numerous letters to me the many good times, nice trips, happy occasions and innocent love affairs into a diary, it would make a salable book and be a joy to you to peruse when clouds of age shut out the sunshine. So far though, my all but 59 years has not changed my tastes for the things I enjoyed at 25 and on. When I do go out, things look as beautiful to me as they ever did, though people have changed, especially the young boys and girls.

Goodnight and love a thousand fold,

"Mam"

This letter from Mam headed twenty-four pages of excerpts Lilburn took from 1911-12 letters returned by Mam. Possibly he was too busy "girling" and writing fresh letters to continue this diary project. Whatever the reason, he did save the returned letters, possibly intending to do something with them eventually.

Later on he did write some for publication (mostly about family and Boonslick Country history) but never got back to excerpting Mam's letters and putting the excerpts into diary form. Vicariously, I have attempted to do this for him in A Man of Many Letters.

Occasionally I fantasize. In one of my fantasies, I see Lilburn and Mam well inside the "Pearly Gates of Heaven." They are sitting on a bench of gold, looking at a copy of A Man of Many Letters. Lilburn is pointing to an illustration, accompanying the excerpt of "I've Been to a Wonderful Party." He says. "Wasn't that the beatin'est thing?"

Mam looks at him a little sadly, shakes her head and replies, "I'd have died much happier, and rested much more comfortably, if I you had only been happily married."

I regret not having a Lilburn letter to his Uncle Tom or to his Cousin (Sis) Alma Smith Armstrong telling what Mam had meant to him and the many contributions she had made to his life. I'm sure such letters were written. There is no doubt but that Mam's death created a large void in Lilburn's life. She was a very significant person to him, one he could confide in, jest with, and seek advice from. In talking with Lilburn when he gave me Mam's letters, he talked of her fondly and reverently as a very special person who refused to let her disability, pain and suffering spoil her enjoyment of life. He said that for several years after her death, when something amusing or outrageous came to his attention, he would think, "How Mam would enjoy hearing about that."

Perhaps unconsciously, Lilburn sought to fill the void Mam left by assuming greater responsibility for Fairview Farm and Orchards and by devoting loving care and attention to his aging parents. Whether this was the case, Mam's death coincided with development of new interests and activities leading to Lilburn achieving increased stature and respect in the Boonslick Country. His letters about many of these activities are now being excerpted for future publications.

—Warren Taylor Kingsbury

Scottsdale, Arizona

September 1, 1990

FOOTNOTES

¹McDaniel, Lynn, "Daniel Boone—Boonslick Pioneer," *Bicentennial Boonslick History* (Boonville, Mo.: Boonslick Historical Society, 1976), pp. 10-11.

²*Ibid*, p. 11.

³*Ibid.*

⁴Boone's Lick State Historic Site [*informational sheet*] (Jefferson City, Mo.: Missouri Department of Natural Resources Division of Parks and Historic Preservation).

⁵Brunda, Mrs. N.A., "Boonslick's Incredible Cooper Family," *Bicentennial Boonslick History* (Boonville, Mo.: Boonslick Historical Society, 1976), pp. 14-15.

⁶*Ibid*, p. 14.

⁷Brunda, Mrs. N.A., "Old Boonslick Trail Brought Settlers Overland," *Bicentennial Boonslick History* (Boonville, Mo.: Boonslick Historical Society, 1976), p. 37.

⁸Dooley, Mrs. Van, "Old Franklin—First Town West of St. Louis." *Bicentennial Boonslick History* (Boonville, Mo.: Boonslick Historical Society, 1976), pp. 22-23.

⁹*Ibid*, p. 23.

¹⁰*Ibid.*

¹¹Kingsbury, Lilburn, "Boonslick Heritage," *Bulletin—Missouri Historical Society* (St. Louis, Mo.: Jan. 1966), pp. 158-9.

¹²*Ibid*, pp. 162-3.

¹³Kingsbury, Lilburn, "Boonslick Heritage," *Bulletin—Missouri Historical Society* (St. Louis, Mo.: April 1966), pp. 333-8.

¹⁴*Ibid*, pp. 338-40.

[In 1976 the Boonslick Historical Society, as their official U.S. bicentennial project, published a *Bicentennial Boonslick History*. It was reprinted in August 1987. It is a well-illustrated compilation of interesting highlights and human sidelights of the history of the Boonslick Country. Twelve of the articles were written by Lilburn Kingsbury, first president of the Boonslick Historical Society. Copies may be obtained from: Friends of Historic Boonville, P.O. Box 1776, Boonville, Mo. 65233.]

APPENDIX I

LILBURN'S BOONSLICK FOLKS

Lilburn loved people. He found them interesting not for who they were, but for the things they did and said. When actions and words were amusing or seemed out of the ordinary to him, he wrote about them in his letters. In excerpting these, I have not changed or delated any names. These were real people. He wrote of them as he saw them. Names of most can be found on grave markers at Mount Pleasant, Clark's Chapel, Walnut Grove, and Fayette Cemeteries. They have long been lying at rest.

Many of these people were known to me personally; others, I have identified from family connections, friends, and context of the letters excerpted. In some instances, I only know them as residents of New Franklin or the area. To help readers associate the individual's relationship to the subject written about I often interposed in the text, a bracketted explanatory comment; e.g., Ruth *[a dressmaker, living in while making Anna Rose's college wardrobe]*.

For individuals written of more frequently and extensively I have tried in the listing below to indicate their place in the community and/or the nature of their family link with Lilburn.

KINGSBURYS: (LILBURN'S LINEAGE)

Jeremiah (Jere). Progenitor of the Boonslick Kingsburys. Sixth generation of Joseph Kingsbury, who came from England to Dedham, Massachusetts, in 1628. Jere was born in New York on November 5, 1784; moved to Randolph County, North Carolina, as a young man and came to Howard County, Missouri, in 1816. He had eleven children.

Horace, Dr. Oldest son of Jere. Owner of Cedar Grove. Eleven children; seven by his first wife; two by his second; and two by his third.

Robert Taylor (called by his middle name). Ninth child of Horace. Owner of Fairview Farm and Orchards. Married Sallie Diana Smith, who died March 16, 1871. Married Alice Virginia Smith (Sallie's sister) April 1, 1872. Seven children; five sons, then two girls. Lilburn was the fifth son.

Lilburn Adkin Kingsbury. *Man of Many Letters.*

LILBURN'S SIBLINGS AND THEIR SPOUSES AND CHILDREN

Horace Milton. Orchardist and farmer, New Franklin. Married Minnie Delice Stinson. One daughter, Xena Yetive, who married Herman Bragg of Huntsville.

William Wallace (Billie). Attorney and banker in Boonville. Married Julia Taylor. Four children: W.W., Jr. (Bill), Warren Taylor, (Little) Julia Taylor, and Jere.

Ernest Lilburn. Orchardist and farmer, Woolridge, Cooper County. Married Hazel Hartman.

Robert Taylor (Bob). Orchardist and farmer, New Franklin. Married Margeret Mills. Three children: Alice Virginia (Ginger), Jean Marie, and Robert (Bobbie) Taylor, III.

Alice Lillian. Married Carl Allan Edmonston. They had three children: Carl Allan, Jr., Taylor Kingsbury, and Lilburn Adkin (Babe).

Anna Rose. Married Will Darneal, a Richmond, Missouri, merchant. Two children: Alice Kathryn and Mary Sue (Susie).

OTHER HOWARD COUNTY KINGSBURYS

John Alnut. Grandson of Jere. Wife, Beatrice (Bea) Smith. Children: Robert Leonard and Martha Palmer

Noah Jerry. Grandson of Jere. Wife, Eva Woods. Children: Kathryn, Martha Jane, Louise, and Leonard.

Montana Kingsburys

Lilburn Scotten (from whom came Lilburn's first name), a son of Dr. Horace. Married to Minerva (Minnie) Smith. Their daughter, Alice Lillian Agnew, became a principal correspondent of Lilburn. She and her daughter, Elizabeth, were Fairview visitors. A son, Ferdinand Davis, became a prominent Montana rancher.

Akinson Wallis, a son of Dr. Horace, who went to Montana and became one of the state's most successful cattlemen. He is one of the state's two representatives in the National Cowboy Hall of Fame at Oklahoma City. He married Margeret Britt and they had two children, Adkin Wallace and Mary Margeret. Lilburn's middle name, Adkin, came from this uncle.

Lilburn's Smith Lineage

Lilburn's mother, Alice Virginia Smith, was a daughter of William Jefferson Smith, the ninth son of William Downing Smith. Born in Culpepper, Virginia, he made his way west with relatives into Kentucky, then on to the Boonslick Country where in 1838 he purchased a sizeable tract of land. In 1841 he married Elizabeth Gerhardt. In 1857 Sunnyside was built. W.J. Smith children and their offspring mentioned in this book are:

Minerva (Married to Lilburn Scotten Kingsbury), Alice Lillian Kingsbury Agnew (her daughter, Elizabeth Minerva Agnew).

William Wallace (Billie) (married to Sarah Frances Agnew). Children: Alice Nadine, Fannie, Florence, Charles Albert, and Ethlyn.

Sallie Diana (Grandfather Taylor Kingsbury's first wife).

Alice Virginia (Grandfather Kingsbury's second wife).

Charles Isaac (Charlie). Married Lillie Boggs (a sister of Will Boggs, President of he Bank of New Franklin.) Children: Helen Webb Duval (Bill), Harris. Robert Taylor, Charles Isaac, III. (C.I), Margaret Lavinia.

Earl Thomas (Tom). Married Ida (Mam) Casey. Children: Evylyn, Lynn, Alma (Sis) Armstrong.

Betty. Married Dr. Dye.

Rose Smith Seidenadel. Son: Wolfgang William Smith (Smitty)

THE ESTILLS

About a mile to the north of Fairview on the M.K.&T. railroad branch line was a railroad station called Estill. There passengers might board morning and evening locals going north to Fayette, Moberly, and Hannibal, and to counterpart locals going south to the mainline at New Franklin. At the station, freight (apples, grain, lumber, cattle and hogs etc.) could be shipped from the area and incoming goods received. The station was named for the Estill family, early settlers of the area, and became a little village with a general store and post office. The Wallace Estills were from Kentucky and introduced shorthorn cattle into the state. Their cattle farm was immediately to the north of the Kingsbury orchard/farm and a close relationship existed between the two families. Lilburn was much interested in an Estill daughter,

Etta, who in 1903 inspired him to compose a song, "Jalna," and dedicate it to her. He maintained an off-and-on courtship of Etta until her marriage in 1912. For many years Lilburn continued friendly with Etta and other members of the family about whom he writes:

Robert and Anne
Rodes and Elizabeth (living at Gleneden)
Gentry and Mary

Related to the Howard County Estills and frequently visiting them, were the Sedalia Estills. Mrs. Nannie Estill was the widow of a brother of Wallace Estill. There were two Estill daughters, Mary and Nannie, who a few years after Etta's marriage was seriously courted by Lilburn. After her marriage, he judged other women by her, and found none to measure up.

SOME OTHER GIRL FRIENDS

Estelle Biddle, and **Lenore Dorsey**, teachers. **Hallie Ogle**, a visiting girl from Texas; **Mary Dimmitt**, from Fayette; **Clara Woodson**, a girl from Richmond (Mo.) whom he met through brothers who were classmates of his at Central College. He was engaged to Clara but broke the engagement.

Ruth Berkheimer, who gave interesting parties.

Josephine Pritchett, whom Lilburn visited several times in Webb City.

Gertrude Ramsey, **Mayme Hendrick**, **Gertrude Ramsey**, **Helen Wagoner**, and **Lois Snarr**, some of Anna Rose's friends that Lilburn entertained.

Susanne Herndon, who lived on a farm about halfway between Fairview and New Franklin. She was a good friend and he frequently dated her as a matter of convenience.

Frances McCutcheon, whom he visited at her home near Lone Elm, Cooper County.

Margeret Edwards (Simpich), an early love who married Fred Simpich, who became an editor of the *National Geographic*. Lilburn's friendship with her continued through the years. He was a frequent visitor in the home of her parents, George and Sallie Edwards, in New Franklin.

OTHER FRIENDS

Frank Brickey, an early suitor of Anna Rose, who ran a garage in Fayette.

Bob McGavock, with whom he sometimes double-dated.

Teale Middleton, a friend of convenience.

Josephine and **Henry Tindall**, Fayette Cousins, who interested him in antique collecting and genealogy.

Guy and **Horace Blankenbaker**. Horace became the owner of Cedar Grove. Ada and Nell Blankenbaker. They were cousins.

Henry Kardell, a Reo car dealer in St. Louis, married a niece of Lilburn's parents and lived in Webster Groves.

APPENDIX II
MAM'S MARRIAGE

In 1934 Lilburn Kingsbury did a profile (unpublished) of his grandfather, William Jefferson Smith, his children, and life at Sunnyside. Included in the profile is an account of the wedding of Tom Smith to Ida Casey (Mam), which was printed in the *Boonville Advertiser* November 22, 1878.

Married at the home of the bride's father, Mr. James Casey, Mr. E.T. Smith to Miss Ida E. Casey.

The above familiar form of notice needs no explanation. As to particulars of the happy occasion your reporter gleans the following brief account. When we arrived at the scene of the happy event, a large portion of the guests had assembled, and as your reporter is slightly acquainted, the visitors so many, we will abstain from the mention of names; sufficient to say that the spacious parlor and rooms were literally crowded with the many relatives and friends of the contracting parties. At the appointed hour the happy couple made their appearance, the handsome bride, attired in a travelling dress of seal brown, very tastily trimmed in velvet and hat appropriate for the occasion, leaning gracefully on the left arm of her chosen companion for life.

As they walked in, they presented a picture as graceful, "As the mute swan that floats down the stream." For a moment all was silence personified, when Dr. C.H. Briggs of Boonville, in words appropriate and advice given only as the doctor can, pronounced the fair bride and handsome groom man and wife. After the ceremony the customary congratulations were offered, after which the company were reminded they were not in "fairy land" by being invited to the dining room where a repast awaited them, consisting of a table groaning under its over-weight of the substantials and delicacies that make up the marriage feast of a country wedding in high life.

After the feast was over a short time was spent in the parlor in the merry conversation generally incited by the partaking of a rich banquet, when the bride and groom, accompanied by a number of their friends, started for Franklin, where they took the train for St. Louis, where they will spend a few days.

May their sojourn through life be one of happiness and sunshine, is the wish of of your reporter for ourself and the paper.

"May thy pathway gentle friends
Ever with sweet flowers be shining."

Lilburn quotes his Aunt Rose, Tom's youngest sister.

"Tom, had a team of high-stepping gray horses and they, when hitched to the family carriage, made a swanky looking outfit. No one remembers just when the family carriage was brought to Sunnyside at a cost of $1200... it was about the swellest thing on wheels that travelled around there. Something like a sedan of today, two doors. The front seat was open and there were seats for five passengers. There were two glass windows that opened by letting down into the doors. There was a seat on the back that unscrewed and let down for a footman or little negro to ride on, to open gates and such. Two horses or mules were hitched to it."

Tom and Ida lived at Sunnyside for several years after their marriage. When Mr. Casey died, they moved to Glenida place which became something of a second home for Lilburn during his teen years.